# THE PRESIDENCY

# ᴛʜᴇ PRESIDENCY

## A Research Guide

Robert U. Goehlert

Fenton S. Martin

ABC-Clio Information Services
Santa Barbara, California
Denver, Colorado
Oxford, England

© 1985 by Robert U. Goehlert and Fenton S. Martin

*This book is Smyth sewn and printed on acid-free paper to meet library standards.*

**Library of Congress Cataloging in Publication Data**

Goehlert, Robert, 1948–
   The presidency.

   Bibliography: p.
   Includes index.
   1. Presidents—United States—Bibliography.
2. Presidents—United States—Research.  I. Martin,
Fenton S.  II. Title.
Z1249.P7G63   1984   [JK516]   016.35303'1   84-6425
ISBN 0-87436-373-X

10 9 8 7 6 5 4 3 2 1


ABC-Clio Information Services
2040 Alameda Padre Serra, Box 4397
Santa Barbara, California 93103

Clio Press Ltd.
55 St. Thomas Street
Oxford, OX1 1JG, England


Manufactured in the United States of America

# Contents

PART II

# The Oval Office     83

CHAPTER 3

# The Presidents     85

**CHAPTER 4**

# Secondary Sources on the Presidents                      149

**PART III**

# Running For Office 165

**CHAPTER 5**

# Campaigns and Elections 167

**PART IV**

# Researching the Presidency                                    211


**CHAPTER 6**

# Designing and Developing a Strategy                           213

Appendixes

Bibliography

# List of Abbreviations
# and Acronyms

| | |
|---|---|
| ABA | American Bar Association |
| ALR | *American Law Reports* |
| AmJur2d | *American Jurisprudence, Second Series* |
| ASI | *American Statistics Index* |
| Bevans | *Treaties and Other International Agreements of the United States of America, 1776–1949* |
| CCH | Commerce Clearing House |
| CDD | Congressional District Data |
| CEA | Council of Economic Advisors |
| CFR | *Code of Federal Regulations* |
| CIA | Central Intelligence Agency |
| CIS | Congressional Information Service |
| CJS | *Corpus Juris Secumdum* |
| CLI | *Current Law Index* |
| CQ | Congressional Quarterly |
| CR | *Congressional Record* |
| CRS | Congressional Research Service |
| CSI | Capitol Services, Inc. |
| DIALOG | DIALOG Information Services, Inc. |
| DocEx | Documents Expediating Project |
| DSB | *Department of State Bulletin* |
| EAS | Executive Agreement Series |
| EO | Executive Order |
| EPA | Environmental Protection Agency |

| | |
|---|---|
| FACA | Federal Advisory Committee Act |
| FCC | Federal Communications Commission |
| FEC | Federal Election Commission |
| FR | *Federal Register* |
| FRD | *Federal Rules Decisions* |
| FSupp | Federal Supplement |
| GPO | Government Printing Office |
| GSA | General Services Administration |
| HConRes | House Concurrent Resolution |
| Hdoc | House Document |
| HJRes | House Joint Resolution |
| HR | House of Representatives Bill |
| HRes | House Resolution |
| HRp | House Report |
| IHS | Information Handling Services |
| IUSGP | *Index to U.S. Government Periodicals* |
| JCP | Joint Committee on Printing |
| LC | Library of Congress |
| LEd | *United States Supreme Court Reports, Lawyers' Edition* |
| LRI | *Legal Resource Index* |
| MLC | *Major Legislation of the Congress* |
| NSC | National Security Council |
| OCLC | *Online Computer Library Center* |
| OMB | Office of Management and Budget |
| ORBIT | SDC Search Service |
| PAIS | *Public Affairs Information Service Bulletin* |
| PL | Public Law |
| PRF | *Publications Reference File* |
| Proc | Proclamation |
| S | Senate Bill |
| SConRes | Senate Concurrent Resolution |
| SCt | *Supreme Court Reporter* |
| Sdoc | Senate Document |
| SExecrp | Senate Executive Report |
| SJRes | Senate Joint Resolution |
| SRes | Senate Resolution |
| Srp | Senate Report |

| | |
|---|---|
| Stat | *United States Statutes at Large* |
| STreaty doc | Senate Treaty Document |
| SuDocs | Superintendent of Documents |
| TIAS | *Treaties and Other International Acts Series* |
| TIF | *Treaties in Force* |
| TS | Treaty Series |
| USC | *United States Code* |
| USCA | *United States Annotated* |
| USCCAN | *United States Code Congressional and Administrative News* |
| USCS | *United States Code Service, Lawyers' Edition* |
| USLW | *United States Law Week* |
| UST | *United States Treaties and Other International Agreements* |

# Introduction

## AIM AND SCOPE

This book is designed as a guide to primary and secondary resources for students and researchers investigating the presidency. It is not intended to teach the reader how to use documents or how to do legal research, but to describe the specialized and general tools that would be useful in any such investigation. We have also included materials that could be used in a comparative study. The student who is researching a particular topic will find basic texts on methodology, books on the use of the polls, and similar kinds of material to consult. When necessary, we have identified sources to review for additional information. A List of Abbreviations and Acronyms precedes the text.

The book is divided into four parts. The first part describes the presidency as an institution and includes sections on the types of presidential papers, the Federal Register System, finding statutes and administrative laws, treaty making, and secondary sources. The second part addresses the presidency from the point of view of the individual in office. This part includes sections detailing how to locate the papers and publications of individual presidents, the Presidential Library System, and secondary sources. Part three focuses on campaigns and elections and identifies all of the primary and secondary sources available. The final part provides an overview on studying the presidency, i.e., designing a research project and developing a research strategy. In addition, we have provided extensive appendices for your guidance and convenience.

## DIFFICULTIES OF RESEARCH

Unlike the Congress and the Supreme Court, the decision-making process in the White House is closed to the public. While presidential documents and papers are important resources, what appears in the public papers are final decisions, orders, proclamations, and press releases. There is no published record of the discussions or hearings that go on in policy formulation. In addition, much information is privileged from disclosure to Congress. Five categories of information protected by executive privilege are (1) diplomatic and military secrets; (2) information classified as confidential by statute; (3) investigations bearing on pending litigation; (4) information relating to the internal affairs of government; and (5) records of policy-making process. Consequently, unless leaked to the press, interdepartmental memos, advisory opinions and recommendations, or working papers are not available to the public. While memoirs do provide some insights, they can be biased and even distorted by time. Outside of the published papers of the president and some of the offices of the Executive Branch, there is no published record of the White House staffers, such as policy and political advisers, the legislative liaison, press secretaries, and special counsels and consultants. Nor is there any record of the outside network of advisers or of party officials, personal friends, consultants and individuals from advisory institutions who provide information to the president.

While researching the presidency is difficult, it is not impossible. There are more sources of information and data available today than even five years ago. By identifying all relevant research tools and secondary sources, this guide will serve as a starting point for studying the presidency.

# GUIDES TO RESEARCH

This volume provides a discussion of both documents and commercial publications. Because detailed guides to the technical and bibliographical aspects of government publications are readily available, we have kept our discussions of documents brief. For those interested in such research, we have provided four annotated entries on the best guides to documents, both for current and historical materials. For those working in specific areas, we have provided a list of specialized research guides. All of these materials can be quite useful, and we suggest the student review them in order to learn when to consult them.

Researchers should also familiarize themselves with the list of general guides to government documents. Although these are general in nature and are not the primary tools for researching the presidency, we will refer to them when it is appropriate to our discussion.

## Commercial Guides

Bitner, Harry, Miles O. Price, and Shirley R. Bysiewicz. *Effective Legal Research*. 4th ed. Boston: Little, Brown, 1969.

This work gives an excellent description of the legislative process and all tools related to legal research. It provides an in-depth examination and explanation of the reference works and indexes used in legislative tracing. There are also chapters on finding federal statutes, treaties, and other international acts; federal administrative law; and the rules and decisions of federal courts and administrative and regulatory agencies. This volume is an excellent guide to presidential documents, especially those relating to the president as lawmaker.

Morehead, Joe. *Introduction to United States Public Documents.* 3rd ed. Littleton, CO: Libraries Unlimited, 1983.

This work, a textbook for library school students and professional librarians, is a valuable guide for anyone interested in researching federal documents. The chapter on legislative branch materials contains a wealth of information, including an especially detailed description of congressional publications and the reference tools used in tracing legislation. There is a lengthy chapter on the documents of the presidency and the Executive Office of the President. There are also separate chapters on the Executive Branch, Regulatory Agencies, and Advisory Commissions. The book is especially useful for learning about the depository system and for identifying the work of the Superintendent of Documents and the Government Printing Office.

Boyd, Anne Morris. *United States Government Publications.* 3rd rev ed. New York: Wilson, 1949.

Although somewhat outdated, this discussion of presidential publications is still useful for understanding the nature, types, and value of presidential publications. The work is also important for researching presidential publications in the eighteenth and nineteenth centuries.

Schmeckebeir, Laurence F., and Roy B. Eastin. *Government Publications and Their Use.* 2nd rev ed. Washington, DC: The Brookings Institution, 1969.

This is a well-known and respected reference work containing extensive information on all forms of government publications. Like the Boyd volume, this work contains much information not available elsewhere. Though the volume does not include the numerous reference tools published in the last decade, Schmeckebeir does provide an excellent description and analysis of documents published prior to 1900.

Many other research guides to political science and government publications contain sections or chapters on presidential research. Most of these are available in any college or university library.

American Library Association. Education Task Force. *Draft Syllabus of Resources for Teaching Government Publications.* Chicago: Government Documents Roundtable, 1976.

Brock, Clifton. *The Literature of Political Science: A Guide for Students, Librarians and Teachers.* New York: R. R. Bowker, 1969.

Folsom, Gwendolyn B. *Legislative History: Research for the Interpretation of Laws.* Charlottesville: University Press of Virginia, 1972.

Freides, Thelma. "A Guide to Information Sources on Federal Government Agencies." *News for Teachers of Political Science* 18 (Summer 1978): 6–13.

Goehlert, Robert. *Congress and Law-Making: Researching the Legislative Process.* Santa Barbara, CA: ABC-Clio, 1979.

Holler, Frederick L. *The Information Sources of Political Science*. 3rd ed. Santa Barbara, CA: ABC-Clio, 1981.

Jacobstein, J. Myron, and Roy M. Mersky. *Ervin H. Pollack's Fundamentals of Legal Research*. 4th Ed. Mineola, NY: Foundation Press, 1973.

Larson, Donna R. *Guide to U.S. Government Directories*. Phoenix: Oryx Press, 1981.

Lu, Joseph K. *U.S. Government Publications Relating to the Social Sciences: A Selected Annotated Guide*. Beverly Hills: Sage Publications, 1975.

Mason, John Brown. *Research Resources: Annotated Guide to the Social Sciences*. 2 vols. Santa Barbara, CA: ABC-Clio, 1968–1971.

Meyer, Evelyn S. "Reference Guides to Congressional Research." *RQ* 12 (Fall 1972): 30–36.

Nabors, Eugene. "Legislative History and Government Documents—Another Step in Legal Research." *Government Publications Review* 3 (Spring 1976): 15–41.

O'Hara, Frederic J. *Guide to Publications of the Executive Branch*. Ann Arbor: Pierian Press, 1979.

Palic, Vladimir M. *Government Publications: A Guide to Bibliographic Tools*. 4th ed. Washington, DC: U.S. Government Printing Office, 1975.

Shannon, Michael Owen. *To Trace a Law: Use of Library Materials in a Classroom Exercise*. Bronx, NY: City University of New York, Herbert H. Lehman College Library, 1975. (ERIC Document ED 111 341)

Vose, Clement E. *A Guide to Library Resources in Political Science: American Government*. Washington, DC: American Political Science Association, 1975.

Weinhaus, Carol, ed. *Bibliographic Tools: Volume II, Legislative Guide*. Cambridge: Harvard University, Program on Information Technologies and Public Policy, 1976.

Wynar, Lubomyr R. *Guide to Reference Materials in Political Science*. Rochester: Libraries Unlimited, 1967.

Zwirn, Jerold. *Congressional Publications: A Research Guide to Legislation, Budgets and Treaties*. Littleton, CO: Libraries Unlimited, 1983.

# Document Guides

The following are general guides to government publications. The first six are especially useful for identifying documents of the eighteenth and nineteenth centuries.

Poore, Ben Perley. *Descriptive Catalog of the Government Publications of the United States, September 5, 1774–March 4, 1881.* Washington, DC: U.S. Government Printing Office, 1885.

    This publication, known as *Poore's Descriptive Catalogue,* attempted to list all governmental publications, but omitted many department publications. It is a chronological, annotated list of government publications dated from September, 1774 to March, 1881. Materials on presidents are listed under the names of the presidents.

Ames, John Griffith. *Comprehensive Index to the Publications of the United States Government, 1881–1893.* 2 vols. Washington, DC: U.S. Government Printing Office, 1905.

    This is known as *Ames Comprehensive Index.* Entries are arranged alphabetically by subject. There is an index of names. Some departmental publications were omitted. For information on the presidency, look under the names of the presidents.

Greely, Adolphus Washington. *Public Documents of the First Fourteen Congresses, 1789–1817. Papers Relating to Early Congressional Documents.* Washington, DC: U.S. Government Printing Office, 1900.

    This is a chronological list of government publications. It includes messages and state papers of presidents that were omitted from Richardson's *Compilation of Presidential Papers.* There is an index of names. Additional information is provided in *Supplement, 1904.* It includes a preliminary list of papers of the first two congresses.

*Checklist of United States Public Documents, 1789–1975.* Arlington, VA: U.S. Historical Documents Institute, 1976.

    This is the single most comprehensive bibliographical source for U.S. government documents. All entries provide full bibliographic citations. The work includes all of the entries in the *1789–1910 Checklist,* the *Document Catalog,* the *Monthly Catalog, 1895–1976,* and the shelflist of G.P.O.'s Public Documents Library.

Lester, Daniel, and Sandra Faull, comps. *Cumulative Title Index to United States Public Documents, 1789–1976.* Arlington, VA: U.S. Historical Documents Institute, 1978.

    This lists all of the titles in the *Checklist of United States Public Documents, 1789–1976.*

*Catalog of the Public Documents of the [53rd to 76th] Congress and of all Departments of the Government of the United States [for the Period of March*

*4, 1893 through December 31, 1940*]. Washington, DC: U.S. Government
Printing Office, 1896–1945.

Known as the *Document Catalog,* this was the first truly systematic record
of U.S. public documents and is the only complete list of executive orders
from 1893 to 1940. It also contains proclamations. The entries are in
alphabetical order. There are entries for authors, subjects, and some titles. To
find materials on presidents, look under "President of U.S." This catalog has
been discontinued.

U.S. Superintendent of Documents. *Monthly Catalog of United States Government Publications.* Washington, DC: U.S. Government Printing Office,
1895– .

The *Monthly Catalog* is the *Reader's Guide* of U.S. government publications. While it does not include all publications, it does index the majority of
the most important ones issued by the federal government. The *Monthly
Catalog* can best be used when searching for information related to electoral
reform, election laws, campaign contributions, etc. The *American Statistics
Index* or the *Bureau of the Census Catalogue* are more useful guides to
statistical sources. Presidential messages are listed under the president or the
agency the message concerns. Look under "President of the U.S." for
information on the presidency.

The following publications serve as indexes to the *Monthly Catalog* during
the years it had no indexing.

*Cumulative Subject Index to the Monthly Catalog of U.S. Government Publica-
tions, 1895–1899.* 2 vols. Compiled by Edna A. Kanley. Arlington, VA:
Carrollton Press, 1978.

*Cumulative Subject Index to the Monthly Catalog of United States Government
Publications, 1900–1971.* Compiled by William W. Buchanon and Edna A.
Kanley. Arlington, VA: Carrollton Press, 1975.

*The Declassified Documents, Retrospective Collection.* 2 vols. Executive ed.,
Annadel Wile. Operations ed., Elizabeth Jones. Arlington, VA: Carrollton
Press, 1976–1977.

The first part of this work is a catalog of abstracts; the second part is a
cumulative subject index.

U.S. Library of Congress. *Popular Names of U.S. Government Reports: A
Catalog.* 3rd ed. Washington, DC: U.S. Government Printing Office, 1974.

The selected entries in this work are photographic reproductions of Library
of Congress catalog cards and are arranged alphabetically by popular name.
It is especially useful for finding Presidential Commission and Advisory
Reports, known by their popular names, such as the Warren Report.

*Bibliographic Guide to Government Publications: U.S.* Boston: G. K. Hall, 1975– .

This guide includes entries for documents cataloged by the Research Libraries of the New York Public Libraries and from the Library of Congress. The annual editions serve as a supplement to the *Catalog of Government Publications* of the Research Libraries of the New York Public Libraries (40 volumes, G. K. Hall, 1972).

# PART I

# The Presidency as an Institution

# CHAPTER 1

# The Presidency

## PRESIDENTIAL PUBLICATIONS

The term presidential papers encompasses all of the material associated with a president; those papers written prior to, during, and after his term. It includes the public papers issued while in office, the papers under the control of the Executive Office (such as interdepartmental reports), official papers (often referred to as the "private papers" or "White House papers"), and personal papers (such as letters).

All of these are the president's personal property and, as such, are not published by the government. Many of them are in the Library of Congress and in presidential libraries. Access to these materials will be discussed in Chapter 4. Nor does the government publish the papers that are under the control of the Executive Office. These are passed on to succeeding administrations. Some of this material is available because a president has released it or because it has come to light under the Freedom of Information Act, a Congressional investigation, or a Court decision.

This section details the kinds of materials contained in the published papers of a president. In the following sections, we will describe how to use a variety of government and commercial reference tools to identify these materials.

## Legislative and Administrative Papers

Under statutory law, Congress has authorized the president to take certain actions expressed as proclamations and executive orders.

### EXECUTIVE ORDERS

Executive orders are claimed by virtue of the office, by the power authorized under the Constitution, as Commander-in-Chief, or under statutory law and have the effect of law. They have never been defined by statute, but in effect, any act of the president authorizing an action is an executive order. While they can deal with a wide variety of matters, generally they relate to the conduct of government business and the organization and procedures of the executive branch.

## PROCLAMATIONS

Legally, there is no distinction between an executive order and a proclamation, but not all proclamations have the effect of law. A call for a public observance does not have the force of law. Proclamations are issued by virtue of the office, existing laws, or as a response to a joint resolution. Proclamations are generally issued for matters of widespread interest, but proclamations and executive orders can overlap in content.

## REORGANIZATION PLANS

Reorganization plans are essentially presidential orders. Issued under prior Congressional authority, they enable the president to change the structure of the executive branch by combining, abolishing, or switching agencies under the level of department.

# Foreign Affairs

Treaties and executive agreements are issued under the power of the Constitution and existing legislation.

## TREATIES

The Constitution declares that a "President . . . shall have power, by and with Advice and Consent of the Senate, to make Treaties provided two thirds of the Senators present concur . . . ." Thus, a treaty is a compact with a foreign nation made by the president and approved by the Senate. Treaties can also be referred to as conventions, contracts, or protocols.

## EXECUTIVE AGREEMENTS

Executive agreements are made by the president under the Constitutional authority invested in the president as the chief executive and under existing legislation. They do not require the approval of the Senate.

# Messages

Presidential messages include all communications made to the Congress, whether written or oral. Most, but not all, messages are consequently published by the Congress. While messages vary in content, they can be divided into the following categories.

## APPROVAL OF BILL

The Constitution states that "every Bill which shall have passed the House of Representatives and the Senate, shall, before it becomes a Law, be presented to the President of the United States." Though the only constitutional requirement is that he sign a bill, a president may include a message as well.

## VETO

The Constitution states that if a president does not sign a bill, "he shall return it, with his Objections to that House in which it shall have originated." While a veto is considered a message, it also represents an important type of legislative power.

## ADDRESSES TO CONGRESS

The President can address the Congress in person, as he does, for example, in the annual State of the Union Address. Addresses need not be made on a regular basis and are more likely to be made upon a special occasion.

## TRANSMITTAL OF REPORTS

The president is required to submit to Congress a number of documents. Among the best known are the *Budget* and *Economic Reports of the President.*

## SPEECHES AND SPECIAL MESSAGES

This category includes speeches made by the president on television, radio, or before official and unofficial gatherings. It includes press conferences, press releases, and other miscellaneous materials issued officially.

# THE FEDERAL REGISTER SYSTEM

The General Services Administration, established in 1949 as an independent agency, was set up to oversee the management of federal documents. The GSA consists of five services, including the National Archives and Records Administration whose chief objective is to preserve and manage federal records. Within the NARS is the Office of the Federal Register. This office publishes several series relating to presidential action. The publication of these documents is what is referred to as the Federal Register System. In the following pages, we will describe these documents and explain how to use them to find particular kinds of information.

## Publications of the U.S. Office of the Federal Register

*Federal Register.* Washington, DC: U.S. Government Printing Office, 1936– .
    The first section of the *Federal Register* includes executive orders, proclamations, and other presidential materials—memoranda from the president to the heads of departments or agencies, directives for officials, letters, and reorganization plans for agencies. New Federal Advisory Committees are also recorded. Notices of each meeting of advisory bodies are published.

*Code of Federal Regulations.* Washington, DC: U.S. Government Printing Office, 1938– .
   The *Federal Register* is codified in the *Code of Federal Regulations.* It includes executive orders, proclamations, and administrative regulations.

*The Federal Register: What It Is and How to Use It: A Guide for the User of the Federal Register—Code of Federal Regulations System.* Washington, DC: U.S. Government Printing Office, 1980.
   This guide explains the *Federal Register* and the *Code of Federal Regulations.* It contains dozens of illustrations depicting all of the relevant parts of the two publications.

*Title 3, The President.* Washington, DC: U.S. Government Printing Office, 1938– .
   This annual work is referred to as "The President." The full texts of executive orders and proclamations are given in one chapter. Another chapter documents the Executive Office of the President.

*Title 3A.* Washington, DC: U.S. Government Printing Office, 1972– .
   This annual volume is known as "The President Appendix." It contains the text of proclamations, executive orders, and other presidential documents.

*United States Statutes at Large.* Washington, DC: U.S. Government Printing Office, 1789– .
   This is a compilation of public and private laws. There are some presidential materials included, such as a list of proclamations, full texts of these proclamations, and a list of reorganization plans. A subject index to these materials is provided.

*Weekly Compilation of Presidential Documents.* Washington, DC: U.S. Government Printing Office, 1965– .
   Published every Monday, this work covers the previous week. It contains texts of messages to the Congress (budget, economic, and State of the Union Addresses), texts of proclamations and executive orders, and transcripts of presidential news conferences. It also provides presidential speeches, statements, letters, remarks of welcome to foreign leaders, and similar materials made in public in the form of White House Press Releases. Letters, memos, and reports to the President from Cabinet members and other officials released by the White House Press Office are included. This provides an up-to-date source for presidential policies and activities. There is an index of contents and a cumulative index to prior issues. There are semiannual and annual indexes as well.

*Public Papers of the Presidents of the United States.* Washington, DC: U.S. National Archives and Records Administration, 1958– .
   Materials in this annual publication are arranged in chronological order with a subject index. It contains texts of President's Messages to Congress, public addresses, messages to heads of state, released statements on various

subjects, and transcripts of news conferences. Reports of presidential task forces, awards for Congressional Medals of Honor and Presidential Unit Citations, and presidential reports to Congress are not included in the main portion of the text. These are located in several appendices at the end of the volumes. Proclamations and executive orders and materials to other officials are listed in "Appendix B" of each volume. Many of the items are annotated, and each volume has an index. The series begins with President Truman, but there are volumes available on President Hoover's administration.

*United States Government Manual.* Washington, DC: U.S. Government Printing Office, 1935– .

This annual manual is the official handbook of the federal government. It gives information on the agencies and departments of all three branches of government, as well as on quasi-official agencies, international organizations and boards, committees, and commissions. Programs and activities of these agencies are described. This manual includes a section summarizing the duties and functions of the Executive Branch. There is a separate name index and a subject index. Its earlier title was *U.S. Government Organization Manual.*

# FEDERAL LEGISLATION

A primary role of a president is that of a legislator. Historically, the president has sponsored bills presented to Congress. Today, one indicator of a president's effectiveness is his success in having his legislative programs passed by Congress. Consequently, researching the presidency entails knowing how to research the Congress, including its Constitutional origins, how a bill proceeds through Congress, and the interpretation of statutes.

## The Constitution

Any analysis of statutes and the rules, regulations, and orders that constitute administrative law must start with the Constitution. The powers of the president are specified in the Constitution. While there are gray areas of legality, executive orders and proclamations are not to supersede statutes. Consequently, it is important to have an understanding of the Constitution to know what the powers of the president are, as well as how statutes are made. In a later section we will list several bibliographies that can be used to identify primary and secondary sources on the origin, history, development and interpretation of the Constitution. The best single source for understanding the Constitution is what is commonly referred to as the *Constitution Annotated.*

U.S. Congress. Senate. *Constitution of the United States of America, Analysis and Interpretation: Annotations of cases decided by the Supreme Court of the United States to....* Washington, DC: U.S. Government Printing Office, 1913– .

This publication is updated every ten years, and supplements are issued every two years. As it contains extensive case annotations and scholarly analysis and interpretations, this work is the best compendium on the Constitution. It includes over one hundred pages on the presidency, covering tenure, succession, pardons, executive agreements, removal power, impeachment, and his role as commander in chief and as a legislator.

Casebooks shed light on the Constitution and the major cases that have altered its interpretation. Literally hundreds provide commentary on the Constitution and annotated cases. We have listed below a few of the general casebooks. There are also casebooks available on specific topics, such as economic themes, civil liberties, etc.

Corwin, Edward. *Corwin on the Constitution.* Edited by Richard Loss. Ithaca: Cornell University Press, 1981– .

Costanzo, Joseph F. *Political and Legal Studies.* 2 vols. West Hanover, MA: Christopher Publishing House, 1982.

Kutler, Stanley I., comp. *The Supreme Court and the Constitution: Reading in American Constitutional History.* 2nd ed. New York: Norton, 1977.

Lockhart, William B., Yale Kamisar, and Jesse Choper. *Constitutional Law: Cases, Comments, Questions.* 4th ed. St. Paul: West Publishing Co., 1975.

Mason, Alpheus T., and William M. Beaney. *American Constitutional Law: Introductory Essays and Selected Cases.* 6th ed. Englewood Cliffs, NJ: Prentice-Hall, 1978.

Stofing, Herbert J., ed. *The Complete Anti-Federalist.* 7 vols. Chicago: University of Chicago Press, 1981.

# Legislative Histories

This section is designed to assist users in tracing legislation and to familiarize them with the major sources of information about legislative process. It provides a basic introduction to the tools of research and how they can be used to gain a better insight into the legislative process. Comprehension of legislative decision making requires considerable effort and probing, and only firsthand examination of the tools cited in this guide will help the researcher overcome the bewildering complexity of bibliographical resources. There is no substitute for the use of reference tools and diligent research. This section does not detail all of the complexities involved in legislative research, but acquaints the user with the information necessary to begin an independent pursuit of his own educational needs.

# THE LEGISLATIVE PROCESS

The passage of a bill through Congress is an intricate process. To understand it fully requires a knowledge of law-making procedures and an awareness of the informal politics that influence congressional decision making, e.g., lobbying and logrolling. The concessions and compromises involved in drafting legislation, some of which take place outside Capitol Hill, are as important as the debates within both chambers of Congress. Thus, a description of the formal steps by which a bill becomes law is not a complete picture of the legislative process. Nevertheless, it is fundamental in tracing legislation. An understanding of the legislative process is necessary to track a law through Congress. The following minimal outline traces a bill as it passes through Congress.

1. A bill is introduced by a member(s) of Congress either in the House or the Senate.
2. The bill is assigned a number and referred to the committee or committees having jurisdiction over the legislation. Bills are increasingly subject to multiple referrals, which complicates the task of legislative tracing.
3. The bill is either considered by the committee or refused further study. While in committee, the bill may be amended or even entirely rewritten. In addition, hearings may be held concerning the ramifications of the bill.
4. A committee mark-up is scheduled and the bill is analyzed.
5. After deliberation by the committee, the bill is referred to the chamber calendar. Bills favorably recommended by a committee are accompanied by a report.
6. The terms of floor consideration are framed and approved.
7. The bill is submitted to the floor of the chamber for possible debate on the merits of the legislation. In the House, legislation is brought up on the floor by "privileged status" or by adoption of a "rule" by the Rules Committee; in the Senate, by negotiation or unanimous consent.
8. If the bill is passed, it is then sent to the other chamber for consideration. Much legislation, however, starts as similar bills in both houses.
9. The bill undergoes the same process as in the original chamber in which it was introduced (steps 1–7).
10. If the House and Senate versions of the bill differ, the bill is sent into conference, where a compromise is hammered out and amendments are agreed to.
11. A conference report is drafted.
12. The conference report is debated by each chamber and approved.
13. The president either signs the bill and it becomes law or he may veto it. The president has ten days (excepting Sunday) to act upon a bill; if a president does not act within ten days, the bill becomes law without his signature, providing Congress is in session. If Congress adjourns before the ten day limit, the bill does not become law; this is what is referred to as a "pocket veto."

The key to legislative tracing is recognizing the relationship between the steps of the legislative process and ensuing congressional publications. In tracing legislation it is indispensible to know which publications emanate from each stage of the law-making process. For each level in the legislative process, there are corresponding publications. For example, when a committee holds hearings, the researcher must automatically begin searching to ascertain if the hearings were published. After becoming familiar with the essential movements in the legislative process, the researcher can then examine in more detail the precise pathways by which bills journey through Congress. Having the steps by which all bills must proceed firmly in mind, the researcher will be able to learn through actual tracing some of the variations that may occur in the course of legislation. The key to tracing a bill is realizing that for each step in the legislative process, there is a corresponding access tool for congressional publications.

Several good sources provide extended treatments and rich background material:

Congressional Quarterly. *Guide to Congress.* 3rd ed. Washington, DC: Congressional Quarterly, 1982.

Cummings, Frank. *Capitol Hill Manual.* Washington, DC: Bureau of National Affairs, 1976.

U.S. Congress. House. *How Our Laws are Made.* 97th Cong., 1st sess., Washington, DC: U.S. Government Printing Office, 1981. H. Doc. 97–120.

U.S. Congress. Senate. *Enactment of a Law.* 96th Cong., 1st sess., Washington, DC: U.S. Printing Office, 1979. S. Doc. 96–1.

The parliamentary procedures used in the House and the Senate can be found in the various compilations of rules published by each body. See Appendix 1, p. 221, for a selected list of House and Senate rules and manuals.

## Congressional Publications

In order to trace legislation, a researcher must become well versed in the terminology he will encounter. The following definitions are those a student should be able to immediately recognize and understand. Congress publishes a copious amount of material, much more than just bills and laws. It disseminates many different kinds of works, including directories, manuals, and legislative calendars. These publications can either be of Congress as a whole or the product of a particular committee or subcommittee. Those that directly result from the legislative process, the documents that accrue as a bill passes through Congress, are the most significant for legislative tracing.

### BILLS

This form is used for most legislation, whether permanent or temporary, general or specific, public or private. They may originate in either chamber, except revenue-raising bills which must be introduced in the House. Appropriations bills, by convention, all originate in the House. H.R. prefixes bills introduced in the House and S. those in the Senate. Bills are numbered consecutively as they are introduced from the beginning of each two-year congressional term.

## JOINT RESOLUTIONS

These are designated H.J. Res. or S.J. Res. In reality there is little difference between a bill and a joint resolution, since a joint resolution goes through the same procedure as a bill and has the force of law. Joint resolutions, however, usually address limited matters, such as a single appropriation. Like a bill, a joint resolution requires the approval of both houses and the signature of the president, except when it is used to propose an amendment to the Constitution.

## RESOLUTIONS

These are designated by H. Res. or S. Res. and are often referred to as a "simple resolution," for they concern only the business of a single house, e.g., creating and appointing committees or instigating a special investigation. For the most part, resolutions deal with the rules of one house or are used to express the sentiments of a house. They have no legislative effect outside the house in which they originate. Resolutions become operative upon passage by that house and do not require approval by the other house or the signature of the president.

## CONCURRENT RESOLUTIONS

These are designated H. Con. Res. or S. Con. Res. Concurrent resolutions are used for matters affecting the business of both houses. Unlike a bill or joint resolution, they do not require the signature of the president. Like simple resolutions, concurrent resolutions do not have the effect of law.

## HEARINGS

These contain the oral testimony and written materials submitted to committees of Congress in public sessions designated for hearing witnesses. Witnesses before hearings include specialists, experts, important government officials, prominent private citizens, and spokespersons for organizations and groups that may be affected by the bills under consideration. Hearings are designated by a alphanumeric notation known as the SUDOCS (Superintendent of Documents) class number.

## COMMITTEE PRINTS

These are documents requested by committees and compiled by their research staffs, outside consultants, or the Congressional Research Service. Committee prints are authorized by a particular committee at the time of a hearing. Used for background information in consideration of a bill, they are usually of a technical or research nature and often give the summation of staff findings, histories of previous legislation and congressional efforts, and the implications of the bill should it pass. Committee prints are also given a SUDOCS classification number. Because not all of these documents are offered to the depository libraries or are for sale by the Superintendent of Documents, often the researcher must request the print directly from the committee or write his or her Congressman for assistance. To say the least, the distribution of committee prints is unpredictable. Since they are usually printed in a limited quantity, it is sometimes difficult to obtain them.

## REPORTS

These are designated as H. Rept. or S. Rept. A committee submits a written report containing the justification for its action with each bill it sends to the floor. The report denotes the scope and purpose of the bill and includes any amendments or written communications submitted by departments or agencies of the executive branch. A report favors the passage of a bill; a committee does not report its recommendations when it disapproves of a bill. As a congressional term, "report" refers to the actual document. As a verb, "report" refers to the process of "reporting a bill," i.e., submitting the committee's findings and recommendations to the parent chamber. Reports are an extremely important element in legislative tracing, for they provide an explanation of a bill's intent and aim.

## PROCEEDINGS

These include the daily printed debates, statements, and actions taken by each house. The *Congressional Record* is the printed account of the proceedings of both the House and Senate. There are also separate *Journals* for the House and Senate, which are the printed proceedings for each house. These are published at the end of each session.

## CONFERENCE REPORTS

If the two chambers cannot agree on the provisions of a bill, conferees appointed by the House and Senate work to hammer out a compromise. When the conferees have harmonized the House and Senate versions of the bill, a conference report is prepared. The compromise bill must then be approved by each house before it is sent to the president. Conference Reports use the imprint of the chamber where the bill originated, e.g., H.R. 1234.

## SLIP LAWS

When a bill has been enacted into law, it is officially published as a slip law, a separately published law in unbound single-sheet or pamphlet form. Once a bill has received presidential approval, it takes two or three days for the slip law to become available.

## STATUTES AT LARGE

This publication is a chronological arrangement of all the laws enacted by Congress for each session. While the laws are not arranged by subject matter, they are indexed.

## UNITED STATES CODE

The general and permanent laws of the United States are consolidated and codified under fifty titles. These titles are arranged by subject: the first six titles identify general subjects; the remaining forty-four are arranged alphabetically by broad subject area. Every six years the code is revised, and after each session of Congress a supplement is issued.

## PRESIDENTIAL MESSAGES

When a president signs or vetoes a piece of legislation, he usually issues a brief statement concerning its value or deficiencies. While the bill proceeds through Congress, the president may also make statements concerning the merits of the bill or criticizing or praising Congress for its handling of the bill.

# Compiling a Legislative History

We have seen how a bill passes through Congress and the publications that result from the sequence. We will now describe the tools used to trace the course of a bill and to identify what publications exist. Some of these are published by the federal government and others are produced by private commercial companies. The intent of this section is not to provide an elaborate discussion of how to use these tools, but to acquaint the user with their existence and purpose. The best way to gain a full knowledge and command of how to employ this material is through repeated use. Reading descriptions of the tools can never be substituted for examining them firsthand. At the end of this section, we will present a detailed strategy of how to trace legislation utilizing these bibliographic guides.

It is advantageous to keep in mind the distinction between guides to legislative action and guides to printed publications. A guide to legislative action allows the user to reconstruct a history of a bill's passage through Congress, to find the date it was introduced, referred to committee, reported to chamber, voted upon, etc. Guides to printed publications enable the user to identify the proper citations necessary for finding the documents related to a bill. In reality this distinction is only a conceptual one, for many tools do both. The *Congressional Record* is both a guide to legislative action and an index to the floor proceedings it contains. Nevertheless, the distinction is useful, for it reminds the user of the procedure of first tracing the steps of a law and then finding specific citations to publications.

## GUIDES TO CONGRESSIONAL ACTIVITY

*Congressional Index.* Washington, DC: Commerce Clearing House, 1937/ 38– .

This weekly publication indexes congressional bills and resolutions and lists their current status. It is designed to enable the user to follow the progress of legislation from initial introduction to final disposition. A section on voting records reports all roll-call votes. Vetoes and subsequent congressional actions are recorded. The guide provides a sequential history of legislation and is a good tool for following a bill through Congress.

*Digest of Public General Bills and Resolutions.* U.S. Library of Congress, Congressional Research Service. Washington, DC: U.S. Government Printing Office, 1935– .

Normally published each session in five cumulative issues with biweekly supplements, it provides a brief synopsis of public bills and resolutions and records the introduction of a bill or resolution, the committee referred to, and the last action taken. Arrangement is by bill number, with a subject index.

*Congressional Record: Proceedings and Debates of the 43rd Congress.* Washington, DC: U.S. Government Printing Office, 1873– .

This is a daily record of the proceedings of Congress, including a history of legislation. It consists of four sections (1) proceedings of the House; (2) proceedings of the Senate; (3) extensions and remarks; and (4) the *Daily Digest* of the activities of Congress. The Proceedings are indexed by subject and name. The "History of Bills and Resolutions" section is arranged by bill and resolution number. While the *Congressional Record* provides a sequential history, it does not provide as much informafion as the *Congressional Index.* Consequently, the *Congressional Index* is often more helpful. The *Congressional Record* is important for finding roll-call votes and congressional action on vetoed bills. It is not a literal transcription of the floor debates. Legislators or their staffs have a chance to edit it before it goes into print and again before it goes into the bound volumes. Consequently, the daily edition is more accurate than the bound volume. Normally this distinction makes little difference, but in hard-fought debates, as in final passage of legislation, there may be considerable editing. Prior to the publication of the *Congressional Record,* the floor proceedings were published in the *Annals of Congress, Register of Debates in Congress,* and the *Congressional Globe.* See Appendix 2, p. 222, for specific years covered by each series.

*House Journal.* U.S. Congress. Washington, DC: U.S. Government Printing Office, 1789– .
*Senate Journal.* U.S. Congress. Washington, DC: U.S. Government Printing Office, 1789– .

These are the official minutes of each chamber of Congress, published at the end of a session. Both *Journals* have a "History of Bills and Resolutions" in which legislative actions are arranged by number, title and action. Each has a name, subject and title index.

*Calendars of the United States House of Representatives and History of Legislation.* U.S. Congress. Washington, DC: U.S. Government Printing Office, 1951– .

The *Calendar* is published daily when the House is in session and each issue is cumulative. Each Monday a subject index to all legislative action to date in both the House and Senate is published. Bills passed or pending are arranged numerically in a table. Because this series is cumulative, it is a useful guide to legislative action.

*Congressional Monitor.* Washington, DC: Congressional Quarterly, 1965– .

The *Congressional Monitor* is published each day Congress is in session.

Each issue of the *Monitor* provides committee actions and witnesses scheduled for the day. A "Weekly Legislative Status Report" is issued every Friday, and bills are indexed by bill number. This is the fastest reporting service covering congressional action. The Congressional Quarterly also publishes *Congress in Print: A Weekly Alert to just-released Committee Hearings, Prints and Staff Studies,* an up-to-minute listing of new publications.

*United States Statutes at Large: Containing the Laws and Concurrent Resolutions Enacted....* Washington, DC: U.S. Government Printing Office, 1789– .
   The *Statutes at Large* is a record of all laws published in their final form, giving the full text of congressional acts and resolutions passed during a congressional session. Slip laws, the texts of individual acts, are published separately as they are passed. Slip laws contain legislative histories on the inside back cover and are indexed in the *U.S. Monthly Catalog.* Since 1963 the *Statutes at Large* contains a section entitled "Guide to Legislative History of Bills enacted into Public Law."

*United States Code.* Washington, DC: U.S. Government Printing Office, 1926– .
   The *Code* is a compilation of all federal laws in force, arranged by subject under fifty "titles." The index volume contains a table of all title and chapter headings and a subject index to all sections. The Office of the Federal Register has published two useful guides for learning how to use the *Statutes* and *Code: How to Find U.S. Statutes and U.S. Code Citations* and *The Federal Register: What it is and How to Use It; A Guide for the User of the Federal Register-Code of Federal Regulations System.*

## GUIDES TO THE LEGISLATIVE PROCESS

*CIS/Index: Congressional Information Service/Index to Publications of the United States Congress.* Washington, DC: Congressional Information Service, 1970– .
   An inclusive monthly index to all congressional publications, this abstracts all forms of publications emanating from the legislative process. Materials are indexed by subject, names, committees, bill numbers, report numbers, document numbers, and names of committee chairmen. The *CIS/INDEX* abstracts of reports, hearings, and other congressional documents saves the researcher time and many check it first when tracing legislation. There are quarterly cumulative indexes and the *CIS/ANNUAL* is issued at the end of the year. There is also the *CIS Five-Year Cumulative Index, 1970–1974* and the *Four-Year Cumulative Index, 1975–1978.* A guide to using *CIS/INDEX* and *Abstracts,* the *CIS/INDEX User Handbook,* is available in most libraries that subscribe to *CIS/INDEX* or can be obtained from the Congressional Information Service. A CIS/INDEX database is also available on-line through ORBIT (System Development Corporation) for computer searching.

*Monthly Catalog of United States Government Publications.* Washington, DC: U.S. Government Printing Office, 1895– .

An important index for identifying many congressional publications, it is especially useful for finding committee hearings and reports. The *Monthly Catalog* has a subject index as well as an index arranged by government author. Carrollton Press has published a *Cumulative Subject Index to the Monthly Catalog of U.S. Government Publications, 1900–1971.*

*GPO Sales Publications Reference File.* Washington, DC: U.S. Government Printing Office, 1977– .

The *Publications Reference File* is a "Documents in Print," for it catalogs all federal publications currently sold by the Superintendent of Documents. Documents are arranged by subjects, titles, agency, series and report numbers, key words, authors, stock numbers, and SUDOCS classification numbers. The *PRF* is issued on 48X microfiche and is available to depository libraries. The *PRF* is easy to use and is the first place to look to identify new or recent documents.

*Cumulative Index of Congressional Committee Hearings.* Washington, DC: U.S. Government Printing Office, 1935– .

The *Cumulative Index* and its supplements can be used for tracing hearings prior to the publication of *CIS/INDEX*. The *Cumulative Index* provides access by bill number, subject, and committee. Greenwood Press has published on microfiche a *Witness Index to the United States Congressional Hearings 25th–89th Congress (1839–1966)*. See Appendix 3, p. 223, for a more complete list of the indexes to committee hearings and Appendix 4, p. 224, for indexes to committee prints.

*United States Code Congressional and Administrative News.* St. Paul: West Publishing Co., 1939– .

This monthly service reprints the full text of all public laws and reproduces the *U.S. Statutes at Large*. It includes selected presidential messages, executive orders and proclamations, listed by number, date and subject. It also reprints selected House and Senate Documents. In addition, this service provides seven tables on the status of legislation. One of the tables provides a complete legislative history of all bills passed as law. This series is cumulative and is an excellent tool for legislative tracing.

*Weekly Compilation of Presidential Documents.* Washington, DC: U.S. Government Printing Office, 1965– .

Published every Monday, it covers the preceding week and is an up-to-date source of information, including the full text of messages, speeches, press conferences, executive orders, and statements made by the president. All bills signed or vetoed are listed. A cumulative index is published with each issue.

*Public Papers of the Presidents of the United States.* Washington, DC: U.S. National Archives and Records Administration, 1958– .

Published annually, the text of the volumes include oral and written statements of the president. Materials are selected from communications to Congress, public speeches, press conferences, public letters, messages to heads of states, and executive documents. Since this series is edited, there are some discrepancies between the *Public Papers* and *Weekly Compilation of Presidential Documents*. KTO Press has published *The Cumulated Indexes to the Public Papers of the Presidents*. At present the six-volume set spans the Truman to Carter presidencies. KTO Press expects to issue volumes as each president's administration is completed. Besides containing the texts of documents, each volume indexes the complete public papers of a presidential administration. Formerly it was necessary to use each individual volume of the government's annual series *The Public Papers of the Presidents of the United States*.

*Presidential Vetoes: List of Bills Vetoed and Action Taken Thereon by the Senate and House of Representatives, 1789–1976*. Washington, DC: U.S. Government Printing Office, 1978.

This is a handy reference work listing vetoes chronologically by congressional session and presidential administration. The vetoes are entered by bill number and include the citation to the *Congressional Record* where the message is printed.

Appendix 5, p. 225, provides a summary of the two sections by listing sources of legislative actions for each step in the legislative process.

## LEGISLATIVE TRACING

Only after you have worked through several legislative tracing exercises will you feel confident of knowing the best strategy to use. Often a researcher is not sure where to begin or becomes lost somewhere in the process. The following outline is designed as a step-by-step guide through legislative tracing. The most important step is attaining a bill's or statute's number. Once you have the bill or statute number, it is relatively easy to compile a legislative history and identify all of the relevant documents. You can also trace legislation by subject. But it is best to isolate a group of bills on a particular subject and trace the bills by their numbers.

These are the steps to follow in tracing a bill through Congress. If the bill has been passed into law, get the statute number and go to any of the following indexes to get the legislative history:

1. *Congressional Quarterly Almanac* or *Congressional Quarterly Weekly Report*
2. *CIS/ANNUAL* — "Index of Bill, Report and Document Numbers"
3. *U.S. Code Congressional and Administrative News* — "Table of Legislative History"
4. *Congressional Record, Daily Digest* — "History of Bills Enacted into Law"
5. *Digest of Public General Bills and Resolutions* — "Public Law Listing"

6. *Calendars of the House and History of Legislation* — "Index Key and History of Bill"
7. *Statutes at Large* — "Guide to Legislative History of Bills Enacted into Public Law"
8. *House Journal* — "History of Bills and Resolutions"
9. *Senate Journal* — "History of Bills and Resolutions"
10. *Slip Law* — "Legislative History"

If a bill is still in Congress, get the bill number and go to the following guides to determine the present status of the bill:

1. *Congressional Quarterly Weekly Report*
2. *Congressinal Index* — "Status Tables"
3. *Digest of Public General Bills and Resolutions* — "Status Tables"
4. *Congressional Record* — "History of Bills and Resolutions"
5. *CIS/INDEX* — "Index of Bill, Report and Document Numbers"
6. *Calendars of House and History of Legislation* — "Index Key and History of Bill"
7. *U.S. Code Congressional and Administrative News* — "Public Laws Table"

If the bill number or statute number is not known, go to the subject, author or other category indexes in the following guides to determine the bill number or statute number:

1. *CIS/INDEX*
2. *Congressional Quarterly Weekly Report* or *Congressional Quarterly Almanac*
3. *Congressional Index*
4. *Congressional Record*
5. *Calendars of House and History of Legislation*
6. *Digest of Public General Bills and Resolutions*
7. *Statutes at Large*
8. *U.S. Code Congressional and Administrative News*

Follow the bill through Congress recording what actions transpired and what publications were issued.

1. Committee activities and publications, hearings, and prints, can be traced through
   *CIS/INDEX*
   *Congressional Quarterly Weekly Report*
   *Congressional Monitor*
   *Cumulated Index of Congressional Committee Hearings*
   *Monthly Catalog of U.S. Government Publications*
2. House, Senate, and Conference Committee reports can be traced through

*CIS/INDEX*
*Congressional Quarterly Weekly Report*
*Congressional Index*
*Calendars of House and History of Legislation*
*Congressional Record*
*Monthly Catalog of U.S. Government Publications*
*U.S. Code Congressional and Administrative News*

3. Floor proceedings and debates can be followed through
   *Congressional Record*
   *Congressional Quarterly Weekly Report*
   *Congressional Monitor*
   *Congressional Digest*

4. Roll-call votes are recorded in
   *Congressional Quarterly Almanac*
   *Congressional Quarterly Weekly Report*
   *Congressional Roll Call*
   *Congressional Record*
   *Congressional Index*

5. Presidential statements are printed and indexed in
   *Weekly Compilation of Presidential Documents*
   *Public Papers of the Presidents of the United States*
   *Cumulated Indexes to the Public Papers of the Presidents*

6. Slip law approval is recorded in
   *CIS/INDEX*
   *Congressional Quarterly Weekly Report*
   *National Journal*
   *Congressional Record*
   *Congressional Index*
   *Calendars of House and History of Legislation*
   *U.S. Code Congressional and Administrative News*
   *Congressional Monitor*

7. Laws are printed in
   *U.S. Code Congressional and Administrative News*
   *Statutes at Large*
   *United States Code*

8. Veto messages are referenced in
   *CIS/INDEX*
   *Congressional Quarterly Weekly Report*
   *Congressional Record*
   *Calendars of House and History of Legislation*
   *Weekly Compilation of Presidential Documents*
   *Monthly Catalog of U.S. Government Publications*

9. Congressional votes on vetoes are recorded in
   *Congressional Quarterly Almanac*
   *Congressional Quarterly Weekly Report*
   *Congressional Record*
   *Congressional Index*
   *Congressional Roll Call*

For analysis and commentary of bills as they pass through Congress, proceed to (1) *Congressional Quarterly Weekly Report;* (2) *National Journal;* (3) *Washington Post;* or (4) *The New York Times.*

A complete legislative history would include the following:

1. A history of legislative activities and publications, both prior and subsequent to the particular bill. This information is useful in charting changes in social trends and congressional attitudes.
2. A chronological list of how a bill is passed through Congress, including dates, committees, actions taken, and votes.
3. An examination of documents relating to the passage of a bill, including

   Bills
   Committee hearings and prints
   Committee reports
   Debates and proceedings
   Presidential messages
   Slip laws
   Veto and congressional action
4. Materials and recommendations made by executive departments concerning the bill.
5. Materials and recommendations made by special interest groups participating in the legislative process.
6. Any relevant court cases and decisions that relate to the interpretation of the law.
7. Useful secondary analyses and histories.

Finally, access to a library that subscribed to the *CIS Legislative History Service* saves an enormous amount of time and energy. Starting with the first session of the 97th Congress, the CIS service covers all significant legislation of each Congress. Each legislative history includes the full texts of all publications relating to the passage of a bill. This includes the slip law, all reports, bills and related bills, debates, hearings and prints, documents, and miscellaneous materials. Subscribers to the service can acquire certain citations for each law or obtain all publications, either on subscription or individually, to each law's history.

CIS published *Annotated Directories* as a looseleaf service to an entire session of Congress. The directories provide legislative history citations for all major laws. Each directory includes a table of contents listing the items contained in the history, a summary of the law, full citations to all the items and abstracts of reports, hearings, committee prints, and documents. Unfortunately, CIS discontinued the *CIS Legislative History Service* and *Annotated Directories* in 1984. Consequently, the service only covers the years 1981–1983.

Another useful tool is the journal, *Major Legislation of the Congress,* published fifteen times a year by the Congressional Research Service. This journal is designed to provide summaries of congressional issues and major legislation.

Each issue is cumulative and the final issue published at the end of each Congress serves as a permanent reference tool.

# Finding Statutes

If the president signs a bill or if it becomes a bill without his signature, the enrolled bill is sent from the White House to the General Services Administration for printing. If a bill is passed by both Houses over the objections of the president, the chamber that last overrides the veto transmits it to the GSA. There it is assigned a public law number and paginated for the *Statutes at Large* volume covering that session of the Congress. The public laws are numbered in sequence starting with the beginning of each Congress. Since 1957, the laws have been prefixed for ready identification by the number of the Congress.

The first official publication of a statute is in the form of a "slip law," a separately published unbound pamphlet. The heading indicates the public law number, the date of approval, and the bill number. Since 1976, the heading also indicates the *United States Statutes at Large* citation. If the statute has been passed over the veto of the president or has become law without his approval, a statement is inserted in place of the usual notation of approval. The Office of the Federal Register also supplies information in the margins giving the citations to statutes mentioned in the text and other explanatory notes. Since 1974, the notes provide the citations to the *United States Code,* enabling a reader to immediately determine where the statute appears in the *Code.* Since 1975, slip laws include a concise legislative history of the law consisting of the committee report numbers, the name of the committees, the date of consideration and passage in each chamber, and the references to the *Congressional Record.* Since 1971, a reference to presidential remarks has been included in the legislative history by citing the *Weekly Compilation of Presidential Documents.*

## USING THE *STATUTES AT LARGE*

In order to provide a permanent collection of the statutes of each session of the Congress, the General Services Administration prepares the *United States Statutes at Large.* Each volume contains a complete index and a table of contents. From 1956 through 1975, the volumes contained a table of earlier laws affected; from 1963 through 1974, they contained a table showing the legislative history of each law. The latter table was discontinued in 1975, since the legislative histories now appear at the back of each slip law.

## USING THE *UNITED STATES CODE*

The *United States Code* is a codification of the statutes of the United States arranged according to subjects under fifty title headings. Its purpose is to present the current status of laws in a concise form as an alternative to the numerous volumes of the *Statutes at Large.* Revised editions are published every six years and cumulative supplements are printed at the end of each session of the Congress.

The research procedure chart for *Statutes at Large* and *U.S. Code* (Appendix 6, p. 231) enables a user to obtain accurate and current citation of the *U.S. Statutes at Large* and the *U.S. Code*. Read the research procedure from left to right. The first column contains the references that require further citing. These are (1) Revised Statutes section, (2) date of law, (3) name of law, (4) number of law, (5) *Statutes* citation, and (6) *Code* citation. The second, third, and fourth columns identify the volumes in which the citations are located. Column five lists other finding aids. These are especially useful for citing recent legislation.

## INDEXES

The *Statutes at Large* and the *United States Code* comprise the official record of statutory law and are the primary sources and indexes for finding laws. But there are several commercial reference series that can also be used to locate statutes, either by number or popular name, and determine the present legality of a statute. These tools can be used by themselves, but it is always best to use them in conjunction with the *Statutes at Large* and the *United States Code*.

*Shepard's Acts and Cases by Popular Names: Federal and State*. Colorado Springs: Shepard's Citations, 1968– .
    Federal statutes are often referred to by their popular names. This service lists statutes in alphabetical order by popular name and cites their location in the *Statutes at Large* and *United States Code*. It provides the same access for state acts. Federal cases referred to by popular names can be accessed by using the section that refers you to the *United States Supreme Court Reports* and *National Reporter System*.

*Shepard's United States Citations: Statute Edition*. Colorado Springs: Shepard's Citations, 1955– .
    By providing citations to earlier and later statutes and cases as well as other legal sources, this work allows one to determine the validity of an act or judicial decision. A student or researcher can determine the current status of a decision or act by identifying which amendments, other enactments, or legal decisions have affected a particular statute or decision.

*United States Code Annotated*. St. Paul: West Publishing Co., 1927– .
    Although this set reprints the *United States Code*, the statutes are accompanied by extensive annotations, legal notes and analytic comments on the specific statute and its legislative history. This supplemental material is invaluable for anyone interested in researching the original intent and later interpretation of the statute.

*United States Code Service*. Rochester: Lawyers Cooperative Publishing Co., 1972– .
    This service is similar to the above item. It reprints the *United States Code* and includes annotations, notes and legislative histories. One of the volumes, the *U.S. Code Guide*, is especially useful for relating the code to several other reference tools, including the *United States Supreme Court Reports, Lawyers Edition*, and *American Jurisprudence*.

These four reference sets are complex tools. The following guides supply a more detailed description of how they work and the various ways they can be used.

Cohen, Morris L. *How to Find the Law.* 3rd ed. St. Paul: West Publishing Co, 1978.

Dickerson, Reed. *The Interpretation and Application of Statutes.* Boston: Little, Brown, 1975.

*How to Use Shepard's Citations.* Colorado Springs: Shepard's Citations, 1968.

Statsky, William P. *Legislative Analysis and Drafting.* 2nd ed. St. Paul: West Publishing Co., 1984.

In addition, *Effective Legal Research* and *Fundamentals of Legal Research,* mentioned earlier in this guide, have excellent chapters on how to use the four services.

## TABLES

In the last section we discussed how a bill becomes a law and the process of compiling a legislative history. Subsequently, we have discussed how to find statutes in the *Statutes at Large, United States Code* and commercial indexes. For the purpose of summation, we have provided a bill status table (Appendix 7, p. 237), information on locating legislative histories (Appendix 8, p. 238), and a list indicating where to locate popular name and subject indexes to federal statutes (Appendix 9, p. 239).

# Interpreting Statutes

Judicial decisions, both by the Supreme Court and lower courts, are important for determining whether a particular statute or presidential action is constitutional or not. Because decisions by the courts affect statutory law and administrative law, it is important to be able to identify decisions and know how to follow judicial interpretations.

## CASEBOOKS

Supreme Court decisions are first issued as "slip opinions." They are published within three days and are available in depository libraries. In addition to the "slip opinions," there are several casebooks a researcher can use for finding Supreme Court decisions.

U.S. Supreme Court. *United States Reports.* Washington, DC: U.S. Government Printing Office, 1790– .
    The *Reports* contain the official text of all opinions of the Supreme Court.

It also includes tables of cases reported, cases and statutes cited, miscellaneous materials, and a subject index. All written reports and most per curiam reports of decisions are printed.

U.S. Supreme Court. *Supreme Court Reporter.* St. Paul: West Publishing Co., 1883– .
   This is a non-governmental publication containing annotated reports and indexes of case names. It includes some material not covered in the *United States Reports,* such as opinions of Justices in chambers.

*United States Law Week.* Washington, DC: Bureau of National Affairs, 1931– .
   This periodical service includes important sections on the Supreme Court. It has four indexes: if you know the subject, you can use the *Topical Index;* if you know the name of the case, you can use the *Table of Cases;* if you know the docket number, you can use the *Docket No. Table;* and if you know the date, you can use the *Proceedings Section.* In addition to containing the full text of all decisions, it also has a number of useful sections, including (1) cases filed last week; (2) summary of cases filed recently; (3) journal of proceedings; (4) summary of orders; (5) arguments before the court; (6) argued cases awaiting decisions; (7) review of the Court's work; and (8) review of the Court's docket.

U.S. Supreme Court. *United States Supreme Court Reports: Lawyers' Edition.* Rochester: Lawyers Cooperative Publishing Co., 1790– .
   While all other casebooks contain the official reports, this service also contains numerous per curiam decisions not found elsewhere and summarizes individually the majority and dissenting opinions and counsel briefs. The Index to Annotations leads one to the legal notes provided for each case.

*West Federal Case News.* St. Paul: West Publishing Co., 1978– .
   This weekly publication not only provides summaries of cases decided in the Supreme Court, but also summaries of other courts, including the U.S. Court of Appeals; the U.S. Court of Claims; the U.S. District Courts; and selected cases from state courts.

   Decisions of lower courts (District Courts and Courts of Appeals) are not reported officially by the government. However, they are printed unofficially. The National Report System is a privately published edition of law reports covering most of the lower Federal courts. The *Federal Reporter* contains the decisions of Federal intermediate appellate courts and some selected district courts, and the *Federal Supplement* contains mainly the decisions of the U.S. District Courts.
   Besides publishing the decisions of the Supreme Court, the government also publishes the decisions of the following courts on a regular basis: Court of Claims; Court of Customs and Patent Appeals; Customs Court; Commerce Court; Tax Court; and United States Court of Military Appeals.

# DIGESTS

Several reference tools list digests that analyze the decisions of the Supreme Court. The digest sets can also be used as indexes for identifying decisions by subject and case name. Because it notes every citation of a court decision, *Shepard's United States Citations* allows you to follow changes in legal interpretation.

Anderson, Nancy. *United States Supreme Court Decisions: An Index to Their Locations*. Metuchen, NJ: Scarecrow Press, 1976.

Blandford, Linda A., and Patricia Russell Evans, eds. *Supreme Court of the United States, 1789–1980: An Index to Opinions Arranged by Justice*. 2 vols. Millwood, NY: Kraus, 1983.

*Digest of United States Supreme Court Reports, Annotated with Case Annotations, Dissenting and Separate Decisions since 1900*. Rochester: Lawyers Cooperative Publishing Co., 1948.

*United States Supreme Court Digest*. St. Paul: West Publishing Co., 1940– .

*Shepard's United States Citations: Case Edition*. Colorado Springs: Shepard's Citations, 1947– .

*Significant Decisions of the Supreme Court*. Washington, DC: American Enterprise Institute, 1969– .

# BRIEFS AND RECORDS

You can use several tools to locate the briefs and oral arguments used by the counsel of both sides. The briefs and records are a valuable resource for understanding the eventual decision of a case and the interpretation of a statute or administrative rule.

*Complete Oral Arguments of the Supreme Court of the United States*. Frederick, MD: University Publications of America, 1980– .

Kurland, Philip, and Gerhard Casper. *Landmark Briefs and Arguments of the Supreme Court of the United States: Constitutional Law*. Washington, DC: University Publications of America, 1975– .

U.S. National Archives. *Tape Recordings of Oral Arguments Before the U.S. Supreme Court*. Record Group 267. Washington, DC: Archives, 1955– .

U.S. Supreme Court. *Records and Briefs*. Washington, DC, 1832– .

## Secondary Sources

The *National Law Journal, Federal Times,* and the *Legal Times of Washington* regularly report on Supreme Court decisions. They also provide a wealth of information on other aspects of the judiciary, including the appointment of new judges and other personnel and judicial behavior in the areas of administrative law, regulatory politics, and legislative-executive relations. *Staff,* published by the Senate Committee on Rules and Administration, also includes a synopsis of important Federal court decisions in each monthly issue. The *Legal Resource Index, Current Law Index* or *Index to Legal Periodicals* can direct you to articles in these newspapers and to those of specific interest in the hundreds of available legal journals.

Finally, the publications of the Justice Department and General Accounting Office provide information about interpretations of the law and legal issues. *Official Opinions of the Attorneys General* and *Opinions of the Office of Legal Counsel* are both issued by the Department of Justice. Each contains opinions of legal issues of relevance to the president and other high level executive officials. In the *Decisions of the Comptroller General,* you can find legal decisions regarding the disbursement of appropriated monies. The last source, *Court Proceedings and Actions of Vital Interest to the Congress,* issued by the House Judiciary Committee, is rather specialized. It focuses primarily on decisions affecting members of Congress, such as immunity, election disputes and the scope of their powers.

# FEDERAL ADMINISTRATIVE LAW

Administrative agencies are often referred to as the fourth branch of government. By delegating authority, Congress gives these agencies administrative, legislative, and judicial power to make and enforce laws. Congress can also authorize the president to make rules and regulations. In turn, the president has delegated much of his authority to the executive agencies under him to make rules and regulations. Therefore, to understand the president as a lawmaker, you must be able to research administrative law.

## Finding Rules and Regulations

The Federal Register System, comprised of the *Federal Register* and the *Code of Federal Regulations,* contains current compilation of all rules and regulations issued by executive departments and agencies. In order to use the Federal Register System effectively, you need to understand each publication and the relationship between the two publications.

### USING THE *FEDERAL REGISTER*

The *Federal Register* is an invaluable tool for monitoring rules and regulations, as it is the only publication that prints all rules adopted by agencies. Issued daily, it contains documents in the following categories:

1. **Presidential Documents**—documents signed by the president and submitted
2. **Rules and Regulations**—documents having general applicability and legal effect

3. **Proposed Rules**—notices to the public of proposed rules
4. **Notices**—documents other than rules that are of interest to the public
5. **Sunshine Act Meetings**—notices of meetings published in accordance with the Government in the Sunshine Act

The *Federal Register* is basically a daily update of the *CFR*. When an agency adopts a new rule, it is published in the *Federal Register*. Every time the *CFR* is updated, all of the adopted rules appearing in the *Federal Register* since the most recent edition are inserted into the proper place in the *CFR*.

## Final Rules and Regulations

The Rules and Regulations section contains regulatory documents keyed to and codified in the *CFR*. The term "rules" and "regulations" are identical in meaning in the *Federal Register*. The Administrative Procedure Act requires agencies to give at least thirty days notice in the *Federal Register* that a rule has been adopted before it has legal effect. Exceptions to this procedure are interpretative rules, statements of policy, rules which grant exceptions, and rules that an agency believes good cause exists for not complying with the thirty day rule.

When an agency publishes a rule in the *Federal Register*, it must include a summary of the comments received in response to the proposed rule and any changes recommended in the comments incorporated into the final rule. Sometimes an agency will adopt a final rule and simultaneously request comments that are not due until after the rule has legal effect. Likewise, an agency will sometimes request comments on a rule that did not go through the proposed rule procedure because the agency believed the Administrative Procedure Act did not require that the proposed rule be issued.

The heading for each document in the *Federal Register* provides the name of the issuing agency, the *CFR* title and parts affected, and a brief synopsis of the contents. A preamble accompanies the text of all proposed and final rules. The purpose of the preamble is to improve the clarity of documents. It must follow this format and contain the following items:

1. The agency proposing the action
2. The type of action
3. Summary of the action
4. Dates for comments
5. Address for sending comments
6. The person in the agency to contact for information
7. Supplementary information, including the background, rationale, and content of the action

## Proposed Rules and Regulations

Proposed rules are generally documents that recommend amendments to regulations in the *CFR* and request public comment on the changes. Most proposed rules are required to be published by authority of the Administrative Procedure

Act or other statutes, but even those exempted from the requirement of notice publish the proposed form anyway. With certain exceptions all rules must be presented to the public in a proposed form before they become final. The publication of proposed rules serves as notices to the public and gives interested citizens the opportunity to participate in the process before the adoption of final rules. The format and preamble requirements for documents in the Proposed Rules Section are identical to the Final Rules Section. The date given in the preamble is usually the final date for submission of comments. An address is provided for sending comments.

One of the first steps in the rule-making procedure is the petition for rule-making. The petition, published in the Proposed Rules Section because it proposes to amend parts of the *CFR*, requests public comment. Another preliminary document published in the Proposed Rules Section is the advance notice of a proposed rule. Agencies issue these notices of intent early in the process to receive public comments as quickly as possible. These documents discuss a problem and the anticipated action of the agency. This step, not required by the Administrative Procedure Act, is used when an agency wants to get public comments before issuing a proposed rule. After reviewing comments received in response to a notice or advance notice, an agency will propose a rule if it decides a new rule is necessary.

Although the Administrative Procedure Act does not require hearings in the rule-making process, the legislation that requires the promulgation of regulations may do so. Even when hearings are not required, most agencies will hold hearings on significant proposals. In order to identify each of its proceedings, agencies assign a specific number to each one. The information the agency receives pertaining to a proceeding is kept on file and is open to the public. These files are referred to as "dockets."

Dockets sometimes include material prepared by the agency staff, but the dockets are not necessarily a complete record of all that has transpired. When the agency staff releases material, a copy is placed in the file for public inspection as well.

## Notices

The *Federal Register* defines notices as "documents other than rules or proposed rules that are applicable to the public." Statutory authority requires some of the documents included in the notices section to be published in the *Federal Register*. Documents in this section are not codified in the *CFR*. The following are types of materials the *Federal Register* publishes as notices:

1. **Advisory Committee Meetings.** The Federal Advisory Committee Act requires that advisory committees publish an announcement stating the date, time, location, and purpose of their meetings.
2. **Petitions and Applications.** These documents represent miscellaneous requests made by an agency for permission for a special authority.
3. **Environmental Impact Statements.** The National Environmental Policy Act requires that an environmental impact

statement be included along with any regulation that may have an effect on the quality of the environment.
4. **Delegations of Authority.** An agency may decide to delegate some of its authority to a different agency.

## Sunshine Meetings

The *Federal Register* publishes the agendas of open agency meetings. The Sunshine Act specifies that agencies hold open meetings and that the public be given a week's notice of the time and place of the meeting. Sunshine meetings are often another way for finding out about proposed rules and final rules before they appear in the *Federal Register*. Agencies also will list those meetings that are closed to the public. Finally, an agency's Office of Information maintains the Sunshine agenda mailing list, and you can try to be included on such lists.

## Finding Aids

The *Federal Register* prints a number of bibliographic tools or "finding aids,' at the beginning and the end of each issue. These finding aids are

1. **Highlights**
   On the front cover and inside front page of the *Federal Register* is a list of the issue's documents that have wide public interest. The Highlights' entries include the beginning page number of the document, a brief subject heading, the issuing agency's name, and a synopsis of the document.
2. **Contents**
   The *Federal Register*'s Contents contains a complete listing of all proposed and final rules, and notices arranged by agency. The documents are arranged under the name of the agencies by Rules, Proposed Rules, and Notices. The entry includes the beginning page number of the document and a brief description. Presidential Documents are listed under the heading "The President."
3. **Meetings Announced in this Issue**
   At the end of the Contents is a section listing meetings announced within the issue. This is arranged by agency name and provides the date of each scheduled meeting.
4. *CFR* **Parts Affected in this Issue**
   This list is similar to the *Cumulative List of CFR Sections Affected (LSA)*, but it is only for that day's issue. This is a listing of Titles and Parts of the *CFR* that have been or will be affected by rules contained within the issue. The proposed and final rules are published under each *CFR* title, arranged by part number, including the beginning page numbers of the documents. *CFR* parts can be affected by such changes as additions, amendments, and deletions.
5. **Reader Aids**
   At the back of each day's issue is the Reader Aids Section to assist the user finding specific information in the *Federal Register*. The Reader Aids include

(a) Information and Assistance
A listing of Office of Federal Register telephone numbers for you to call about specific questions.

(b) *Federal Register* Pages and Dates
This is a parallel table of the inclusive pages and corresponding dates for the current month's *Federal Register.*

(c) *CFR* Parts Affected During [month]
A cumulative monthly list of *CFR* parts affected by proposed and final rules, this list serves the same purpose as the "List of *CFR* Parts Affected in This Issue." This list is necessary for filling in the period between the most recent *LSA* and the accumulated issues of the *Federal Registers.*

(d) Agency Publication on Assigned Days of the Week
Some agencies publish their documents on two assigned days of the week.

(e) Table of Effective Dates and Time Periods
Published in the first issue of each month, this table is used for computing advance notice requirements and the public deadline for comments for *FR* documents published during the current month.

(f) *CFR* Checklist
This is a list of the revision dates and current prices of *CFR* volumes and is published in the first issue each month.

(g) Agency Abbreviations
This contains the abbreviations used in the Highlights and Reminder sections. This is published in the first issue of each month.

(h) Reminders
Every issue concludes with a list of reminders, including Rules Going into Effect Today and the List of Public Laws recently signed by the president. Each Wednesday the list is expanded to include the following information: Next Week's Deadlines for Comments on Proposed Rules, Next Week's Meetings, and Next Week's Public Hearings.

The *Federal Register* publishes an important finding aid separately—The *Federal Register Index.* Indexed by agency, this provides citations to all proposed and final rules and notices that have been printed in the *Federal Register* for the last month, quarter or year. The *Index* also prints a list of Privacy Act publications, a Table of *Federal Register* Pages and Dates, and a Guide to Freedom of Information Indexes. It is published quarterly and annually.

# USING THE *CODE OF FEDERAL REGULATIONS*

The *Code of Federal Regulations* codifies the rules published in the *Federal Register* by all executive departments and agencies. Arranged under fifty titles which represent broad subject areas, the *CFR* is revised annually. Each Title contains regulations pertaining to a single subject area and consists of one or more Chapters. Each chapter contains a single agency's regulations. The chapters are further divided into Parts, Parts into Sections, and if necessary, sections are broken down by paragraph. The following lists terms, symbols, and descriptions of each section:

| Term | Symbol | Description |
|------|--------|-------------|
| Title | 1, 2, 3, etc. | Each title represents an area that is subject to federal regulation. Subtitles are arranged consecutively by capitals and letters, and if it is necessary, distinguishes between the regulations of the agency as a whole and its bureaus. Subtitles are also used to group related chapters. |
| Chapter | I, II, III, etc. | Chapters are arranged by capital Roman numerals and each is normally assigned to a single issuing agency—either an agency or one of its bureaus. Subchapters are arranged by capital letters to group related parts. |
| Part | 1, 2, 3, etc. | Each chapter is divided into parts by Arabic numerals. A part consists of regulations pertaining to a single function of the issuing agency or is devoted to a particular subject under the jurisdiction of an issuing agency. Subparts are also arranged by capital letters to group related sections. |
| Section | 1.1, 1.2, 1.3, etc. | Each section number includes the number.of the part set off by a period preceded by the symbol denoting section. The section is the basic unit of the *CFR* and consists of a brief account of a single proposition. |
| Paragraph | (a), (b), (c), etc. | When further division of a section is needed, sections are divided into paragraphs. |

The *CFR* is revised every three months and issued on a quarterly basis. Consequently, at the end of each year the complete *CFR* has been revised according to the following schedule: January 1, Title 1 through Title 16; April 1, Title 17 through Title 27; July 1, Title 28 through Title 41; and October 1, Title 42 through Title 50.

The revision date is printed on the cover of each volume, and the cover for each volume is a different color for quick reference. Since most Titles include such a broad area, the regulations of any single Title will generally be contained in more than one book. Normally, all of a particular agency's regulations are contained in a single Title. Every volume of the *CFR* includes a "Table of *CFR* Titles and Chapters," listing the subject areas of the regulations contained in each Title and the name of the agency for the corresponding Chapter. The authority citation following the Table of Contents is listed before each part. This citation provides the legislative or presidential authority under which a part or a section is issued. A source note is also provided specifying by volume, page, and date where the codified document was published in its entirety in the *Federal Register.* Every volume of the *CFR* also includes an alphabetical list of agencies whose regulations are codified within the *CFR* and a citation to the Title and Chapter where the agency's regulations are located. And each agency's regulations include the procedures the agency is to follow in making its rules. After the codified material, each *CFR* volume includes several finding aids.

The *CFR Index,* revised semiannually, is a separate volume of the *CFR.* The volume consists of an index arranged by agency names and subject headings covering rules currently codified in the *CFR,* with a citation to the Title and Section of the *CFR* where the rules pertaining to a subject or agency can be found. Also included in the *CFR Index* are:

1. Agency prepared indexes for each *CFR* volume
2. Parallel Table of Statutory Authorities and Rules
   This table lists all sections of the *United States Code* and the *United States Statutes at Large* cited as the authority for rules codified in the *CFR.* A three-part table, it is designed to lead a researcher from a statute to a regulation.
3. List of *CFR* Titles, Chapters, Subchapters, and Parts
   This list is the same as the "Table of *CFR* Titles and Chapters" contained in each *CFR* volume.
4. Alphabetical Listing of Agencies
   The alphabetical listing of agencies is the same as that contained in every *CFR* volume.

Finally, the *Cumulative List of CFR Sections Affected (LSA)* is published monthly amd serves as an update to the *CFR.* The starting date for each Title is the date when the *CFR* volume containing that title was last revised. The *LSA* is intended to assist users in finding amendments published in the *Federal Register.* The entries are arranged by *CFR* title, chapter, part, and section, and denote the change made. Besides these entries, the *LSA* also contains an explanation of how to use the *LSA,* a Checklist of Current *CFR* Volumes, a Parallel Table of Authorities and Rules, and a Table of *Federal Register* Issue Pages and Dates. Instead of going through numerous issues of the *Federal Register* to find out what new rules, amendments, or proposed rules have been promulgated since the *CFR* was last updated, it is best to use the *LSA.*

## COMMERCIAL GUIDES

While the *Federal Register* and *Code of Federal Regulations* are the primary tools and records of rules and regulations, there are several commercial indexes to finding administrative citations. In addition to the three services cited below, the Congressional Information Service issued a *CIS Federal Register Index* in the beginning of 1984.

*Index to the Code of Federal Regulations*. Bethesda: Congressional Information Service, 1977– .

The detailed subject index allows you to search all fifty titles at once. You can search a general or a specific subject and be referred to all the relevant parts and subparts. There are two geographical indexes. The first indexes regulations regarding political jurisdictions (states, counties, and cities). The second cites properties administered by the Federal government (parks, military bases, etc.). There are also two other indexes that can save time if you already have a citation. A list of descriptive headings is assigned to each part of the code. A list of reserved headings indicates which parts of the code have been designated reserved, either for future use or because they are no longer in use.

*IHS Index to the Code of Federal Regulations*. Englewood, CO: Information Handling Service, 1977– .

Like *CIS*'s index, this service provides a subject index that crosses title boundaries. It also contains a geographical index, a list of descriptive headings, and a list of reserved headings.

*Shepard's United States Administrative Citations*. Colorado Springs: Shepard's Citations, Inc., 1967– .

This lists all the decisions of federal agencies, boards, and commissions published in the agencies' own indexes and digests. It also includes citations to articles in law journals and various other reporting series. Some of the more important indexes for particular agencies are identified in the following section.

# Other Sources of Administrative Law

Most federal administrative agencies issue decisions and opinions that are useful for studying the presidency. Some decisions and opinions eventually are contested in the Supreme Court regarding their constitutionality. Below we have listed some of the government decisions most directly related to presidential actions.

## INDEXES

Most independent regulatory agencies and departments of the executive branch publish their own decisions. They also may publish a variety of reports, catalogs, and digests. While the administrative rules and decisions of every agency could be used in researching various aspects of the presidency, we have listed the decisions and reports for only a select number of agencies.

## Federal Communications Commission

*Decisions and Reports, 1st series*. 1934–65.

*Decisions and Reports, 2nd series*. 1965– .

*Reports, 2nd series*.

*Decisions Interpreting the Communications Act of 1934,* 2 vols.
Compiled by the Department of Commerce, 1978.

## General Accounting Office

*Decisions of the Comptroller General of United States.* 1921– .

*Index-Digest of the Published Decisions of the Comptroller General
of the United States.* 1894– .

*Quarterly Digests of Unpublished Decisions of the Comptroller
General of the U.S.* 1965– .

*GAO Documents, Catalog of Reports, Decisions, Opinions,
Testimonies and Speeches.*

## Internal Revenue Service

*Treasury Decisions Under Internal Revenue Laws.* Vols. 1–36,
1898–1942.

*Internal Revenue Bulletin.* 1922– .

## Justice Department

*Official Opinions of the Attorneys General of the United States.*
1789–1851. Vol. 1, 1852– .

*Digest of Official Opinions.* Vols. 1–32, 1789–1921.

## Treasury Department

*Decisions of the First Comptroller.* Vols. 1–6, 1880–85, vol. 7,
1893–94.

*Digest of Decisions of the Second Comptroller.* Vols. 1–4, 1817–94.

*Decisions of the Comptroller of the Treasury.* Vols. 1–27,
1894–1921.

*Synopsis of Decisions.* 1868–98.

*Treasury Decisions.* Vols. 1–101, 1899–1966.

## CASEBOOKS AND TREATISES

As with constitutional law, there are hundreds of casebooks dealing with
administrative law. These identify important decisions, statutory legislation,
and explanations of procedures and practices. In addition to the casebooks
listed below, there are many more that focus on antitrust, transportation, the
environment, and so on.

*Administrative Agencies of the U.S.A.: Their Decisions and Authority.* Dalmas
H. Nelson. Detroit: Wayne State University Press, 1964.

*Administrative Law.* Basil J. Mezines, Jacob A. Stein, and Jules Gruff. New
York: Matthew Bender, 1977.

*Administrative Law.* Bernard Schwartz. Boston: Little, Brown and Co., 1976.

*Administrative Law and Process in a Nutshell.* Ernest Gellhorn and Barry B. Boyer. 2nd ed. St. Paul: West Publishing Co., 1981.

*Bureaucracy in Court: Commentaries and Case Studies in Administrative Law.* Richard C. Cortner. Port Washington, NY: Kennikat Press, 1982.

*Business, Government and the Public.* Murry Weidenbaum. Englewood Cliffs, NJ: Prentice-Hall, Inc., 1977.

*Decisions of Federal Administrative Agencies and of Federal Courts in Agency Cases, Prior to 1958.* Westport, CT: Redgrave Information Services Corp., 1972.

*Economic Regulation of Business and Industry: A Legislative History of U.S. Regulatory Agencies.* Bernard Schwartz. New York: Chelsea Publishers, 1973.

*Federal Administrative Law: Practice and Procedure.* Craig W. Christensen and Roger D. Middlekauf. New York: Practising Law Institute, 1977.

*An Interpretative Guide to the Government in the Sunshine Act.* Richard K. Berg and Stephen H. Klitzman. Washington, DC: U.S. Government Printing Office, 1978.

*Legal Control of Government: Administrative Law in Britain and the United States.* Bernard Schwartz and H. W. R. Wade. New York: Oxford University Press, 1972.

*Working on the System: A Comprehensive Manual for Citizen Access to Federal Agencies.* James R. Michael. New York: Basic Books, 1974.

For a researcher interested in keeping up on administrative law in general or the role of the president in administration law, the best sources to review are the *Legal Times of Washington,* the *National Law Journal,* and the *Administrative Law Review.* You should also consult several legal indexes, including the *Current Law Index, Index to Legal Periodicals,* and *Legal Resource Index.*

# CONGRESSIONAL SERIES

In previous sections we have focused on the publications of Congress as they related to legislative tracing. But Congress also issues many noncongressional publications, especially some documents associated with the presidency. For example, the *Economic Report of the President* is issued as a Congressional Document. The House and Senate Document series issues reports to be made to the Congress by the president. The GAO's annual *Reports to be Made to Congress,* a complete listing of all presidential reports to be made to Congress, is itself issued as a House document. The kinds of presidential documents that can be found in the congressional series follow.

# House and Senate Journals

The *Journals* include presidential addresses, messages, and communications to the Congress in general. Veto messages can be found in the *Journal* of the chamber in which the bill was initiated. The *Journals* use similar, but not identical, subject indexing; for the House of Representatives it is the "President," and for the Senate it is the "President of the United States."

# Congressional Record

The *Congressional Record* includes presidential addresses, executive orders, proclamations, messages, and statements. Presidential documents and actions are indexed under "President of the United States." You can also use a subject approach to find presidential materials.

# The Serial Set

The *Serial Set* is a Congressional series of publications, selected and compiled under the direction of Congress. Begun in 1789, it contains a wealth of information about Congressional activities and constitutes a historical record of the work and accomplishments of the Congress. The *Serial Set* includes documents published by Congress, as well as noncongressional materials originating in executive departments, independent agencies, commissions, and nongovernmental bodies required by their incorporation to submit a report to Congress. Although the documents differ in origin, they are selected because of their value to the Congress in fulfilling its duties and responsibilities. In general, the *Serial Set* collection consists of the following types of publications:

1. Congressional journals
2. Congressional manuals, directories, and other internal documents
3. Congressional reports on public and private bills
4. Special investigatory reports conducted by or commissioned by Congressional committees
5. Recurring reports to be made to Congress by executive departments and agencies
6. Executive publications ordered by Congress for inclusion
7. Memorial addresses
8. Annual or special reports of nongovernmental bodies required by law to report to Congress

The Superintendent of Documents sells some of the documents issued in the *Serial Set,* such as the *Congressional Directory, House Manual,* and *Senate Manual,* to provide for a greater distribution to the public.

The best access to *Serial Set* publications is through Congressional Information Service's *CIS U.S. Serial Set Index.* The twelve-part index covers the period from 1789 to 1969. It includes a comprehensive subject index, an index of names of individuals and organizations named as recipients of private relief or related actions of Congress, a numerical list of reports and documents, and a schedule of Serial volumes. While the *CIS U.S. Serial Set Index* is quite easy to use, the *Serial Set* collection does have a number of idiosyncracies. Seeking the help of a documents librarian when trying to identify a document will often save time.

## Senate Documents

The Senate Executive Document series includes the messages from the president to the Senate Foreign Relations Committee regarding the text of treaties and other international agreements. The Senate Foreign Relations Committee, meeting in closed session, reviews the materials and issues its report and the materials to the Senate as a Senate Executive Document.

## Finding Aids

The best finding aids for the *Congressional Record, House Journal,* and *Senate Journal* are the indexes contained in each of those series. The *Congressional Index, CIS Index,* and *Federal Index* can also be used for identifying presidential materials in the *Congressional Record.* The *Congressional Index* has a "Division" which deals with the response of Congress to presidential treaties, nominations, and reorganization plans. The Senate Executive Documents are indexed in the *Monthly Catalog* and *CIS Index.*

# TREATIES AND AGREEMENTS

This section describes the role of the president in the treaty-making process and foreign affairs in general. Because the president has the power to initiate treaties and conduct negotiations, he has far more latitude than in the legislative process. Since treaties and agreements comprise a special category of presidential documents, we are covering them separately from all of the other kinds of documents.

## State Department

The Department of State, so named in 1789 following the election of George Washington, is the oldest department of the executive branch. The Constitution places the whole of the diplomatic corp under the command of the president. Historically, this department and the Secretary have been an arm of the president.

### GUIDES TO PUBLICATIONS

The Department of State is one of the most voluminous publishers in the executive branch. Its publications cover many aspects of foreign affairs and diplomacy. The best indexes for identifying these are the *Monthly Catalog* and *GPO Sales Publications Reference File*. Two publications put out by the Department of State are especially useful for studying the president's power to enter into treaties and executive agreements.

*Department of State Bulletin*. Washington, DC: U.S. Government Printing Office, 1939– .
   From 1939 to 1977, the *Bulletin* was a weekly publication with semiannual indexes. Since then it has been issued monthly with an annual index. As the official record of foreign policy, it is an invaluable tool for studying treaties. Documents included in the *Bulletin* are presidential addresses; remarks; radio and television excerpts; correspondence and memoranda; exchanges and greetings with foreign dignitaries and official joint communiques; messages and reports to Congress; and news conferences and proclamations relating to foreign affairs. The annual index lists these materials under the entry, "Presidential Documents." There are also sections in each issue devoted to the ratification of treaties and announcing executive agreements. In addition to its own index, the *Bulletin* is also indexed in *Public Affairs Information Service Bulletin,* the *Index to U.S. Government Periodicals,* and *Reader's Guide to Periodical Literature*.

*The Foreign Relations of the United States, Diplomatic Papers*. Washington, DC: U.S. Government Printing Office, 1861– .
   This series, usually published on an annual basis, contains records on foreign policy and diplomatic practice. A variety of materials can be found in this set, including presidential documents, some treaties, and diplomatic correspondence and reports.

## DIPLOMATIC CORRESPONDENCE AND DOCUMENTS

These collections contain some presidential materials and are useful for the study of treaties for the periods covered.

Richardson, James D., comp. *A Compilation of the Messages and Papers of the Confederacy, Including the Diplomatic Correspondence, 1861–1865*. 2 vols. Nashville: United States Publishing Co., 1905.

*Diplomatic Correspondence of the United States: Concerning the Independence of the Latin-American Nations*. 3 vols. Edited by William R. Manning. New York: Oxford University Press, 1925.

*Diplomatic Correspondence of the United States: Inter-American Affairs, 1831–1860*. 12 vols. Edited by William R. Manning. Washington, DC: Carnegie Endowment for International Peace, 1932–1939.

*The Diplomatic Correspondence of the United States of America: From the Signing of the Definitive Treaty of Peace, 10th September, 1783, to the Adoption of the Constitution, March 4, 1789*. 3 vols. 2nd ed. Edited by F. P. Blair and John C. Rives. Washington, DC: Blair and Rives, 1837.

*Journal Index to the Published Volumes of the Diplomatic Correspondence and Foreign Relations of the United States, 1861–1899.* Washington, DC: U.S. Government Printing Office, 1902.

*The Revolutionary Diplomatic Correspondence of the United States.* 6 vols. Edited by Francis Wharton. Washington, DC: U.S. Government Printing Office, 1889.

# Treaties

Whether referred to as an accord, protocol, compact, or convention, any international agreement between two or more nations that is governed by international law submitted to the Senate by the president is a treaty.

## TREATY PUBLICATIONS

Four compilations provide complete texts for all treaties and executive agreements from 1776 to the present. These four works are all a student needs for finding a treaty.

U.S. Department of State. *Treaties in Force.* Washington, DC: U.S. Government Printing Office, 1929– .
This annual publication, referred to as TIF, lists treaties and agreements of the United States when the treaty is still in effect. The first part lists bilateral treaties and other agreements by country and then by topic. The second part lists multinational agreements arranged by subject and then by country under the subject. The series also cites superceding and terminations of treaty articles and notes amendments and supplementary treaties. The monthly *Department of State Bulletin* will keep you up to date.

U.S. Department of State. *Treaties and Other International Acts Series.* Washington, DC: U.S. Government Printing Office, 1945– .
This series, referred to as TAIS, is a continuation of *Treaty Series,* which covers the years 1908–1945 and the *Executive Agreement Series,* which covers the years 1929–1945. Consequently, the serially numbered treaties and agreements begin with the number 1501. Each text is published separately in pamphlet form six to twelve months after it is in force. The text, printed in English and the language of the other country, includes important dates in its development, the president's proclamation, and correspondence.

U.S. Department of State. *United States Treaties and Other International Agreements.* Washington, DC: U.S. Government Printing Office, 1950– .
This annual publication, referred to as UST, provides the text of treaties and agreements proclaimed during the preceding year in the language of the original instrument. It contains a subject and country index. Before 1950, the treaties and agreements were published in the *United States Statutes at Large.* This annual multivolume set (UST) cumulates and replaces TAIS.

Bevans, Charles I. *Treaties and Other International Agreements of the United*

*States of America 1776–1949.* Washington, DC: U.S. Government Printing Office, 1968– .
This compilation contains all of the treaty and agreement texts prior to 1950 and is the most comprehensive collection of treaties. Each volume has an index, and there are cumulative analytical indexes. This set is commonly referred to as "Bevans."

## COMPILATIONS AND LISTS OF TREATIES

The following volumes provide a listing of treaties, agreements, and other international acts for various time periods. While all of these can be found in the four titles just cited, the following may be easier to use for specific time periods or subject matters.

Bioren, John, and W. John Duane. *Laws of the United States.* 10 vols. Philadelphia, 1815–1845.

Bryan, Henry L. *Compilation of Treaties in Force.* Washington, DC: U.S. Government Printing Office, 1899.

Davis, J. C. Bancroft. *Treaties and Conventions Concluded Between the United States of America and Other Powers Since July 4, 1776.* Washington, DC: U.S. Government Printing Office, 1871.

Elliot, Jonathan, ed. *The American Diplomatic Code: Embracing a Collection of Treaties and Conventions Between the United States and Foreign Powers from 1778 to 1834.* 2 vols. Washington, DC: by the editor, 1834.

*Executive Agreement Series.* Washington, DC: U.S. Government Printing Office, 1926–1946.

Hasse, Adelaide R. *Index to United States Documents Relating to Foreign Affairs, 1828–1861.* Washington, DC: Carnegie Institute, 1914–1921.

Haswell, John H. *Treaties and Conventions Concluded Between the United States of America and Other Powers Since July 4, 1776.* Washington, DC: U.S. Government Printing Office, 1889.

*A List of Treaties and Other International Acts of the United States of America in Force on December 31, 1932.* Washington, DC: U.S. Government Printing Office, 1933.

*A List of Treaties and Other International Acts of the United States of America in Force on December 31, 1941.* Washington, DC: U.S. Government Printing Office, 1944.

*List of Treaties Submitted to the Senate, 1789–1934.* Washington, DC: U.S. Government Printing Office, 1935.

*List of Treaties Submitted to the Senate, 1789–1931, Which Have Not Gone into Force, October 1, 1932.* Washington, DC: U.S. Government Printing Office, 1932.

*List of Treaties Submitted to the Senate, 1935–1944.* Washington, DC: U.S. Government Printing Office, 1945.

Miller, David Hunter, comp. *Treaties and Other International Acts of the United States of America.* 8 vols. Washington, DC: U.S. Government Printing Office, 1931–1948.

*Numerical List of the Treaty Series, Executive Agreement Series and Treaties and other International Acts Series.* U.S. Department of State, no. 3787. Washington, DC: U.S. Government Printing Office, 1950.

Rockhill, W. W., ed. *Treaties, Conventions, Agreements, Ordinances, etc., Relating to China and Korea (October 1904–January 1908).* Washington, DC: U.S. Government Printing Office, 1908.

Rockhill, W. W., ed. *Treaties and Conventions with or Concerning China and Korea, 1894–1904, Together with Various State Papers and Documents Affecting Foreign Interests.* Washington, DC: U.S. Government Printing Office, 1904.

*Subject Index of Treaties and Executive Agreement Series, July 1, 1931.* Washington, DC: U.S. Government Printing Office, 1932.

*A Tentative List of Treaty Collections.* Washington, DC: U.S. Government Printing Office, 1919.

*Treaties, Conventions, International Acts, Protocols, and Agreements Between the U.S.A. and Other Powers, 1776–1937.* Washington, DC: U.S. Government Printing Office, 1910–1938.

*Treaty Developments, 1944.* Washington, DC: U.S. Government Printing Office, 1945.

*Treaty Information Bulletin.* 5 vols. Washington, DC: U.S. Government Printing Office, 1929–1939.

*United States Treaty Developments.* Washington, DC: U.S. Government Printing Office, 1947–1951.

*United States Treaty Series.* Washington, DC: U.S. Government Printing Office, 1908–1946.

U.S. Congress. House. Committee on Foreign Affairs. *Collective Defense Treaties.* Committee Print. 91st Cong., 1st sess., 1969.

*United States Department of State Catalogue of Treaties 1814–1918.* Washington, DC: U.S. Government Printing Office, 1919.

## DOCUMENT COLLECTIONS

The following document collections include various kinds of presidential papers, including messages, addresses, statements, reports, treaties and diplomatic notes.

Lowrie, Walter, and Mathew St. Clair Clark, eds. *American State Papers: Documents, Legislative and Executive, of the Congress of the United States. Class 1, Foreign Relations.* Washington, DC: Gales and Seaton, 1832–1859.

Miller, Robert W. *United States Policy Toward Germany, 1945–1955: U.S. Government Documents on Germany.* Frankfort, Germany: Europe Archiv, 1956.

Stebbins, Richard P. *Documents on American Foreign Relations, 1938/39.* New York: Harper & Row, 1838.

U.S. Department of State. *A Decade of American Foreign Policy: Basic Documents, 1941–49.* Washington, DC: U.S. Government Printing Office, 1950.

U.S. Department of State. *American Foreign Policy: Current Documents.* Edited by Peter V. Curl. Washington, DC: U.S. Government Printing Office, 1956.

U.S. Department of State. *American Foreign Policy, 1950–1955: Basic Documents.* Washington, DC: U.S. Government Printing Office, 1957.

# Reference Guides

In the following two sections we identify some of the most useful commercial guides to treaty information.

## FINDING AIDS

While TIF, TIAS, UST, and Bevans are the primary sources for finding treaties, there are several commercial guides that also provide useful information.

Kavas, Igor I., and M. A. Michael, comps. *United States Treaties and Other International Agreements Cumulative Index, 1776–1949.* Buffalo: William S. Stein, 1975.
    This four-volume set can be used to identify treaties and agreements by their TIAS number, date, country, and subject.

Kavas, Igor I., and Adolph Sprudas, comps. *UST Cumulative Index, 1950–1970.* Buffalo: William S. Stein, 1973–1977.

This five-volume set provides the same kind of access as the above entry. This series is also updated by a looseleaf service, which is cumulated every five years.

Wiktor, Christian L. *Unperfected Treaties of the United States, 1976–.* Dobbs Ferry, NY: Oceana, 1976.
This set is an annotated compilation of treaties that were not approved by the Senate or ratified by the president.

As we mentioned earlier, Senate Executive Documents are issued by the Congress and indexed and abstracted in *CIS/INDEX* and *CIS/ANNUAL*. Also, *Shepard's United States Citations: Statute Edition* contains a section entitled "United States Treaties and Other International Agreements." This can be used to determine what modifications, renewals, terminations, revisions, and court decisions have affected a treaty.

In Appendices 9 and 10, we have summarized where to look to find information regarding the treaty-making process. The tools listed in Appendix 10, p. 240, include both publications and bibliographic tools. Appendix 11, p. 243, identifies where one can find information regarding modifications of treaties as well as legislative and judicial histories. The best sources for finding information about current treaty developments are the *Department of State Bulletin*, the *Weekly Compilation of Presidential Documents, TIAS, Shepard's United States Citations, CIS/INDEX,* and the *Monthly Catalog.*

## BIBLIOGRAPHIES

The bibliographies and guides listed below are useful in a variety of ways. In addition to providing citations to secondary materials, especially books and articles, they also contain information on many of the treaty compilations previously cited. They also contain references to other sources of information relating to the study of foreign affairs such as archives, manuscript collections, documentary collections, yearbooks, atlases, oral histories, and special collections. All three of these guides are superb reference tools and should be consulted in any study of the role of the president in foreign affairs.

Burns, Richard Dean, ed. *Guide to American Foreign Relations Since 1700.* Santa Barbara, CA: ABC-Clio, 1983.

Bemis, Samuel Flagg. *Guide to the Diplomatic History of the United States, 1775–1921.* Washington, DC: U.S. Government Printing Office, 1935.

Plishke, Elmer. *U.S. Foreign Relations: A Guide to Information Sources.* Detroit: Gale Research Co., 1980.

# EXECUTIVE OFFICE

The offices of the Executive Office of the President provide another source of information about the activities of the presidency. In this section we will identify some of the major publications of the Office of Management and Budget, the Central Intelligence Agency, the National Security Council, and the Council of Economic Advisors. Additional divisions in the Executive Office of the President we will not discuss are the White House Office; the Office of Federal Procurement Policy; the Office of Policy Development; the Office of the United States Trade Representatives; the Council on Environmental Quality; the Office of Science and Technology Policy; and the Office of Administration. For a complete list of the offices that have been under the Executive Office, see Appendix 12, p. 244.

In general the best tools for identifying publications of the Executive Office are the *Monthly Catalog, GPO Publications Reference File*, and *CIS/INDEX*. *CIS/INDEX* is especially useful for finding testimony given before committees by individuals in the Executive Office, such as the Director of the OMB and the Chair of the CEA.

# Office of Management and Budget

The Office of Management and Budget (OMB) issues the following publications. All executive budget publications are noted in the *Weekly Compilation of Presidential Documents* and are indexed in the *Monthly Catalog*.

*The Budget of the United States Government*. Washington, DC: U.S. Government Printing Office, 1972– .
   This annual publication contains the president's message on the budget. It summarizes his proposed plans for the budget and any recommended taxes.

*The Budget of the United States Government, Appendix*. Washington, DC: U.S. Government Printing Office, 1972– .
   This annual publication accompanies the OMB publication, *The Budget of the United States Government*. It gives detailed estimates for the budget arranged by agency and account. It is a line item identification of the budget.

*The U.S. Budget in Brief*. Washington, DC: U.S. Government Printing Office, 1972– .
   This is an abridged version of OMB's *Budget of the United States Government*. For quickly finding information on the budget, this publication is the one to consult.

*Major Themes and Additional Budget Details*. Washington, DC: U.S. Government Printing Office, 1983– .
   This annual publication describes how the budget affects the president's program.

*Special Analyses, Budget of the United States Government*. Washington, DC: U.S. Government Printing Office, 1969– .
   This publication provides an analysis of presidential programs in terms of the budget. This series contains statistical data, charts, and tables.

Other Office of Management and Budget publications are listed below.

*Catalog of Federal Domestic Assistance Program.* Washington, DC: U.S. Government Printing Office, 1965– .

*Social Indicators.* Washington, DC: U.S. Government Printing Office, 1973– .

*Statistical Services of the United States Government.* Washington, DC: U.S. Government Printing Office, 1975.

*Federal Statistical Directory.* Washington, DC: U.S. Government Printing Office, 1955– .

For information concerning the Office of Management and Budget the following work is most helpful.

Berman, Larry. *The Office of Management and Budget and the Presidency, 1921–1979.* Princeton: Princeton University Press, 1979.

# Central Intelligence Agency

The CIA publishes maps and atlases, National Foreign Assessment Center publications, as well as *The World Factbook.* There are no bibliographies, indexes, or catalogs that list all documents published by the CIA. Many of the publications, such as directories, technical reports, journals, and dictionaries, are released by the Document Expediting Project (DOCEX) of the Library of Congress. Some publications, such as the *National Basic Intelligence Factbook,* are available from the Government Printing Office. The researcher may check the *GPO Sales Publications Reference File* (PRF) to ascertain what CIA documents are available from the Government Printing Office. The Public Affairs Office of the CIA will provide general information, and you can also consult a publication of the National Foreign Assessment Center, *CIA Publications Released to the Public Through Library of Congress DOCEX: Listing for 1972–1977.* Annual updates of this bibliography have also been published. To identify background materials concerning the CIA and documents of the CIA, review the following works:

Cline, Marjorie W., Carle E. Christiansen, and Judith M. Fontaine. *Scholar's Guide to Intelligence Literature: Bibliography of the Russell J. Bowen Collection.* Frederick, MD: University Publications of America, 1983.

Goehlert, Robert, and Elizabeth R. Hoffmeister. *The CIA: A Bibliography.* Monticello, IL: Vance Bibliographies, 1980.

Leary, William M., ed. *The Central Intelligence Agency, History and Documents.* University: University of Alabama Press, 1984.

# National Security Council

While most NSC publications are still classified, some have been made available to the public. University Publications of America has collected many of the public documents and published them as microfilm sets. Each set includes a printed guide. The following four collections have been published:

*Documents of the National Security Council, 1947–1977.* Frederick, MD: University Publications of America, 1980. Microfilm.

*Documents of the National Security Council: First Supplement.* Frederick, MD: University Publications of America, 1981. Microfilm.

*Documents of the National Security Council: Second Supplement.* Frederick, MD: University Publications of America, 1983. Microfilm.

*Minutes of Meetings of the National Security Council, with Special Advisory Reports.* Frederick, MD: University Publications of America, 1983. Microfilm.

## Council of Economic Advisors

The Council of Economic Advisors (CEA) consists of three members apppointed by the president with Congressional consent. They serve the president by providing economic advice based on their analysis of the national economy and federal economic programs and assist in preparing the president's economic reports to Congress. They issue the following publications:

*Economic Report of the President.* Washington, DC: U.S. Government Printing Office, 1947– .
    This publication is the president's economic report to Congress and the annual report of the Council of Economic Advisors. It covers economic developments, trends, and recommendations.

*International Economic Report of the President.* Washington, DC: U.S. Government Printing Office, 1973– .
    This annual publication deals with the economic aspects of the United States in relation to the rest of the world.

*Economic Indicators.* Washington, DC: U.S. Government Printing Office, 1948– .

# PRESIDENTIAL ADVISORY COMMISSIONS

Advisory commissions and committees are established to assist the president and are listed in the *U.S. Government Manual* in the section, "Guide to Boards, Committees and Commissions." The commissions and committees issue reports that cover their findings. Information on publications of these bodies appears in the *Monthly Catalog.* The publications are indexed by key word, title, and subject, but not by popular name. When a report of a presidential commission or committee is known under a popular name its official title can be identified in *Popular Names of U.S. Government Reports Catalog,* which lists reports alphabetically under popular name. Androit's *Guide to U.S. Government Publications* (McLean, VA: Documents Index, 1973– ) also includes names of commissions and committees in its index.

# Guides to Reports

Information on presidential commissions and committees can be located in the following works.

U.S. Office of Management and Budget. *Federal Advisory Committees.* Washington, DC: U.S. Government Printing Office, 1973–1974.

This Office of Management and Budget report gives information on every advisory committee in the executive branch. For each entry the committee name, date, authority for citation, reporting date, functions, publications, meeting dates, and cost of funding the committee are given. It is abstracted in the *CIS/INDEX.*

U.S. General Services Administration. *Federal Advisory Committees, Annual Report of the President.* Washington, DC: U.S. Government Printing Office, 1973– .

This annual report lists all of the advisory committees within the White House; Executive Office of the President; departments; independent establishments; committees within committees; commissions; or councils. It is arranged alphabetically by title.

*Federal Register.* Washington, DC: U.S. Government Printing Office, 1936– .

The *Federal Register* publishes notices about the establishment of Federal Advisory Committees and Commissions. It also notes when their meetings are to take place.

Sullivan, Linda, ed. *Encyclopedia of Governmental Advisory Organizations: A Reference Guide to Federal Agency, Interagency, and Government-Related Boards, Committees, Councils, Conferences, and Other Similar Units Serving in an Advisory, Consultative, or Investigative Capacity.* 3rd ed. Detroit: Gale Research Company, 1981.

This work identifies committees, boards, councils, and other advisory groups serving the federal government. It provides the office name, popular name, telephone, address, dates, authority, membership, staff, activities, publications, and subsidiary units for each entry. There is a cumulative index by subject and name.

*New Governmental Advisory Organizations.* Detroit: Gale Research Company, 1976– .

This Gale publication updates their *Encyclopedia of Governmental Advisory Organizations.* It is issued periodically between editions.

Tollefson, Alan M., and H. C. Chang, eds. *A Bibliography of Presidential Commissions, Committees, Councils, Panels, and Task Forces, 1961–1972.*

St. Paul: Government Publications Division, University of Minnesota Libraries, 1973.

This selective bibliography lists alphabetically 243 publications by advisory groups. There are indexes for personal names, titles, and subjects by key word.

Korman, Richard I., comp. *Guide to Presidential Advisory Commissions, 1973–1981.* Westport, CT: Meckler Books, 1982.

This guide is divided into three main sections. The first section is a chronological listing of advisory commissions and provides identifying information for each commission. Section two lists and identifies commission members alphabetically. Section three lists, along with an abstract, reports made by the commissions.

# Selected Commissions

Listed below are some of the recent presidential commissions, boards, and task forces that have issued reports and publications. This small sample gives an idea of the range of commissions. Some commissions are in existence for a relatively short period of time, while others have long histories. The easiest way to determine which commission reports are available is to check the *Monthly Catalog* or *GPO Publications Reference File.* All of the commissions below have published reports since 1979.

### Selected List of Boards, Committees, and Commissions

President's Commission on Drunk Driving

President's Commission for the Study of Ethical Problems in Medicine

President's Commission for a National Agenda for the Eighties

President's Commission on Coal

President's Commission on Foreign Language and International Studies

President's Commission on Housing

President's Commission on Mental Health

President's Commission on the Accident at Three Mile Island

President's Commission on Pension Policy

President's Committee on Employment of the Handicapped

President's Task Force on Regulatory Relief

President's Task Force on Victims of Crime

# CHAPTER 2

# Secondary Sources for the Presidency

This chapter presents all of the secondary resources useful for researching the presidency. While the tools described here deal with the presidency as an institution, they can also be used to research individual presidents as well. We have included as many sources as possible relating to the presidency, drawing upon tools available in the fields of history, political science, law, and the social sciences in general. Though researching the presidency is difficult, especially in regard to primary sources, there is a wealth of secondary material.

## RESEARCH GUIDES

Only two guides attempt to identify sources of information about the presidency. While the first book does contain citations to reference books, it is more of a bibliography about the presidency. The second book focuses on approaches to the study of the presidency, such as conceptualization, quantitative techniques, interviewing, etc.

Davison, Kenneth E. *The American Presidency: A Guide to Information Sources*. Detroit: Gale Research Company, 1982.
    This annotated bibliography of books, articles, and government publications dealing with the presidency and presidents is divided into two parts. The first deals with the presidency; the second deals with the presidents. Part one has eleven chapters: Aids to Research; Office of the President; General Works; First Ladies; Presidential Elections; Functions and Powers of the President; Institutional Presidency; Problems of the Presidency; Presidential Documents; Presidential Libraries; and Museums and Private Organizations and Publishers. The second part includes materials on each of the presidents. There are author, title, and subject indexes.

Edwards, George C., and Stephen J. Wayne. *Studying the Presidency.* Knoxville: University of Tennessee Press, 1983.
  The authors have organized their book into two parts. The first part deals with approaches, cases, concepts, and analyses used in the study of the presidency. Part two describes sources used in researching presidential studies (indexes, congressional documents, legal documents, and presidential libraries). The last two chapters discuss interviewing presidential aides.

# ALMANACS

Most of these annual almanacs can be used as ready reference sources. While they differ in format, they all contain essentially the same information—brief presidential biographies, as well as information on vice-presidents, first ladies, cabinets, etc. Election returns since 1789 are given on a national basis, including the electoral vote, popular vote, and some percentages or pluralities. The most recent election results are broken down by state. These almanacs often vary from year to year in regard to the data presented. Usually, almanacs published following an election year will include somewhat more detailed statistics (such as election results broken down by county). They allow quick and easy checking of statistics on presidential elections, but these should only be regarded as the initial step in scholarly research.

*World Almanac and Book of Facts.* New York: Newspaper Enterprise Association, 1868– .

*Information Please Almanac.* New York: Simon and Schuster, 1947– .

*The Official Associated Press Almanac.* Maplewood, NJ: Hammond Almanac, 1974– .

# RESOURCE MATERIALS

Congressional Quarterly is a major publisher of materials on national affairs. It reports on all aspects of the presidency, Congress, Supreme Court, and the policy process. Congressional Quarterly's publications have the reputation of being factually reliable and up-to-date. Anyone who is unfamiliar with these publications should spend some time browsing through them. Many of these publications are relatively inexpensive to acquire. In addition to their reference works, Congressional Quarterly issues special paperbacks on current topics and has several paperbacks in print related to the presidency. A few examples are

*President Reagan.* Washington, DC: Congressional Quarterly, 1981.

*President Carter 1980.* Washington, DC: Congressional Quarterly, 1981.

*Elections '82.* Washington, DC: Congressional Quarterly, 1982.

*The Politics of Shared Power: Congress and the Executive,* by Louis Fisher. Washington, DC: Congressional Quarterly, 1981.

*The Presidency and the Political System,* by Michael Nelson. Washington, DC: Congressional Quarterly, 1983.

*Invitation to Struggle: Congress, the President and Foreign Policy,* by Cecil V. Crabb and Pat Holt. Washington, DC: Congressional Quarterly, 1980.

*A Tide of Discontent: The 1980 Elections and Their Meanings,* by Ellis Sandoz and Cecil V. Crabb. Washington, DC: Congressional Quarterly, 1981.

*Change and Continuity in the 1980 Elections,* by Paul R. Abraham, John H. Aldrich and David W. Rohde. Washington, DC: Congressional Quarterly, 1982.

Congressional Quarterly also publishes numerous other titles on specific issues and aspects of government. Those related to the study of the presidency are

*Financing Politics,* by Herbert Alexander, 3rd ed. Washington, DC: Congressional Quarterly, 1984.

*The Washington Lobby,* 4th ed. Washington, DC: Congressional Quarterly, 1982.

*Interest Group Politics,* edited by Allan J. Cigler and Burdett A. Lomis. Washington, DC: Congressional Quarterly, 1983.

*Dollar Politics,* 3rd ed. Washington, DC: Congressional Quarterly, 1982.

*Budgeting for America.* Washington, DC: Congressional Quarterly, 1982.

*Mass Media and American Politics,* by Doris A. Graber. Washington, DC: Congressional Quarterly, 1980.

*Interest Groups, Lobbying and Policymaking,* by Norman J. Ornstein and Shirley Elder. Washington, DC: Congressional Quarterly, 1978.

A catalog of publications is available on request from Congressional Quarterly, 1414 22nd St. N.W., Washington, DC, 20037.

*Congressional Quarterly Almanac.* Washington, DC: Congressional Quarterly, 1945– .
This annual edition is published each spring. The *Almanac* is more than a synthesis of material issued in the *Weekly Reports,* for it summarizes and cross-indexes the previous year in Congress. It includes accounts of major legislation enacted, presidential programs and initiatives, analyses of Supreme Court decisions, election results of any federal elections contested in

the last year, an examination of lobbying activities, and other special reports. Like the *CQ Weekly Report,* the *Almanac* records the roll-call vote for every member of Congress.

*Congress and the Nation, 1945–1980.* 5 vols. Washington, DC: Congressional Quarterly, 1965–1981.
This multivolume reference set spans thirty-five years and seven presidential administrations. A well-organized reference work, it provides quick access to descriptions of major legislation, national, and international events. The set is an excellent chronological history of major legislative programs and political developments during each Congress and executive administration, including biographical information, major votes, key judicial decisions, and election issues. Additional volumes in the series are issued at the end of each presidential term in office.

*Guide to Current American Government.* Washington, DC: Congressional Quarterly, 1968– .
This series serves as a handbook to current developments in the American political system. Issued each spring and fall, it covers the general areas of the presidency, Congress, the judiciary, intergovernmental relations, and lobbies. This series can be used as an up-to-date supplement to both the *Almanac* and *Congress and the Nation.*

*Editorial Research Reports.* Washington, DC: Congressional Quarterly, 1923– .
This series follows a journal format and is issued four times a month. The *Reports* provide documented research on a full range of current affairs, from the arts to welfare. Each *Report* gives the reader the pros and cons of the issue being discussed. It includes bibliographies for further study. The *Reports* are indexed in *Public Affairs Information Service Bulletin.*

*Congressional Roll Call.* Washington, DC: Congressional Quarterly, 1970– .
This special series of CQ publications began with the first session of the 91st Congress. The volumes begin with an analysis and legislative description of key votes on major issues followed by special voting studies, such as freshman voting, bipartisanship, voting participation, etc. The remainder of the volume is a member-by-member analysis, in chronological order, of all roll-call votes in the House and Senate. There is also a roll-call subject index. In the compilation of roll-call votes, there is a brief synopsis of each bill, the total vote and vote by party affiliation. The indices record whether the member voted for or against, paired for or against, announced for or against, was polled by CQ as for or against, voted "present," voted "present" to avoid a conflict of interest, or did not vote or make his position known. The *CQ Weekly Report* and *CQ Almanac* present voting indexes in the same format.

*Guide to Congress.* 3rd ed. Washington, DC: Congressional Quarterly, 1982.
Concentrating on Congress, this handbook explains how that body works,

beginning with an account of its origins and history. There are chapters on the structure and procedures of Congress and its relations with the other branches of government. The volume is most valuable to the student or researcher who is seeking a basic and thorough understanding of how Congress operates. Several sections in this guide relate to the presidency—constitutional beginnings, power of impeachment, power to elect the president, foreign affairs and defense powers, and congressional-executive relationships.

*Historic Documents.* Washington, DC: Congressional Quarterly, 1972– .
    This annual series reprints important documents in chronological order. The volume includes significant presidential statements and messages, speeches, treaties, debates, court decisions, proclamations, government reports, and documents and includes a detailed subject index.

Commager, Henry Steel. *Documents on American History.* New York: Appleton-Century-Crofts, 1968.
    This single-volume reference book contains an excellent selection of historical documents, including presidential messages and speeches, treaties, Supreme Court decisions and other documents. Each document is accompanied with explanatory notes and citations to secondary sources.

# DICTIONARIES

Dictionaries can be used in a variety of ways for studying the presidency. They are good tools for finding the answers to reference questions, such as a date, a definition, the name of an individual, etc. The more scholarly and detailed dictionaries provide short essays rather than dictionary style entries.

## Political Science

These dictionaries contain a variety of facts. In addition to definitions of political terms and concepts, you can find entries for legal cases, court decisions, histories of government agencies, and biographical sketches. Most dictionaries in political science contain hundreds of entries relevant to the study of the presidency.

Dunner, Joseph. *Dictionary of Poltical Science.* New York: Philosophical Library, 1964.

Elliot, Jeffrey M., and Sheikh R. Ali. *The Presidential-Congressional Political Dictionary.* Santa Barbara, CA: ABC-Clio, 1984.

Heimanson, Rudolph. *Dictionary of Poltical Science and Law.* Dobbs Ferry, NY: Oceana, 1967.

Holt, Sol. *The Dictionary of American Government.* Rev ed. New York: Woodhill Press, 1970.

McCarthy, Eugene J. *Dictionary of American Politics*. New York: Macmillan, 1968.

Plano, Jack C., and Milton Greenberg. *The American Political Dictionary*. 6th ed. New York: Holt, Rinehart and Winston, 1982.

Smith, Edward C., and Arnold J. Zurcher. *Dictionary of American Politics*. 2nd ed. New York: Barnes and Noble, 1968.

Tallman, Marjorie. *Dictionary of American Government*. Paterson, NJ: Littlefield, Adams and Co., 1968.

Whisker, James B. *A Dictionary of Concepts on American Politics*. New York: John Wiley, 1980.

# Legal

Legal dictionaries are especially useful for finding brief definitions and pronunciations, legal terms and phrases, judicial opinions, major statutes, and biographies. They are particularly good sources for finding information on the role of the president in the judicial process, such as relations with the Supreme Court, constitutional issues, and significant legal decisions.

Anderson, William S., ed. *Ballentine's Law Dictionary, with Pronunciations*. San Francisco: Bancroft-Whitney Co., 1969.

Black, Henry C. *Black's Law Dictionary*. 5th ed. St. Paul: West Publishing Co., 1979.

Bouvier, John. *Law Dictionary*. Cleveland: Banks-Baldwin Law Co., 1948.

Gifis, Steven H. *Law Dictionary*. Rev ed. Woodbury, NY: Barron's Educational Series, Inc., 1983.

Kling, Samuel G. *The Legal Encyclopedia and Dictionary*. New York: Pocket Books, 1970.

Radin, Max. *Radin Law Dictionary*. Rev ed. Dobbs Ferry, NY: Oceana Publications, 1970.

Chandler, Ralph C., Richard A. Enslen, and Peter G. Renstrom. *The Constitutional Law Dictionary: Individual Rights*. Santa Barbara, CA: ABC-Clio, 1984.

Volkell, Randolph Z. *Quick Legal Terminology*. New York: Wiley, 1979.

# History

These dictionaries can be used to find important dates, biographies, and significant historical events. When you run across an event, name, or issue with which you are unfamiliar, the fastest way to access basic information is to refer to a dictionary.

Adams, James T. *Dictionary of American History.* Rev ed. New York: Scribner's, 1976.

Martin, Michael, and Leonard Gelber. *Dictionary of American History.* Totowa, NJ: Littlefield, Adams and Co., 1978.

# ENCYCLOPEDIAS

Most students and researchers tend to overlook encyclopedias in their search for information, but these are excellent sources of information on the presidency. The encyclopedias cited below contain essays for each entry. The entries are usually written by experts in the field and provide concise overviews and histories. The political science encyclopedias are useful not only for finding information about the presidency, but for information on research concepts and methodologies as well. The legal encyclopedias are especially useful for students and researchers whose knowledge of legal studies is limited. These encyclopedias are the first place to look before searching for documents, legal cases, etc.

## Political Science

Greenstein, Fred I., and Nelson W. Polsby. *The Handbook of Political Science.* 8 vols. Reading, MA: Addison-Wesley Publishing Co., 1975.
> The volumes in this work are arranged according to eight major classifications: Volume 1: Political Science: Scope and Theory; Volume 2: Micropolitical Theory; Volume 3: Macropolitical Theory; Volume 4: Nongovernmental Politics; Volume 5: Governmental Institutions and Processes; Volume 6: Policies and Policymaking; Volume 7: Strategies of Inquiry; and Volume 8: International Politics. A cumulative subject index is provided in the last volume.

*Encyclopaedia of the Social Sciences.* Edited by Edwin Seligman. New York: Macmillan, 1930–1935.
> This encyclopedia contains scholarly articles on the concerns of the social sciences. The articles supply bibliographies and are signed by the author. The entries are arranged alphabetically.

*International Encyclopedia of the Social Sciences.* 17 vols. Edited by David L. Sills. New York: Macmillan, 1968.
> Articles with a general subject matter are arranged alphabetically in this encyclopedia. There are cross-references and an index to aid the reader in

finding materials. The articles, written by social scientists, provide material
on the presidency relating to the disciplines of political science, law, history,
economics, and sociology. This encyclopedia is not a revision of the earlier
*Encyclopaedia of the Social Sciences.*

# Legal

*American Jurisprudence.* 2nd ed. San Francisco: Bancroft-Whitney, 1962– .
This encyclopedia contains treatises covering U.S. federal and state law.
Each volume is indexed, and there is also an index to the whole set. There are
annual supplements.

*Corpus Secundum Secumdum.* New York: American Law Book Co., 1937–
1960, 1961.
Over 400 articles on U.S. law are arranged under topical headings in this
work. Citations are given to law cases. They are indexed in each volume, as
well as in a separate index. There are annual supplements.

*The Guide to American Law: Everyone's Legal Encyclopedia.* 12 vols. St. Paul:
West Publishing Co., 1983.
This encyclopedia contains entries for over 5,000 topics, including articles
on legal cases, statutes, terms and concepts, and notable persons. Each
volume is individually indexed, and the last volume indexes and cross-
references the entire set.

# History

Morris, Richard B., and Graham W. Irwin. *Encyclopedia of American History.*
New York: Harper and Row, 1970.
This single-volume work chronologically covers the important events in
American history. One section is devoted to biographies of important U.S.
figures.

DeConde, Alexander, ed. *Encyclopedia of American Foreign Policy: Studies of
the Principal Movements and Ideas.* 3 vols. New York: Scribner's, 1978.
This encyclopedia contains articles on U.S. foreign policy written by
scholars in that field. There are articles on Eisenhower, Nixon, and the
Truman Plan as well as many other articles on the presidency. An appendix
lists important persons in American diplomatic history. There is also an
index.

# NEWSPAPERS AND INDEXES

Newspapers are unrivaled for their ability to provide almost instantaneous
reporting on presidential activities. They provide vivid day-by-day reports. The
two best newspapers for following presidential politics are *The New York Times*
(indexed in the *New York Times Index*) and the *Washington Post* (indexed in the
*Washington Post Index*).

The NEW YORK TIMES INFORMATION BANK, begun in 1969, is a unique on-line database service. Articles published in *The New York Times*, as well as articles from over seventy additional periodicals, are indexed and abstracted in the database. You can use the database to retrieve the bibliographic citations or the abstracts of the articles. While the indexing and abstracting is selective, there is a strong emphasis on political issues and officials.

The *National Newspaper Index* indexes *The New York Times, The Wall Street Journal* and the *Christian Science Monitor.* This microfilm index is cumulative and kept up-to-date regularly. Since this index covers more than a single calendar, it is easier to use than the annual indexes to the three newspapers. For research on current and recent issues, the *National Newspaper Index* is the first place to look.

Most major newspapers will reprint in full or selected excerpts of presidential speeches, news conferences, and addresses. All newspapers generally cover the presidency extensively, reporting on the national implications and local reactions.

# Single Newspaper Indexes

*Chicago Tribune Index.* Wooster, OH: Bell and Howell, 1971– .

*Christian Science Monitor. Index to . . .* Wooster, OH: Bell and Howell, 1951– .

*Dallas Morning News Index.* Dallas: Dallas Morning News Communications Center, 1960– .

*Detroit News Index.* Wooster, OH: Bell and Howell, 1976– .

*Houston Post Index.* Wooster, OH: Bell and Howell, 1976– .

*Los Angeles Times Index.* Wooster, OH: Bell and Howell, 1972– .

*Milwaukee Journal Index.* Wooster, OH: Bell and Howell, 1976– .

*New Orleans Times-Picayune Index.* Wooster, OH: Bell and Howell, 1972– .

*New York Times Index.* Glen Rock, NJ: Microfilming Corp. of America, 1851– .

*Palmer's Index to the Times Newspapers, 1790–1941.* London: Samuel Palmer, 1869–1943.

*San Diego Union.* Riverside, CA: Custom Microfilm Systems, 1930– .

*San Francisco Chronicle Index.* Wooster, OH: Bell and Howell, 1976– .

*Wall Street Journal Index.* Wooster, OH: Bell and Howell, 1955–1957. Princeton: Dow Jones Books, 1958– .

*Washington Post Index.* Wooster, OH: Bell and Howell, 1971– .

## Multinewspaper Indexes

*California News Index.* Claremont, CA: Center for California Public Affairs, 1970– . (Indexes the *Los Angeles Times,* the *San Diego Union,* the *Sacramento Bee,* and the *San Francisco Chronicle.*)

*The Newsbank Urban Affairs Library.* Spring Valley, NY: Arcata Microfilm, 1971– . (Indexes over 150 major newspapers in more than 100 cities.)

In addition, both *Public Affairs Information Service Bulletin* and the *Business Periodicals Index* selectively index stories from *The New York Times* and *The Wall Street Journal.*

# NEWS MAGAZINES

Weekly and monthly news magazines provide an excellent source for current information about the presidency. They not only include news stories, but editorials and feature articles. *Newsweek* and *Time* supply weekly reports on presidential activities and actions. The *Washington Monthly* and *Human Events* are particularly useful, as both focus specifically on politics in the Capitol, on the presidency, congressional activities, and developments in the executive branch and other agencies. *Human Events* contains sections entitled "Capitol Briefs" and "This Week's News in Washington." The *Washington Monthly,* in addition to several feature articles per issue, has information on new appointments, news briefs on all activities of the government, and book reviews on American politics. The magazines listed below regularly carry articles on the presidency or stories related to the presidency. The journals listed include a variety of philosophical viewpoints, from liberal to conservative.

While a variety of indexes include many of these magazines, the best indexes to consult to locate articles are *Reader's Guide to Periodical Literature* and the *Magazine Index.* Though these magazines do publish some scholarly articles on the presidency, they are not usually thought of as research journals. They are most useful for keeping up on current events and as a record of public opinion, as evidenced in their editorials and opinion articles. While they have limited value for serious research, they are valuable resources nonetheless.

*American Spectator.* Bloomington, IN: Saturday Evening Club, 1967– .

*Atlantic Monthly.* Boston: Atlantic Monthly Co., 1857– .

*Center Magazine.* Santa Barbara, CA: Center for the Study of Democratic Institutions, 1967– .

*Commentary: Journal of Significant Thought and Opinion on Contemporary Issues.* New York: American Jewish Committee, 1945– .

*Commonweal.* New York: Commonweal Publishing Company, 1924– .

*Conservative Digest.* Falls Church, VA: Viguerie Communications Corp., 1975– .

*Current.* Washington, DC: Heldref Publications, 1960– .

*Harper's Magazine.* New York: Harper's Magazine Co., 1851– .

*Human Events; The National Conservative Weekly.* Washington, DC: Human Events, Inc., 1944– .

*National Review: A Journal of Fact and Opinion.* New York: National Review, Inc., 1955– .

*New Republic: A Journal of Opinion.* Washington, DC: New Republic, 1914– .

*Newsweek.* New York: Newsweek, Inc., 1933– .

*Progressive.* Madison: Progressive, Inc., 1909– .

*Society: Social Science and Modern Society.* New Brunswick, NJ: Transactions Periodicals Consortium, Rutgers University, 1963– .

*Time: The Weekly News Magazine.* New York: Time-Life, 1923– .

*U.S. News and World Report.* Washington, DC: U.S. News and World Report, Inc., 1933– .

*Washington Monthly.* Washington, DC: Washington Monthly Co., 1969– .

# NEWSLETTERS

There are hundreds of newsletters and reports published by public interest and lobbying groups, representing almost every industry, business and professional association, and organization throughout the country. These newsletters range from just a few pages to lengthy reports. Intended for specific audiences, such as unions, political organizations, professions, etc., their news coverage is selective and reflects the interests of the publishing agency. They can include feature articles, editorials, news briefs, background studies, ratings of legislators, and lobbying information. While their formats differ, all attempt to report any important developments related to their area of interest, whether it be presidential actions, new or proposed legislation, a Supreme Court decision, or changes in regulatory rules and decisions.

Listed below are selected titles reflecting a wide range of interests. Generally, most of these newsletters are not indexed, but the *Business Periodicals Index* and *Applied Science and Technology Index* index some of the major ones.

The best way to determine if an organization, whether it is a public interest group or industrial or business association, publishes a newsletter focusing on national politics is to write to the organization. Many newsletters are distributed free. Academic and public libraries also subscribe to a variety of newsletters. But some publications are only available to members of the group. For the student and researcher, newsletters can be a source of information on lobbying activities or a resource for studying a particular interest group. Many newsletters give ratings of legislators and other leaders; these can generate data for a research design. Depending on how they are used, newsletters can be considered as primary source material and secondary source material.

| Title | Publisher |
|---|---|
| *ADA Legislative Newsletter* | Americans for Democratic Action<br>1411 K Street, N.W.<br>Washington, DC 20005 |
| *AFL-CIO News* | American Federation of Labor and<br>Congress of Industrial<br>Organizations<br>815 16th Street, N.W.<br>Washington, DC 20006 |
| *AGA Monthly* | American Gas Association<br>1515 Wilson Boulevard<br>Arlington, VA 22209 |
| *ALA Washington Newsletter* | American Library Association<br>110 Maryland Ave, N.E.<br>Washington, DC 20002 |
| *American Political Report* | American Political Research Corp.<br>4720 Montgomery Avenue<br>Bethesda, MD 20014 |
| *DSG Legislative Reports* | Democratic Study Group<br>Room 1422 Longworth House Office<br>Building<br>Washington, DC 20515 |
| *Congressional Round-up* | National Rural Housing Coalition<br>1346 Connecticut Avenue, N.W.<br>Washington, DC 20036 |
| *Consumer Newsweekly* | Consumer News, Inc.<br>813 National Press Building<br>Washington, DC 20045 |
| *Dateline Washington* | National Conference of State<br>Legislatures<br>444 N. Capitol St., N.W.<br>Washington, DC 20001 |
| *Energy Legislative Service* | McGraw-Hill<br>1221 Avenue of the Americas<br>New York, NY 10020 |
| *Federal Legislative Roundup* | National Association of Life<br>Underwriters |

|  | 1922 F. Street, N.W.<br>Washington, DC 20006 |
|---|---|
| *Federal Times* | Army Times Publishing Co.<br>475 School Street, S.W.<br>Washington, DC 20024 |
| *First Monday* | Republican National Committee<br>310 First Street, S.E.<br>Washington, DC 20003 |
| *For the People* | Congressional Black Caucus<br>306 House Annex<br>Washington, DC 20515 |
| *In Common* | Common Cause<br>2030 M Street, N.W.<br>Washington, DC 20036 |
| *Legislative Bulletin* | American Mining Congress<br>1100 Ring Building<br>Washington, DC 20036 |
| *Legislative Lookout* | American Association of University<br>Women<br>2401 Virginia Avenue, N.W.<br>Washington, DC 20037 |
| *NLC Washington Report* | National League of Cities<br>1620 Eye Street, N.W.<br>Washington, DC 20006 |
| *National Farmers Union<br>Washington Newsletter* | National Farmers Union<br>600 Continental Building<br>1012 14th Street, N.W.<br>Washington, DC 20005 |
| *National News Report* | Sierra Club<br>530 Bush Street<br>San Francisco, CA 94108 |
| *Republican Research Committee<br>Reports* | House Republican Research<br>Committee<br>1616 Longworth House Office<br>Building<br>Washington, DC 20515 |
| *Report from the Hill* | League of Women Voters of the<br>United States<br>1730 M Street, N.W.<br>Washington, DC 20036 |
| *View from the Hill* | National Grange Legislative News<br>Service<br>1616 H Street, N.W.<br>Washington, DC 20006 |
| *The Voice of Small Business* | National Small Business Association<br>1225 19th Street, N.W.<br>Washington, DC 20036 |
| *Washington Action* | Veterans of Foreign Wars of the<br>United States |

| | 200 Maryland Ave., N.E.<br>Washington, DC 20002 |
|---|---|
| *Washington Actions on Health* | Terry Schmidt Assoc., Inc.<br>1701 Pennsylvania Ave., N.W.<br>Washington, DC 20006 |
| *Washington Developments* | American Hospital Association<br>840 North Lake Shore Drive<br>Chicago, IL 60611 |
| *Washington Edition* | Association of National Advertisers<br>1725 K Street, N.W.<br>Washington, DC 20006 |
| *Washington Report* | Chamber of Commerce of the United<br>States<br>1615 H Street, N.W.<br>Washington, DC 20062 |
| *Washington Report* | National Association of Regional<br>Councils<br>1700 K Street, N.W.<br>Washington, DC 20006 |
| *Washington Report of the*<br>*American Security Council* | American Security Council<br>1101 17 Street, N.W.<br>Washington, DC 20036 |
| *Washington Report on Medicine*<br>*and Health* | McGraw-Hill<br>457 National Press Building<br>Washington, DC 20045 |
| *Washington Situation* | The National Council of Farmer<br>Co-operatives<br>1129 20th Street, N.W.<br>Washington, DC 20036 |
| *Washington Social Legislative*<br>*Bulletin* | Social Legislation Information<br>Service of the Child Welfare<br>League of America<br>1346 Connecticut Avenue, N.W.<br>Washington, DC 20036 |
| *Washington Week* | National Industrial Council<br>1776 F. Street, N.W.<br>Washington, DC 20006 |
| *What's Next* | Congressional Clearinghouse on the<br>Future<br>3692 HOB Annex II, U.S. House of<br>Representatives<br>Washington, DC 20515 |
| *The Word from Washington* | Wilson E. Hamilton and Associates<br>2000 L Street, N.W.<br>Washington, DC 20036 |

# NEWS SERVICES

While newspapers provide day-to-day coverage of political events, one of the most frustrating things that researchers encounter is the time lag for published indexes. Indexes to newspapers generally are three or more months behind. Consequently, if you are interested in finding some information about an event that took place a month ago, you may not be able to search newspapers through an index. This is when news services can be most useful, for they are only about two weeks behind in their publication. *Facts on File* and *Keesing's Contemporary Archives* are the only indexed sources you can use to find information about very recent events. For example, you can use them to research political campaigns in progress or to research an event shortly after it has happened, such as a convention, summit meeting, or press conference.

*Facts on File. Weekly News Digest and Index*. New York: Facts on File, 1940– .
This weekly digest of world events places an emphasis on the United States. It is thus a good service for presidential politics. The entries are grouped under topics, such as world affairs or national affairs. There is a cumulative index.

*Facts on file Yearbook [1941–1979]*. New York: Facts on File, 1946– .

Set 1: *America in World War II (1941–1945)*.
Set 2: *The Truman Administration and the Growth of the Cold War (1946–1952)*.
Set 3: *The Eisenhower Decade (1953–1960)*.
Set 4: *The Kennedy/Johnson Years (1961–1968)*.
Set 5: *The Nixon/Ford Years (1969–1976)*.

These yearbooks offer world events in a chronological order. The volumes essentially provide a "year in review" analysis of significant events.

*Keesing's Contemporary Archives: Weekly Diary of World Events*. Edited by W. Rosenberger and H. C. Tobin. London: Keesing's Publications, Ltd., 1931– .
This publication offers summaries of news reports for the week and provides strong coverage of news events in the United Kingdom and Europe. It is indexed cumulatively every two weeks, three months, each year, and every two years. *Keesing's* is a useful tool for studying American foreign policy, international relations, and the role of the president in treaty making.

*Editorials on File: Semi-Monthly Compilations from 140 U.S. and Canadian Newspapers*. New York: Facts on File, 1977– .
Editorials are reproduced and indexed in this semimonthly reference work. This tool can be used to study public opinions and attitudes toward the presidency, as well as reactions to presidential programs and announcements. It is especially useful for studying campaigns and elections and determining the newspaper endorsements of candidates.

# LEGAL NEWSPAPERS

We have identified legal newspapers as a separate category as they are indeed a special kind of publication. Though these newspapers are written with the legal profession in mind, they contain valuable information for anyone studying the presidency. They include stories about major issues, appointments of new officials, budget increases and cutbacks, and political developments and controversies surrounding the president. For anyone following the nation's politics, these newspapers are required reading.

*Legal Times of Washington.* Washington, DC: Legal Times of Washington, 1978– .
This weekly periodical contains accounts of current developments in the legal world.

*The National Law Journal.* New York: New York Law Publishing Company, 1978– .
This publication is a legal newspaper geared for a general audience. It offers a weekly selective index to legal materials.

*U.S. Law Week.* Washington, DC: Bureau of National Affairs, Inc., 1931– .
This weekly newspaper has four major sections. Section one gives summaries and analyses of major court decisions. The second section deals with new court decisions and agency rulings. The third section contains information on Supreme Court decisions. The last section contains information on Supreme Court opinions.

# BIBLIOGRAPHIES

Anyone interested in presidential politics will have no difficulty in finding materials. Perhaps the only problem the researcher will face is focusing in on a particular topic and weeding through citations and sources. The bibliographies mentioned in this section cover all kinds of materials, including books, periodical literature, and government documents. These bibliographies will give the researcher thousands of citations from which to choose.

## General

*Bibliographic Index: A Cumulative Bibliography of Bibliographies.* New York: H. W. Wilson, 1937– .
This work lists bibliographies by subject. These are further divided into books, parts of books, periodical articles, or pamphlets. There is a semiannual index and a cumulative index each December.

## Presidency

Greenstein, Fred I., Larry Berman, and Alvin S. Felzenberg. *Evolution of the Modern Presidency: A Bibliographic Survey.* Washington, DC: American Enterprise Institute for Public Policy Research, 1977.

This bibliography contains about 2,500 entries arranged topically in twenty-one chapters. Some of the entries are annotated. Separate chapters give lists of materials on presidents from Franklin D. Roosevelt to Gerald Ford. There is an author index.

*The American Presidency: A Historical Bibliography.* Santa Barbara, CA: ABC-Clio, 1984.

This bibliography consists of more than 3,000 abstracts from journals in the social sciences and humanities published between 1973 and 1982. It covers the lives of presidents, elections, and the growth of the executive branch. It features a multiterm subject index.

Heslop, David A. *The Presidency and Political Science: A Critique of the Work of Political Scientists in Three Areas of Presidential Politics.* Ann Arbor: University Microfilms, 1969.

Both books and articles dealing with presidential studies are included in this work.

# Federal Government

Smith, Dwight L., and Lloyd W. Garrison, eds. *The American Political Process: Selected Abstracts of Periodical Literature (1954–1971).* Santa Barbara, CA: ABC-Clio, 1972.

This work supplies numerous citations on presidential politics. Since the Abstracts in this work were drawn from *Historical Abstracts* and *America: History and Life,* the work is a good source for materials published in journals in the humanities, especially history. It also includes excellent author and subject indexes.

Garrison, Lloyd W., ed. *American Politics and Elections.* Santa Barbara, CA: ABC-Clio, 1968.

This work contains selected abstracts of periodical literature between 1964 and 1968. The abstracts cover more than 500 U.S. and Canadian periodicals. They are divided into four subject areas: (1) political parties, (2) the electoral process, (3) voting behavior, and (4) presidential elections (between 1800 and 1968). Within each category, these abstracts are arranged topically and chronologically in alphabetical sequence by author.

# Constitutional Law

Chambliss, William J., and Robert B. Seidman. *Sociology of the Law: A Research Bibliography.* Berkeley: Glendessary Press, 1970.

This bibliography provides material on the Supreme Court and constitutional law, but it is most useful for finding citations to jurisprudence, judicial review, and more theoretic aspects of judicial behavior.

Andrews, Joseph L. *The Law in the United States of America: A Selective Bibliographical Guide.* New York: New York University Press, 1965.

This bibliography selectively lists and annotates legal publications. There are two parts: The first lists primary materials and the second lists secondary works. The entries are found under broad subject headings.

Millet, Stephen M. *A Selected Bibliography of American Constitutional History.* Santa Barbara, CA: ABC-Clio, 1975.
  This bibliography contains citations to the origins and development of the Constitution, the history of amendments, the role of the Supreme Court, Congress, and the president in the judicial system.

Mason, Alpheus T., and D. Grier Stephenson. *American Constitutional Development.* Arlington Heights, IL: AHM Publishing Corporation, 1977.
  This is an excellent guide to the literature on constitutional law and statutory interpretation. The citations in this bibliography are taken mostly from the field of legal studies, but it does have some citations from the social sciences and humanities.

McCarrick, Earlean M. *The U.S. Constitution: A Guide to Information Sources.* Detroit: Gale Research Co., 1980.
  This guide covers all aspects of constitutional law, including its development, amendments, and the role of the Supreme Court and individual justices. It is better for finding citations to books than to journal literature.

# JOURNALS

Researchers interested in presidential activities will have no difficulty in finding journal articles. Journal articles are important because they are published faster than books and treat narrow topics. Every researcher should learn how to engineer his own literature search, including the use of indexes and abstracting services. Many journals contain articles on the presidency; we have cited only those that have such articles regularly. We have identified some of the major journals in political science, law, and history, but six journals deserve special mention, for they focus on the presidency itself or closely related subjects.

## Special Focus

### PRESIDENCY

*Congress and the Presidency: A Journal of Capitol Studies.* Washington, DC: School of Government and Public Administration, American University, 1983– .
  Formerly *Congressional Studies,* this journal now covers both the presidency and Congress, the interaction between the two and national policymaking in general. Published twice a year, it contains a mix of articles from both political science and history. Besides research articles, it includes research notes, review essays, and book reviews.

*Presidential Studies Quarterly.* New York: Center for the Study of the Presidency, 1972– .

This journal focuses solely on the presidency. It regularly includes ten or more feature articles addressing a single theme. While most of the articles are written by historians or political scientists, it does include articles from other fields. Current and former political officials contribute articles as well. The journal also contains a lengthy book review section.

## FEDERAL GOVERNMENT

*CQ Weekly Report*. Washington, DC: Congressional Quarterly, 1946– .
This journal recounts important congressional and political activities for the previous week, including developments in committees and on the floor. When covering major pieces of legislation, it provides voting records and excerpts of testimony in hearings. Full or selected texts of presidential press conferences, major statements, and speeches are reprinted. Lobbying activities are given considerable coverage, with special reports on the relationship between congressional voting and interest groups. Each issue usually contains an article on special issues or major legislation pending in Congress. The *CQ Weekly Report* quickly publishes the unofficial returns for elections the following week. CQ indexes the *Weekly Report* both quarterly and annually and it is indexed in *Public Affairs Information Service Bulletin*.

*National Journal: The Weekly on Politics and Government*. Washington, DC: Government Research Corporation, 1969– .
The *National Journal,* a weekly publication, covers all areas of federal decision making. It provides excellent analyses of presidential activities as well as the Executive Office. Each issue contains at least two or more feature articles on some aspect of presidential politics. Although in some respects similar to the *CQ Weekly Report,* the *National Journal* differs in its emphasis on developments in the executive branch. Using both the *CQ Weekly Report* and the *National Journal* will provide excellent coverage of current political events. The *National Journal* is self-indexed quarterly and annually by subject, name, and organization. It is also indexed in *Public Affairs Information Service Bulletin*.

## ELECTIONS

*Campaigns and Elections: The Journal of Political Action*. Washington, DC: National Press Building, 1980– .
Though this journal is intended for individuals involved in campaign management, politicians, and interest groups, it is useful to students and researchers. It covers a wide variety of topics, including polling, political action committees, election demographics, fund-raising and financing, media relations, and campaign techniques and strategies.

*Electoral Studies*. Guild Ford, England: Butterworth, 1982– .
This journal is international in scope, but it does include American election studies. As it is the first journal to exclusively cover elections, it is invaluable for anyone interested in electoral analysis, either on a comparative basis or for the United States.

# Political Science

Virtually every journal in political science at one time or another will contain an article on the presidency. The journals listed below either publish articles on a regular basis or are useful for specialized areas of study, such as public opinion. Throughout this guide, we will mention when a particular journal is important for that area of research. Journals in the fields of economics, sociology, psychology, and policy studies also publish articles related to the presidency. Again, the best method for locating articles from journals in those disciplines is to use a variety of indexes and abstracting services.

*American Academy of Political and Social Sciences, The Annals.* Philadelphia: American Academy of Political and Social Science, 1890– .

*American Journal of Political Science.* Detroit: Midwest Political Science Association, 1957– .

*American Political Science Review.* Washington, DC: American Political Science Association, 1907– .

*American Politics Quarterly.* Beverly Hills: Sage Publications, 1973– .

*British Journal of Political Science.* New York: Cambridge University Press, 1971– .

*Bureaucrat.* Alexandria, VA: Bureaucrat, Inc., 1970– .

*Foreign Affairs.* New York: Council on Foreign Relations, 1922– .

*Foreign Policy.* Washington, DC: Carnegie Endowment for International Peace, 1970– .

*Journal of Politics.* Gainesville, FL: Southern Political Science Association, 1939– .

*Law and Contemporary Problems.* Durham, NC: Duke University, School of Law, 1933– .

*Legislative Studies Quarterly.* Iowa City: University of Iowa, 1976– .

*Micropolitics.* New York: Crane, Russak and Co., Inc., 1981– .

*Policy Review.* Washington, DC: Heritage Foundation, Inc., 1977– .

*Political Behavior.* Albany, NY: Agathon Press, 1979– .

*Political Communication and Persuasion.* New York: Crane, Russak and Co., Inc., 1980– .

*Political Psychology.* New Brunswick, NY: International Society of Political Psychology, 1979– .

*Political Science Quarterly.* New York: Academy of Political Science, 1886– .

*Polity.* Amherst: Northeastern Political Science Association, 1968– .

*Public Administration Review.* Washington, DC: American Society for Public Administration, 1940– .

*Public Interest.* New York: National Affairs, Inc., 1965– .

*Public Opinion Quarterly.* New York: American Association for Public Opinion Research; Columbia University, 1937– .

*Public Opinion.* Washington, DC: American Enterprise Institute, 1978– .

*Review of Politics.* Notre Dame: University of Notre Dame, 1938– .

*Social Science Quarterly.* Austin: Southwestern Social Science Association, 1920– .

*Western Political Quarterly.* Salt Lake City: Western Political Science Association, 1948– .

*Wilson Quarterly.* Washington, DC: Woodrow Wilson Center for Scholars, 1976– .

# Legal

Most students and researchers tend to overlook law journals unless they are doing work on some topic from a legal point of view. Yet they can be useful for other approaches, for law journals contain an enormous number of articles on all aspects of the presidency. It is impossible to cite all the journals that would be useful; therefore, we have selected only a few representative titles. University journals (for example, *Harvard Law Review, Georgetown Law Journal*), state journals (for example, *Illinois Bar Journal, Maryland Law Review*), and specialized journals (for example, *Antitrust Law and Economic Review*, *Tax Law Review*) can provide essential information on topics in these areas. You should take the time to see what specialized journals exist, for they may be a primary source of information.

*American Bar Association Journal.* Chicago: American Bar Association, 1915– .

*American Journal of Legal History.* Philadelphia: American Society for Legal History, 1957– .

*Administrative Law Review*. Chicago: American Bar Association, 1973– .

*Federal Bar Journal*. Washington, D.C.: Federal Bar Association, 1931– .

*Federal Communications Law Journal*. Los Angeles: University of California, Los Angeles, School of Law, 1977– .

*Federal Rules Decisions*. St. Paul: West Publishing Co., 1940– .

*Harvard Journal on Legislation*. Cambridge: Harvard Legislative Research Bureau, 1964– .

*Supreme Court Review*. Chicago: University of Chicago Press, 1960– .

*United States Law Week: A National Service of Current Law*. Washington, DC: Bureau of National Affairs, 1933– .

# History

Obviously, anyone doing research of a historical nature will want to use history journals; but history journals should not be overlooked regardless of the topic or time frame of your research. These journals publish articles on current events and offer analyses of broad themes. They provide a wealth of information for anyone doing research from an institutional perspective.

In addition to the major journals listed below, all of the state historical journals (for example, *Annals of Iowa*, *Kansas Historical Quarterly*, *Ohio History*, *Wisconsin Magazine of History*) print articles related to the study of the presidency, expecially those journals published where one or more presidents were born or resided. They also publish articles on presidential actions, appointments, or policies that significantly affected their state. Finally, there are two journals that are devoted to specific presidents, the *Lincoln Herald* and the *Hayes Historical Journal*.

*American Heritage: The Magazine of History*. New York: American Heritage Publishing Co., 1949– .

*American Historical Review*. Washington, DC: The American Historical Association, 1895– .

*American Studies*. Lawrence, KS: Midcontinent American Studies Association, 1960– .

*Current History*. Philadelphia: Current History, Inc., 1943– .

*Diplomatic History*. Wilmington, DE: Scholarly Resources, Inc., 1977– .

*Historian: A Journal of History*. Allentown, PA: Alpha Theta International Honor Society in History, 1938– .

*Journal of American History*. Bloomington, IN: Organization of American Historians, 1914– .

*Journal of Southern History*. New Orleans: Southern Historical Association, 1935– .

*Pacific Historical Review*. Berkeley: American Historical Association, Pacific Coast Branch, 1932– .

*Prologue: The Journal of the National Archives*. Washington, DC: U.S. National Archives and Records Service, 1969– .

# JOURNAL INDEXES

Indexes and abstracting services are crucial research tools for studying the presidency. They are the key to locating journal literature. While almost every index will include citations to articles on the presidency, we have selected the indexes most likely to be used in the study of the presidency. But students and researchers should always check to see if other indexes prove useful to their research. For example, if you were interested in the role of women in the Executive Office, you would consult *Women Studies Abstracts*. If you were focusing on presidential initiatives in urban problems, you would check *Sage Urban Studies Abstracts* and *Urban Affairs Abstracts*; or if you were researching presidential efforts in the area of law and order, you would use the *Abstracts on Criminology and Penology*, and *Criminal Justice Periodical Index*, as well as several other indexes in the field of criminal justice. In the final chapter of the book, we discuss how to conduct a search of indexes and how they can be incorporated into an overall search strategy.

## General

*ABS Guide to Recent Literature in the Social and Behavioral Sciences*. Beverly Hills: The American Behavioral Scientist, Sage, 1965– .
 This guide abstracts periodical articles in the social sciences, including political science. The entries are classified by subject. This abstracting service includes behavioral and psychological studies on the presidency.

*British Humanities Index*. London: Library Association, 1963– .
 This work indexes articles from over 275 periodicals in the humanities and social sciences. The entries in the quarterly issues are arranged by subject. In addition to indexing all of the major British political science journals with articles on the presidency, it also indexes journals such as *New Society*, the *Guardian*, etc. These journals can be used as a source for studying British views of the presidency and American politics.

*Business Periodicals Index*. New York: H. W. Wilson, 1958– .
 This work indexes articles occurring in English-language business periodicals published in the United States. It covers accounting, advertising,

finance, labor, management, public administration, and general business. This index can be used in two ways for studying the presidency. First, it can help you locate articles that reflect what the business and industrial sectors think of presidential policies and actions. Secondly, because it indexes a considerable number of trade and professional magazines, it can be used to follow the views and actions of interest groups and associations.

*Magazine Index.* Menlo Park, CA: Information Access Company, 1978– .
This indexes articles and reviews appearing in general U.S. magazines and is most useful for following current events relating to the presidency and finding articles reflecting various opinions on issues.

*Public Affairs Information Service Bulletin.* New York: The Service, 1915– .
This is a weekly subject guide to the field of American politics in general, indexing government publications, books, and periodical literature. It includes citations to many hearings. Additionally, it indexes the *National Journal*, *CQ Weekly Report, Congressional Digest*, and selections from the *Weekly Compilation of Presidential Documents*. All of these journals are invaluable guides to studying the presidency on a current basis. A fifteen volume *Cumulative Subject Index to the P.A.I.S. Annual Bulletins, 1915– 1974* has been published by Carrollton Press. *P.A.I.S.* is cumulated quarterly and annually.

*Reader's Guide to Periodical Literature.* New York: H. W. Wilson, 1905– .
This guide indexes articles in popular periodicals published in the United States by author and subject. Annual indexes include hundreds of citations about the presidency, campaigns and elections. Although you would not begin your scholarly work here, you should take the time to see what it does say about the presidency. For research focusing on events within the past few years, it is a vital reference tool.

*Social Sciences Citation Index.* Philadelphia: Institute for Science Information, 1973– .
Items appearing in the *SSCI* have been cited in footnotes or bibliographies in the social sciences. These works include books, journal articles, dissertations, reports, proceedings, etc. There are four separate indexes: a source (author) index, a citation index, a corporate index, and the Permuterm subject index. Though difficult to use, it does have several unique features useful for studying the presidency. The corporate index enables you to identify publications issued by particular organizations (such as the Center for the Study of the Presidency or the Brookings Institution). The source and citation indexes allow you to identify the works of a particular scholar who has written extensively on the presidency and to identify other researchers who have cited his writings.

*Social Sciences Index.* New York: H. W. Wilson, 1975– .
This work indexes articles found in about 150 social science journals. It covers all of the major journals in political science as well as the other social

sciences and should be used for all studies of the presidency, regardless of the topic.

## Political Science

*ABC POL SCI: A Bibliography of Contents: Political Science and Government*. Santa Barbara, CA: ABC-Clio, 1969– .
    This lists and indexes tables of contents from approximately 300 selected journals, both U.S. and foreign. This bibliography is especially useful for finding very recent articles on the presidency and subjects related to political science.

*American Political Science Research Guide*. New York: IFI/Plenum Data Co., 1977– .
    This is an annotated list of books and articles dealing with federal, state, and local government. It covers the executive branch as well as the legislative and judicial branches of government. There is an author index and a broad subject index. The entries were selected from the Universal Reference System database.

*Combined Retrospective Index to Journals in Political Science, 1886–1974*. 8 vols. Arlington, VA: Carrollton Press, 1978.
    This work indexes articles from approximately 180 English-language political science periodicals appearing since 1886. It indexes by subject and author and publishes annual supplements. Since most such indexes were only started in the last twenty years, this index is invaluable for anyone interested in articles published about the presidency in the nineteenth century and early twentieth century.

*International Bibliography of Political Science*. Chicago: Aldine Publishing Co., 1962– .
    This bibliography lists books, articles, reports, and other research publications. The entries are classified under six sections: political science, political thought, government and public administration, governmental process, international relations, and area studies. Entries are selected from over 2,000 journals. This is another source for foreign-language materials on the presidency. It also includes many English-language citations as well.

*International Political Science Abstracts*. Oxford: Basil Blackwell, 1952– .
    This work abstracts articles published in 600 English-language and foreign-language political science journals. The abstracts for the English-language journals appear in English; the foreign-language articles are abstracted in French. This is the best source for finding foreign-language articles about the presidency. You should check it for citations on the presidency that may have not appeared in other indexes.

*Sage Public Administration Abstracts*. Beverly Hills: Sage Publications, 1974– .

This work abstracts articles selected from approximately 200 English-language journals as well as books, pamphlets, and government publications dealing with public administration. Though this service does not have a large number of citations about the presidency, it should be consulted when searching for information related to policy analysis, public management, bureaucratic studies, and federal programs. It is most useful to the researcher interested in the president as a manager and administrator.

*United States Political Science Documents*. Pittsburgh: University Center for International Studies, University of Pittsburgh, 1976– .
This work indexes and abstracts about 120 political science journals and appears annually in two volumes. The first volume contains indexes by the author, subject, geographic area, proper name, and journal title. The second volume abstracts the articles indexed in volume one. This is another index that should be used for studying the presidency, regardless of the topic. Because it indexes many of the new journals in political science, it covers journals not indexed elsewhere.

# Legal

*Annual Legal Bibliography*. Cambridge: Harvard University Law School, Library, 1961– .
This is a bibliography covering books and articles acquired by the Harvard University Law School Library. The entries are classified in the following groups: common law, civil law and other jurisdictions, private international law, and public international law. The entries are not annotated. This bibliography provides excellent coverage of administrative law and presidential relations with the Congress and Supreme Court.

*Contents of Current Legal Periodicals*. Los Angeles: Law Publications, 1975– .
Tables of contents are provided for legal journals in this work. The articles are also indexed by subject. The virtue of this service is the currency of its indexing. It is most useful for finding recent legal studies on the presidency.

*Current Law Index*. Menlo Park, CA: Information Access Corp., 1980– .
This index covers legal periodicals and newspapers. Its microfilm counterpart, *Legal Resources Index*, cumulates the information found in the paper copy. It also indexes books and documents. These two indexes provide extensive coverage of the presidency and related topics. While mostly reviewed in connection with legal issues, they should be consulted regardless of the subject.

*The Federal Index*. Cleveland: Predicasts, Inc., 1976– .
This monthly index covers the congressional, executive, and judicial branches of government. It indexes the *Federal Register*, the *Congressional Record*, the *Weekly Compilation of Presidential Documents*, and *U.S. Law Week*. It is also cumulated annually. Presidential announcements, regulations, and laws are covered. This index is enormously useful for keeping up-to-date on federal policies, rules, and decisions. As a commercial index to

documents and selected secondary sources, it can save you time when you are searching for presidential documents.

*Index to Legal Periodicals*. New York: H. W. Wilson, 1908– .
This work indexes articles appearing in legal periodicals of the U.S., Canada, Great Britain, Northern Ireland, Australia, and New Zealand. Articles are indexed by author, subject, and cases. This is another legal index that should be used in almost every search on the presidency. As it is the oldest legal index, it can serve as a tool for historical research as well.

*Index to Periodical Articles Related to Law*. Dobbs Ferry, NY: Glanville Publications, 1958– .
This indexes by author and subject articles found in journals published by law schools, lawyers' associations, and law institutes. It contains some citations relevant to the study of the presidency, but it should be used only after consulting the other legal indexes.

*Monthly Digest of Legal Articles*. Greenville, NY: Research and Documentation Corp., 1969– .
This service is most useful for finding recent journal literature on the presidency.

# History

*America: History and Life*. Santa Barbara, CA: ABC-Clio 1964– .
There are four parts to this bibliography: Part A, *Article Abstracts and Citations* abstracts the entries; Part B, *Index to Book Reviews*, gives book reviews published in journals; Part C, the annual *American History Bibliography (Books, Articles, and Dissertations)*, includes the articles in Part A, book entries not cited from Part B, and dissertations; Part D, the annual *American History Index*, indexes by subject and author all of the entries from the other parts. This abstracting service provides excellent coverage of historical materials. Anyone conducting historical research on the presidency should include this index.

*Arts and Humanities Citation Index*. Philadelphia: Institute for Scientific Information, 1978– .
This work indexes books, journal articles, theses, dissertations, reports, proceedings, congresses, and other unpublished papers cited in footnotes or bibliographies in the humanities. It provides an author index, citation index, subject index, and corporate index and can be used to find citations to the presidency from history journals as well as the arts. For anyone interested in presidential activities and actions related to the arts, culture, and humanities, this index is most helpful. Though limited as an index for studying the presidency, for most topics it is the best source for the disciplines it covers.

*Combined Retrospective Index to Journals in History, 1838–1974*. 11 vols. Arlington, VA: Carrollton Press, 1978.
This work indexes over 150,000 articles published in over 200 English-language journals in history since 1838. Five of the eleven volumes cover

United States history. There is an author index in addition to the subject index. Besides providing indexing of journals for the nineteenth century, it is very good for biographical research on presidents.

*Humanities Index*. New York: H. W. Wilson Company, 1974– .
This cumulative index to English-language journals in the humanities indexes articles by author and subject. Covering the major journals in history, it is an excellent resource for locating citations related to the history of the presidency.

*Writings on American History: A Subject Bibliography of Articles*. Millwood, NY: KTO Press, 1974– .
This is a bibliography of journal articles published on American history from approximately 500 periodicals. The entries are arranged chronologically, geographically, and by subject. There is an author index, but no subject index. It includes journals from political science, economics, and other social sciences. Though most researchers do not think of using this index unless they are looking for citations to history journals, it usually contains many useful citations on almost every topic related to the presidency.

# DATABASES

Information retrieval services are available at most university and research libraries. Bibliographic databases that cover all areas of the social sciences are available for retrieving information quickly and efficiently. Many libraries subscribe to on-line bibliographic databases such as Lockheed's DIALOG Information Retrieval Service, the Bibliographic Retrieval Service (BRS), or the Systems Development Corporation's ORBIT. The two legal database systems are LEXIS and Westlaw. The Information Bank of The New York Times has materials from *The New York Times* as well as selected materials from other newspapers and magazines. Librarians are trained to use these databases and can advise the researcher about the cost and effectiveness of the various systems.

For anyone interested in on-line databases, there are two journals, *Online* and *Database: The Magazine of Database Reference and Review*, that report on new databases, new searching techniques, and possible future developments. There are also two directories to database services.

## Directories

Williams, Martha E. *Computer-Readable Data Bases: A Directory and Data Sourcebook*. Washington, DC: American Society for Information Service, 1976– .
This directory, updated by looseleaf supplements, identifies databases that conduct searches and other reference services. It includes information about the producer of the database, availability and charge rates, scope of subject

matter, the indexing, search programs, services offered, and any available user aids.

Schmittroth, John J., ed. *Encyclopedia of Information Systems and Services*. 5th ed. Detroit: Gale Research Co., 1982.
This reference volume gives descriptions of over 2,000 organizations in the U.S. and sixty other countries that produce, process, store, and use bibliographic and nonbibliographic data. It also identifies and discusses on-line vendors, videotext and teletext systems, telecommunication networks, and library systems.

# Selected Databases

## CURRENT AFFAIRS

NATIONAL NEWSPAPER INDEX. Menlo Park, CA: Information Access Corporation, 1979– .
This indexes the *Christian Science Monitor*, *The New York Times*, and *The Wall Street Journal*. It covers all items except weather charts, stock market tables, crossword puzzles, and horoscopes. It provides good coverage of government relations and is especially useful for finding articles related to current presidential activities, press conferences, campaigns, and electioneering.

NEWSEARCH. Menlo Park, CA: Information Access Corporation, 1978– .
This is a daily index of more than 2,000 news stories, information articles, and book reviews from over 1,400 newspapers, magazines, and periodicals. It indexes articles for the current month. At the end of the month the magazine article data is transferred to the MAGAZINE INDEX, and the newspaper data is transferred to the NATIONAL NEWSPAPER INDEX. NEWSEARCH is another excellent source for keeping up-to-date on presidential stories. It is also useful for finding reports on presidential spokesmen, such as members of the Council of Economic Advisors, the National Security Council, and other individuals in the Executive Office of the President.

MAGAZINE INDEX. Menlo Park, CA: Information Access Corporation, 1976– .
This database indexes articles from over 370 general magazines and provides good coverage of current affairs. While not as extensive in scope as the previous two, this resource is useful for researching headline stories about the president and current issues and controversies surrounding the president.

## DOCUMENTS

CONGRESSIONAL RECORD ABSTRACTS. Washington, DC: Capitol Services, Inc., 1976– .
This contains abstracts of items appearing in the *Congressional Record*. It

covers bills, resolutions, committee and subcommittee reports, public laws, executive communications, speeches, and inserted materials. This database can speed up the process of compiling a legislative history and identifying presidential speeches and messages.

GPO PUBLICATIONS REFERENCE FILE. Washington, DC: U.S. Government Printing Office, 1971– .
Essentially an on-line version of the *GPO Sales Publications Reference File* described earlier, this is best suited for finding citations to new publications, especially those that have not yet been cited in the *Monthly Catalog* or for determining whether a particular document is still available for purchase.

FEDERAL INDEX. Washington, DC: Capitol Services, Inc., 1976– .
This indexes the *Washington Post, Congressional Record, Federal Register*, presidential documents, and other federal documents, including rules, regulations, bills, speeches, hearings, roll calls, reports, vetoes, court decisions, and executive orders. It is the best single source for finding information about the federal government. Because it indexes a wide scope of legislative and executive documents, it is extremely useful for researching the president, especially his role as a legislator and administrator.

FEDERAL REGISTER ABSTRACTS. Washington, DC: Capitol Services, Inc., 1977– .
This database abstracts materials in the *Federal Register*. It covers government regulations, proposed rules, and legal notices, such as presidential proclamations, executive orders, and presidential determinations. For anyone studying the president as an administrator, this is indispensable, for it is an excellent index to presidential documents and administrative law in general.

GPO MONTHLY CATALOG. Washington, DC: U.S. Government Printing Office, 1976– .
This contains records of reports, studies, etc., issued by all U.S. federal government agencies, including Senate and House hearings, and is useful for finding documents issued through the Office of the President and the Executive Office. While it is better suited for finding documents issued by departments of the executive branch, it can also be used in compiling a legislative history.

## SOCIAL SCIENCES

AMERICA: HISTORY AND LIFE. Santa Barbara, CA: ABC-Clio, 1964– .
This reference, available both in hardcover and on-line through DIALOG, provides comprehensive coverage of all areas of U.S. history, international relations, and politics and government. This is the best database for finding articles dealing with the history of the presidency, biographical materials on each president, and campaign and election studies.

COMPREHENSIVE DISSERTATION INDEX. Ann Arbor: Xerox University Microfilms, 1861– .
This database indexes American dissertations (from 1861 onward) by subject, title and author. For anyone doing in-depth research on the presidency or a specific president, a search of this database will yield dozens of citations on particular topics, for there are thousands of dissertations written about various aspects of the presidency.

HISTORICAL ABSTRACTS. Santa Barbara, CA: ABC-Clio, 1964– .
This reference is a guide to the literature of world history and the related social sciences and humanities. It contains article abstracts and annotations from more than 2,000 journals published worldwide. *HISTORICAL ABSTRACTS'* database contains approximately 145,000 records, and approximately 15,000 new bibliographic records are added to the database each year. Covers the historical period from 1450 to the present.

PAIS INTERNATIONAL. New York: PAIS, Inc., 1976– .
Each year approximately 25,000 citations found in over 1,200 journals and over 800 books, pamphlets, government documents, and agency reports are added to this database. It covers all fields of the social sciences—political science, public administration, international relations, law, and public policy—and is useful not only for finding materials related to current events, but for doing research on specific topics as well. Because it indexes books, documents, and articles from journals (such as the *CQ Weekly Report* and the *National Journal*), a search can yield a wide variety of citations to both primary and secondary sources.

PSYCINFO. Washington, DC: American Psychological Association, 1967– .
Each year citations covering psychology and related areas are chosen from over 900 journals, 1,500 books, and technical reports for this database. A search can result in numerous citations to psychological and behavioral studies of the presidency. It is especially useful for finding citations to articles analyzing the president as a political actor or as part of an elite. It is particularly useful for anyone studying the presidency on a micro level.

SOCIAL SCISEARCH. Philadelphia: The Institute for Scientific Information, 1972– .
This covers all areas of the social and behavioral sciences. Entries are chosen from the 1,000 most important social science journals, as well as from 2,200 others in the natural, physical, and biomedical sciences. Its scope, both in terms of the number of journals and disciplines covered, is larger than any other data base and it provides citations to almost any facet of presidential studies.

SOCIOLOGICAL ABSTRACTS. San Diego: Sociological Abstracts, Inc., 1963– .
Abstracts covering sociology and related areas in the social and behavioral sciences are included in this database. Entries are chosen from over 1,200

periodicals and other serial publications. In addition to citations to sociological and behavior studies of the presidency, it also includes citations to
campaigning, elections, public opinion, and political communication and the
impact of presidential policies and programs.

USPSD. Pittsburgh, PA: University of Pittsburgh Press, 1975– .
    Articles from approximately 120 major political science journals pub-
lished in the U.S. are abstracted and indexed. This database can be best used
to find citations from the major journals in the field of political science. It is
also the best for identifying articles on the presidency from the growing
number of policy studies journals.

## LEGAL

LEXIS. Dayton, OH: Mead Data Central, Inc., 1973– .
    This system searches through legal documents to retrieve needed informa-
tion. Using a LEXIS terminal and telephone, text is retrieved from a computer storing the documents in Dayton, Ohio. You can use this system to find
citations to several different perspectives on the presidency, including legal
analyses of policies, administrative decision making, and regulatory politics.

WESTLAW. St. Paul: West Publishing Co., 1978– .
    All recent U.S. State and Federal Court decisions are abstracted in this
database. It covers judicial decision making and the court system and can be
used most effectively to find citations related to the interpretation of public
laws and the relationship of the president to the Supreme Court.

LEGAL RESOURCE INDEX. Menlo Park, CA: Information Access Corporation, 1980– .
    This database provides the best overall coverage to legal materials, for it
indexes over 660 law journals, 5 law newspapers, legal monographs, and
government publications from the Library of Congress MARC database. It
can be used for researching almost any topic related to the presidency, from
constitutional history to the vice-presidency.

Appendix 13, p. 247, a list of databases and indexes, identifies the form(s) in
which these sources of information are available.

# DISSERTATIONS

Hundreds of dissertations from various disciplines in the humanities and social
sciences examine the presidency and individual presidents. To get an idea of the
kinds of dissertations that are available, you need only glance through a catalog.
Dissertations are not systematically acquired by libraries; you must borrow
them through interlibrary loan, purchase them directly, or see whether they can
be purchased by a library. Consequently, students may not want to include
dissertations in their search strategy, but for the serious researcher, these are a
major source of secondary information.

*Presidents: A Catalog of Doctoral Dissertations*. Ann Arbor: University Microfilms International, 1983.

This catalog records 915 titles of dissertations and theses completed between 1939 and 1982 and included in *Dissertation Abstracts International* or *Masters Abstracts*. The entries give the following information: author, title, degree of author, school name, date of degree, pages, the citation to the DAI or MA, and the order number. Topics covered are campaigns, elections, candidates, election and the media, power and political behavior, and the vice-presidency. There are no entries for Presidents Harrison, Taylor, Pierce, or Arthur.

*Comprehensive Dissertation Index*. Ann Arbor: Xerox University Microfilms, 1973– .

This work indexes by author and keywords the entries found in the *American Doctoral Dissertations* and *Dissertation Abstracts International*. This thirty-seven volume set covers dissertations done between 1861 and 1977, and publishes annual five-volume supplements. This is the best index to use for identifying a particular dissertation or for conducting a subject search.

*Dissertation Abstracts International*. Ann Arbor: Xerox University Microfilms, 1938– .

This monthly index abstracts dissertations completed at American and some foreign universities. While the *Comprehensive Dissertation Index* is a better tool for searching by subject, the *DAI* is indispensable for finding recent dissertations.

*American Doctoral Dissertations*. Ann Arbor: Xerox University Microfilms, 1955/56– .

This is a supplement to *Dissertation Abstracts International*. Entries of additional dissertations are listed each year.

*Doctoral Dissertations Accepted by American Universities, 1933/34–1954/55*. New York: Wilson, 1934–1956.

This work lists dissertations from United States and Canadian universities from 1933–1955. The entries are arranged by subject. There is an author and a subject index.

*Masters Abstracts*. Ann Arbor: Xerox University Microfilms, 1962– .

Masters theses of some U.S. colleges and universities are abstracted in this work. The entries are arranged by subject discipline.

*Index to American Doctoral Dissertations*. Ann Arbor: University Microfilms International, 1957– .

Issued each year as a part of *Dissertations Abstracts*, this index has been published as a separate work since 1963.

# PART II

# The Oval Office

# CHAPTER 3

# The Presidents

We will now focus on identifying primary source materials relating to individual presidents, including official documents, writings, and other resources. We have developed special tables useful for determining where to look for specific kinds of presidential documents. We have designed a table (Appendix 14, p. 250) which summarizes the tools you can use for all types of materials and more specific tables (Appendices 15–18, p. 252) for actions, proclamations and executive orders, messages, and speeches. Secondly, we have compiled a list of writings by each president. While these listings are not exhaustive, we have provided the most complete bibliography to be found anywhere.

## PRESIDENTIAL DOCUMENTS AND WRITINGS

We have discussed various kinds of presidential documents as they are issued in the legislative process, in the process of administrative policy making and treaty making. At this point, it would be useful to reiterate which sources can be used to find presidential materials.

### Compilations

#### CURRENT SOURCES

There are basically five tools that can be used to identify the texts of presidential documents on a current basis:

*Weekly Compilation of Presidential Documents*. Washington, DC: U.S. National Archives and Records Service, 1965– .
   This work includes messages, statements, public speeches, remarks, press conferences, and other material released by the White House.

*Federal Register.* Washington, DC: U.S. National Archives and Records Service, 1936– .

*Code of Federal Regulations.* Washington, DC: U.S. National Archives and Records Service, 1949– .
These include executive orders, reorganization plans, and presidential proclamations of legal significance. *Title 3*, *CFR* is a compilation of presidential documents.

*U.S. Code Congressional and Administrative News.* St. Paul: West Publishing Co., 1939– .
This includes selected presidential messages, executive orders, and proclamations.

Many presidential messages and reorganization plans are published separately as House and Senate documents.

## RETROSPECTIVE SOURCES

There are basically four places, other than the *United States Code* and the sources cited previously for treaties, where you can find the texts of presidential documents that are more than a year old:

*Public Papers of the Presidents of the United States.* U.S. National Archives and Records Service. Washington, DC: U.S. Government Printing Office, 1958– .

*The Cumulated Indexes to the Public Papers of the Presidents.* Washington, DC: KTO Press, 1977.
This set combines and integrates all of the separate indexes to the *Public Papers of the Presidents* for each individual president into one alphabetical listing covering that administration. The indexes can be used to locate all the statements of a president on a particular topic during his administration. Presently there are volumes for Hoover, Truman, Eisenhower, Kennedy, Johnson, Nixon, Ford, and Carter.

*A Compilation of Messages and Papers of the Presidents, 1789–1927.* 20 vols. James D. Richardson. New York: Bureau of National Literature, 1928.
This work is an unofficial compilation of papers and materials from Washington to Coolidge. No official compilation of presidential papers has been published for the years 1929–1945.

*Presidential Messages and State Papers.* 10 vols. New York: Review of Reviews, 1917.
This is a selection of presidential papers from Washington to Wilson.

# INDIVIDUAL PRESIDENTS

We have listed two kinds of materials relating to individual presidents. The first is a listing of the indexes prepared as part of the Presidential Papers Series. These are indexes to the papers of presidents available at the Manuscript Division of the Library of Congress. They have been prepared by the Manuscript Division. In the section on Archives and Manuscript Collection, we will describe in more detail the collection at the Library of Congress. The second part lists the writings of each president and other works that contain selected writings, speeches, correspondence, etc. This list of writings is valuable for several reasons. It supplements the public papers published by the government. Since most of these are memoirs, they contain material and analysis not found in official sources.

## Documents

*Index to the George Washington Papers*. Washington, DC: U.S. Government Printing Office, 1964.

*Index to the Thomas Jefferson Papers*. Washington, DC: U.S. Government Printing Office, 1976.

*Index to the James Madison Papers*. Washington, DC: U.S. Government Printing Office, 1965.

*Index to the James Monroe Papers*. Washington, DC: U.S. Government Printing Office, 1967.

*Index to the Andrew Jackson Papers*. Washington, DC: U.S. Government Printing Office, 1960.

*Index to the John Tyler Papers*. Washington, DC: U.S. Government Printing Office, 1961.

*Index to the James K. Polk Papers*. Washington, DC: U.S. Government Printing Office, 1969.

*Index to the Zachary Taylor Papers*. Washington, DC: U.S. Government Printing Office, 1960.

*Index to the Franklin Pierce Papers*. Washington, DC: U.S. Government Printing Office, 1962.

*Index to the Abraham Lincoln Papers*. Washington, DC: U.S. Government Printing Office, 1963.

*Index to the Andrew Johnson Papers*. Washington, DC: U.S. Government Printing Office, 1963.

*Index to the Ulysses S. Grant Papers.* Washington, DC: U.S. Government Printing Office, 1965.

*Index to the James A. Garfield Papers.* Washington, DC: U.S. Government Printing Office, 1973.

*Index to the Chester A. Arthur Papers.* Washington, DC: U.S. Government Printing Office, 1961.

*Index to the Benjamin Harrison Papers.* Washington, DC: U.S. Government Printing Office, 1964.

*Index to the Grover Cleveland Papers.* Washington, DC: U.S. Government Printing Office, 1965.

*Index to the William McKinley Papers.* Washington, DC: U.S. Government Printing Office, 1963.

*Index to the Theodore Roosevelt Papers.* Washington, DC: U.S. Government Printing Office, 1970.

*Index to the William H. Taft Papers.* Washington, DC: U.S. Government Printing Office, 1972.

*Index to the Woodrow Wilson Papers.* Washington, DC: U.S. Government Printing Office, 1973.

*Index to the Calvin Coolidge Papers.* Washington, DC: U.S. Government Printing Office, 1965.

# Writings

## George Washington
*The Agricultural Papers of George Washington.* Edited by Walter Edwin Brooke. Boston: R.G. Badger, 1919.

*The Autobiography of George Washington, 1753–1799.* Edited by Edward C. Boykin. New York: Reynal & Hitchcook, 1935.

*Basic Writings of George Washington.* Edited by Saxe Commins. New York: Random House, 1948.

*Correspondence Concerning the Society of the Cincinnati.* Edited by Edgar Erkine Hume. Baltimore: John Hopkins Press, 1941.

*The Diaries of George Washington.* 6 vols. Edited by Donald Jackson. Charlottesville: University Press of Virginia, 1976– 80.

*Diaries, 1748–1799*. 4 vols. Edited by John C. Fitzpatrick. Boston: Houghton Mifflin, 1925.

*George Washington and Mount Vernon; A Collection of Washington's Unpublished Agricultural and Personal Letters*. Edited by Moncure Daniel Conway. Brooklyn: Long Island Historical Society, 1889.

*The George Washington Papers*. Edited by Frank Donovan. New York: Dodd, Mead, 1964.

*George Washington's Accounts of Expenses While Commander-in-Chief of the Continental Army, 1775–1783*. Edited by John C. Fitzpatrick. Boston: Houghton Mifflin, 1917.

*The Journal of Major George Washington; An Account of His First Official Mission, Made as Emissary from the Governor of Virginia to the Commandant of the French Forces on the Ohio, October 1753–January 1754*. New York: Holt, 1959.

*Letters from His Excellency George Washington, President of the United States, to Sir John Sinclair, Bart. M. P., on Agricultural and Other Interesting Topics*. London: W. Bulmer, 1800.

*The Letters of George Washington in the Robert Hudson Tannahill Research Library*. Edited by Jerome Irving Smith. Dearborn, MI: Greenfield Village and Henry Ford Museum, 1976.

*Masonic Correspondence as Found Among the Washington Papers in the Library of Congress*. Compiled by Julius F. Sachse. Philadelphia: New Era Printing Co., 1915.

*Maxims of Washington: Political, Social, Moral, and Religious*. Rev ed. Edited by John Frederick Schroeder. Mount Vernon, VA: The Mount Vernon Ladies' Association, 1942.

*Papers of George Washington*. 2 vols. Edited by William W. Abbot. Charlottesville: University Press of Virginia, 1982.

*President Washington's Diaries, 1791 to 1799*. Compiled by Joseph A. Hoskins. Summerfield, NC: The Compiler, 1921.

*The Washington Papers; Basic Selections From the Public and Private Writings of George Washington*. Edited by Saul K. Padover. New York: Harper, 1955.

*Washington Speaks for Himself*. Lucretia Perry Osborn. New York: Scribner's, 1927.

*The Washington-Crawford Letters, Being the Correspondence Between George*

*Washington and William Crawford, From 1767 to 1781, Concerning Western Lands*. Edited by Consul W. Butterfield. Cincinnati: R. Clerke, 1877.

*Washington-Irvine Correspondence; The Official Letters Which Passed Between Washington and Brig. Gen. William Irvine and Between Irvine and Others Concerning Military Affairs in the West from 1781 to 1783*. Edited by Consul W. Butterfield. Madison, WI: D. Atwood, 1882.

*The Writings of George Washington from the Original Manuscript Sources, 1745–1799*. 39 vols. Edited by John C. Fitzpatrick. Washington, DC: U.S. Government Printing Office, 1931–1944.

*Writings*. 14 vols. Edited by Worthington Chauncey Ford. New York: Putnam, 1889–1893.

*Writings*. Edited by Lawrence B. Evans. New York: Putnam, 1908.

*The Writings of George Washington*. Edited by Jared Sparks. Boston: American Stationer's Co., 1837.

### John Adams

*The Adams-Jefferson Letters; The Complete Correspondence Between Thomas Jefferson and Abigail and John Adams*. Edited by Lester J. Cappon. Chapel Hill: University of North Carolina Press, 1959.

*The Adams Papers*. Edited by Lyman H. Butterfield. Cambridge: Harvard University Press, 1961.

*A Collection of State Papers, Relative to the First Acknowledgement of the Sovereignity [sic] of the United States of America, and the Reception of Their Minister Plenipotentiary, by Their High Mightinesses the States-General of the United Netherlands*. London: J. Fielding, 1782.

*Correspondence Between the Hon. John Adams and the Late William Cunningham, esq., Beginning in 1803, and Ending in 1812*. Boston: E. M. Cunningham, 1823.

*Correspondence of the Late President Adams*. Boston: Everett and Munroe, 1809–1810.

*Deeds and Other Documents Relating to the Several Pieces of Land, and to the Library Presented to the Town of Quincy, by President Adams, Together With a Catalogue of the Books*. Cambridge: Hilliard and Metcalf, 1823.

*A Defence of the Constitutions of Government of the United States of America*. 3 vols. London: Printed for C. Dilly, 1787–1788.

*Diary and Autobiography*. 4 vols. Edited by Lyman H. Butterfield. Cambridge: Harvard University Press, 1961.

*Discourses on Davila: A Series of Papers on Political History. Written in the Year 1790, and then Published in the Gazette of the United States.* Boston: Printed by Russell and Cutler, 1805.

*Familiar Letters of John Adams and His Wife Abigail Adams, During the Revolution.* Edited by Charles Francis Adams. New York: Hurd and Houghton, 1876.

*The John Adams Papers.* Edited by Frank Donovan. New York: Dodd, Mead, 1965.

*Novanglus, and Massachusettensis; or, Political Essays, Published in the Years 1774 and 1775, on the Principal Points of Controversy, Between Great Britain and Her Colonies. The Former by John Adams, the Latter by Jonathan Sewall. To Which are Added, a Number of Letters, Lately Written by President Adams to the Honourable William Tudor; Some of Which Were Never Before Published.* Boston: Hews & Goss, 1819.

*Old Family Letters: Copied From the Originals for Alexander Biddle.* Philadelphia: Lippincott, 1892.

*The Papers of John Adams 1755–1775.* Edited by Robert J. Taylor. Cambridge: Harvard University Press, 1977.

*The Political Writings of John Adams: Representative Selections.* Edited with an introduction by George A. Peek, Jr. New York: Liberal Arts Press, 1954.

*Statesman and Friend; Correspondence of John Adams with Benjamin Waterhouse, 1784–1822.* Edited by Worthington Chauncey Ford. Boston: Little, Brown, 1927.

*Thoughts on Government, Applicable to the Present State of the American Colonies. In a Letter from a Gentleman to His Friend [George Wythe].* Philadelphia: J. Dunlap, 1776.

*The Selected Writings of John and John Quincy Adams.* Edited by Adrienne Koch and William Peden. New York: Knopf, 1946.

*Twenty-Six Letters, Upon Interesting Subjects, Respecting the Revolution of America, written in Holland, in the year 1780.* London: Printed for the Subscribers, 1786.

*The Works of John Adams, Second President of the United States; With a Life of the Author, Notes and Illustrations, by His Grandson, Charles Francis Adams.* 10 vols. Boston: Little, Brown, 1850–1856.

*Warren-Adams Letters, Being Chiefly a Correspondence Among John Adams, Samuel Adams, and James Warren, 1743–1814.* 2 vols. Boston: Massachusetts Historical Society, 1917–1925.

### Thomas Jefferson

*The Adams-Jefferson Letters: The Complete Correspondence Between Thomas Jefferson and Abigail and John Adams*. Edited by Lester J. Cappon. Chapel Hill: University of North Carolina Press, 1959.

*Autobiography*. New York: Capricorn Books, 1959.

*Autobiography of Thomas Jefferson, 1743–1790, Together With a Summary of The Chief Events in Jefferson's Life*. New York: Putnam, 1914.

*Basic Writings of Thomas Jefferson*. Edited by Philip S. Foner. Garden City, NY: Halcyon House, 1944.

*The Best Letters of Thomas Jefferson*. Edited by J. G. de Rolhac Hamilton. Boston: Houghton Mifflin, 1926.

*The Commonplace Book of Thomas Jefferson, A Repertory of His Ideas on Government*. Baltimore: Johns Hopkins Press, 1926.

*The Complete Anas [1791–1809] of Thomas Jefferson*. Edited by Franklin B. Sawvel. New York: Round Table Press, 1903.

*The Complete Jefferson, Containing His Major Writings, Published and Unpublished, Except His Letters*. Edited by Saul K. Padover. New York: Duell, Sloan and Pearce, 1943.

*The Correspondence of Jefferson and [Pierre S.] Du Pont de Nemours*. Baltimore: Johns Hopkins Press, 1931.

*Correspondence of Thomas Jefferson and Francis Walker Gilmer, 1814–1826*. Edited by Richard Beale Davis. Columbia: University of South Carolina Press, 1946.

*Crusade Against Ignorance: Thomas Jefferson on Education*. Edited by Gordon C. Lee. New York: Bureau of Publications, Teachers College, Columbia University, 1961.

*Democracy*. Edited by Saul K. Padover. New York: Appleton-Century Co., 1939.

*An Essay Towards Facilitating Instruction in the Anglo-Saxon and Modern Dialects of the English Language*. New York: J. F. Trow, 1851.

*The Family Letters of Thomas Jefferson*. Edited by Edwin Morris Betts and James Adam Bear. Columbia: University of Missouri Press, 1966.

*Guide to the Microfilm Edition of the Jefferson Papers of the University of Virginia, 1732–1828*. Charlottesville: University of Virginia Library, 1977.

*The Jefferson-Dunglison Letters*. Edited by John M. Dorsey. Charlottesville: University of Virginia Press, 1960.

*Jefferson Himself, the Personal Narrative of a Many-sided American*. Edited by Bernard Mayo. Boston: Houghton Mifflin, 1942.

*The Jefferson Papers of the University of Virginia*. Charlottesville: University Press of Virginia, 1973.

*The Jefferson Papers [1770–1826]*. Boston: Massachusetts Historical Society Collections, 1900.

*A Jefferson Profile as Revealed in His Letters*. Edited by Saul K. Padover. New York: J. Day, 1956.

*The Jeffersonian Cyclopedia; A Comprehensive Collection of the Views of Thomas Jefferson Classified and Arranged in Alphabetical Order Under Nine Thousand Titles Relating to Government Politics, Law, Education, Political Economy, Finance, Science, Art, Literature, Religious Freedom, Morals, etc.* Edited by John P. Foley. New York: Funk and Wagnalls, 1900.

*Jeffersonian Principles; Extracts From the Writings of Thomas Jefferson*. Edited by James Truslow Adams. Boston: Little, Brown, 1928.

*Jefferson's Ideas on a University Library; Letters from the Founder of the University of Virginia to a Boston Bookseller*. Edited by Elizabeth Cometti. Charlottesville: Tracy W. McGregor Library, University of Virginia, 1950.

*The Life and Selected Writings of Thomas Jefferson*. Edited by Adrienne Koch and William Peden. New York: Modern Library, 1944.

*The Literary Bible of Thomas Jefferson, His Commonplace Book of Philosophers and Poets*. Baltimore: Johns Hopkins Press, 1928.

*The Living Thoughts of Thomas Jefferson*. Edited by John Dewey. New York: Longmans, Green and Co., 1940.

*A Manual of Parliamentary Practice, For the Use of the United States*. Washington City [Washington, DC]: S. H. Smith, 1801.

*Memoir, Correspondence, and Miscellanies, From the Papers of Thomas Jefferson*. 4 vols. Edited by Thomas Jefferson Randolph. Charlottesville: F. Carr, 1829.

*Notes on the State of Virginia*. London: J. Stockdale, 1787.

*Notes on the State of Virginia*. Edited by William Peden. Chapel Hill: University of North Carolina Press, 1955.

*The Papers of Thomas Jefferson*. 20 vols. Edited by Julian P. Boyd. Princeton: Princeton University Press, 1950–1974.

*Political Writings: Representative Selections*. Edited by Edward Dumbauld. New York: Liberal Arts Press, 1955.

*The Portable Thomas Jefferson*. Edited by Merrill D. Peterson. New York: Viking Press, 1975.

*The Proceedings of the Government of the United States, in Maintaining the Public Right to the Beach of the Mississippi, Adjacent to New Orleans, Against the Intrusion of Edward Livingston*. New York: Ezra Sargeant, 1812.

*Reports of Cases Determined in the General Court of Virginia: From 1730, to 1740, and From 1768 to 1770*. Charlottesville: F. Carr, 1829.

*A Summary View of the Rights of British America: Set Forth in Some Resolutions Intended for the Inspection of the Present Delegates of the People of Virginia, Now in Convention*. Williamsburg, VA: Printed by Clementina Rind, 1774.

*Thomas Jefferson and His Unknown Brother Randolph. Twenty-Eight Letters Exchanged Between Thomas and Randolph Jefferson . . . During the Years 1807 to 1815*. Charlottesville: Tracy W. McGregor Library, University of Virginia, 1942.

*Thomas Jefferson and the National Capital; Containing Notes and Correspondence Exchanged Between Jefferson, Washington, L'Enfant, Ellicott, Halet, Thornton, Latrobe, the Commissioners, and Others, Relating to the Founding, Surveying, Planning, Designing, Constructing, and Administering of the City of Washington, 1783–1818*. Edited by Saul K. Padover. Washington, DC: U.S. Government Printing Office, 1946.

*Thomas Jefferson, Architect; Original Designs in the Collection of Thomas Jefferson Coolidge, Junior*. Boston: Riverside Press, 1916.

*Thomas Jefferson's Farm Book*. Edited by Edwin Morris Betts. Princeton: Princeton University Press, 1953.

*Thomas Jefferson's Garden Book, 1766–1824, With Relevant Extracts From His Other Writings*. Edited by Edwin Morris Betts. Philadelphia: American Philosophy Society, 1944.

*Writings*. 10 vols. Edited by Paul Leicester Ford. New York: Putnam, 1892–1899.

*Writings: Memorial edition, containing his Autobiography, Notes on Virginia, Parliamentary Manual, Official Papers, Messages and Addresses, and Other Writings, Official and Private, Now collected in Their Entirety for the First*

*Time*. 20 vols. Edited by Andrew A. Lipscomb. Washington, DC: Thomas Jefferson Memorial Association of the United States, 1903–1904.

*The Writings*. Edited by Saul K. Padover. Luneburg, VT: Stinehour Press, 1967.

## James Madison

*An Address Delivered Before the Agricultural Society of Albemarle, on Tuesday, May 12, 1818*. Richmond: Shephard and Pollard, 1818.

*Calendar of the Correspondence of James Madison*. New York: B. Franklin, 1970.

*The Complete Madison; His Basic Writings*. Edited by Saul K. Padover. New York: Harper, 1953.

*The Federalist: a Collection of Essays, Written in Favour of the New Constitution, as Agreed Upon by the Federal Convention, September 17, 1787*. 2 vols. New York: J. and A. McLean, 1788.

*The Federalist Papers*. James Madison, Alexander Hamilton, and John Jay. New Rochelle, NY: Arlington House, 1966.

*Journal of the Federal Convention, Kept by James Madison*. Edited by E. H. Scott. Freeport, NY: Books for Libraries Press, 1970.

*Letters and Other Writings [1769–1836]*. Philadelphia: Lippincott, 1865.

*Letters and Other Writings of James Madison*. 4 vols. New York: R. Worthington, 1884.

*Letters of Helvidius; Written in Reply to Pacificus, on the President's Proclamation of Neutrality*. Philadelphia: S. H. Smith, 1796.

*Notes of Debates in the Federal Convention of 1787, Reported by James Madison*. Athens: Ohio University Press, 1966.

*The Papers of James Madison*. 13 vols. Edited by William T. Hutchinson, et al. Chicago: University of Chicago Press, 1962–1981.

*The Papers of James Madison, Purchased by Order of Congress; Being His Correspondence and Reports of Debates in the Federal Convention*. 3 vols. Washington, DC: Langtree and O'Sullivan, 1840.

*The Writings of James Madison, Comprising His Public Papers and His Private Correspondence, Including Numerous Letters and Documents Now For the First Time Printed*. 9 vols. Edited by Gaillard Hunt. New York: Putnam, 1900–1910.

**James Monroe**
*Autobiography*. Edited by Stuart Gerry Brown. Syracuse: Syracuse University Press, 1959.

*The Memoir of James Monroe, esq., Relating to his Unsettled Claims Upon the People and Government of the United States*. Charlottesville: Gilmer, Davis, 1828.

*The People of the Sovereigns; Being a Comparison of the Government of the United States With Those of the Republics Which Have Existed Before, With the Causes of Their Decadence and Fall*. Edited by Samuel L. Gouverneur. Philadelphia: Lippincott, 1867.

*A View of the Conduct of the Executive, In the Foreign Affairs of the United States, Connected with the Mission to the French Republic, During the Years 1794, 5, & 6*. Philadelphia: B. F. Bache, 1797.

*The Writings of James Monroe, Including a Collection of His Public and Private Papers and Correspondence Now for the First Time Printed*. Edited by Stanislaus Murray Hamilton. New York: Putnam, 1898–1903.

**John Quincy Adams**
*The Adams Papers*. Edited by Lyman H. Butterfield. Cambridge: Harvard University Press, 1961– .

*Address to His Constituents of the Twelfth Congressional District, at Braintree, September 17th, 1842*. Boston: J. H. Eastburn, 1842.

*Address to the Massachusetts Historical Society, November 22, 1841, on the Opium War Between Great Britain and China*. Edited by Charles Francis Adams. Boston: Massachusetts Historical Society, 1910.

*American Principles: A Review of the Works of Fisher Ames*. Boston: Everett and Munroe, 1809.

*An Answer to Paine's Rights of Man*. London: Stockdale, 1793.

*Argument, Before the Supreme Court of the United States, in the Case of the United States, Appellants, vs. Cinque, and Others, Africans, Captured in the Schooner Amistad, By Lieut. Gedney, Delivered on the 24th of February and 1st of March, 1841*. New York: S. W. Benedict, 1841.

*A Catalogue of the Books of John Quincy Adams Deposited in the Boston Athenaeum, With Notes on Books, Adams Seals and Book-Plates By Henry Adams*. Boston: The Athenaeum, 1938.

*Correspondence Between John Quincy Adams, Esquire, President of the United States, and Several Citizens of Massachusetts Concerning the Charge of a*

*Design to Dissolve the Union Alleged to Have Existed in that State*. Boston: Press of the Boston Daily Advertiser, 1829.

*Correspondence of John Quincy Adams, 1811–1814*. Edited by Charles Francis Adams. Worcester, MA: American Antiquarian Society, 1913.

*Dermot MacMorrogh, or, The Conquest of Ireland; An Historical Tale of the Twelfth Century; In Four Cantos*. Boston: Carter, Hendee, 1832.

*A Discourse on Education, Delivered at Braintree, Thursday, October 24, 1839*. Boston: Perkins and Marvin, 1840.

*Diary of John Quincy Adams, 1794–1845; American Diplomacy and Political, Social, and Intellectual Life from Washington to Polk*. Edited by Allan Nevins. New York: Scribner's, 1951.

*The Duplicate Letters, the Fisheries and the Mississippi, Documents Relating to the Transactions at the Negotiation of Ghent*. Washington, DC: Davis and Force, 1822.

*An Eulogy on the Life and Character of James Madison . . . Delivered at the Request of the Mayor, Aldermen, and Common Council of the City of Boston*. Boston: J. H. Eastburn, City Printer, 1836.

*An Eulogy on the Life and Character of James Monroe, Fifth President of the United States*. Boston: J. H. Eastburn, 1831.

*An Inaugural Oration, Delivered at the Author's Installation, a Boylston's Professor of Rhetorick and Oratory, at Harvard University, in Cambridge, Massachusetts, on Thursday, 12 June, 1806*. Boston: Monroe and Francis, 1806.

*John Quincy Adams and American Continental Empire: Letters, Papers and Speeches*. Edited by Walter LaFeber. Chicago: Quadrangle Books, 1965.

*The Jubilee of the Constitution, A Discourse Delivered at the Request of the New York Historical Society*. New York: S. Colman, 1839.

*Lectures on Rhetoric and Oratory, Delivered to the Classes of Senior and Junior Sophisters in Harvard University*. Cambridge, MA: Hilliard and Metcalf, 1810.

*A Letter to the Hon. Harrison Gray Otis, A Member of the Present State of our National Affairs; With Remarks on Mr. Pickering's Letter to the Governor of the Commonwealth*. Boston: Oliver and Munroe, 1808.

*Letters and Address on Freemasonry*. Dayton, OH: United Brethren Publishing House, 1875.

*Letters From John Quincy Adams to his Constituents of the Twelfth Congressional District in Massachusetts, To Which Is Added his Speech in Congress Delivered February 9, 1837.* Boston: J. Knapp, 1837.

*Letters of John Quincy Adams to his Son, On the Bible and Its Teachings.* Auburn, AL: J. M. Alden, 1850.

*Letters on Silesia; Written During a Tour Through That Country in the Years 1800, 1801.* London: J. Budd, 1804.

*Letters on the Masonic Institution.* Boston: T. R. Marvin, 1847.

*Life in a New England Town: 1787,1788; Diary of John Quincy Adams While a Student in the Office of Theophilus Parsons at Newburyport.* Boston: Little, Brown, 1903.

*Memoirs of John Quincy Adams, Comprising Portions of His Diary from 1795 to 1848.* 12 vols. Edited by Charles Francis Adams. Philadelphia: Lippincott, 1847–1877.

*The New England Confederacy of MDCXLIII; A Discourse Delivered Before the Massachusetts Historical Society, at Boston, on the 29th of May, 1843; In Celebration of the Second Centennial Anniversary of That Event.* Boston: Little, Brown, 1843.

*An Oration Delivered Before the Cincinnati Astronomical Society, on the Occasion of Laying the Corner Stone of an Astronomical Observatory, on the 10th of November, 1843.* Cincinnati: Shepard, 1843.

*An Oration Delivered Before the Inhabitants of the Town of Newburyport, at Their Request, on the Sixty-First Anniversary of the Declaration of Independence, July 4th, 1837.* Newburyport, MA: Morss and Brewster, 1837.

*Oration on the Life and Character of Gilbert Motier de Lafayette, Delivered at the Request of Both Houses of the Congress of the United States . . . on the 31st of December, 1834.* Washington, DC: D. Green, 1835.

*Parties in the United States.* New York: Greenberg, 1941.

*Poems of Religion and Society, With Notices of His Life and Character.* By John Davis and I. H. Benton. New York: W. H. Graham, 1850.

*Report of the Minority of the Committee on Manufactures, Submitted to the House of Representatives of the United States, February 28, 1833.* Boston: J. H. Eastburn, 1833.

*Report Upon Weights and Measures.* Washington, DC: Gales and Seaton, 1821.

*The Selected Writings of John And John Quincy Adams*. Edited by Adrienne Koch and William Peden. New York: Knopf, 1946.

*The Social Compact, Exemplified in the Constitution of the Commonwealth of Masssachusetts; with Remarks on the Theories of Divine Right of Hobbes and of Filmer, and the Counter Theories of Sidney, Locke, Montesquieu, and Rousseau . . . a Lecture, Delivered Before the Franklin Lyceum, at Providence, R.I., November 25, 1842*. Providence: Knowles and Vose, 1842.

*Writings of John Quincy Adams*. 7 vols. Edited by Worthington Chauncy Ford New York: Macmillan, 1913– 1917.

### Andrew Jackson

*Correspondence of Andrew Jackson*. Edited by John Spencer Bassett. Washington, DC: Carnegie Institution of Washington, 1926– 1935.

*Messages to the United States Congress; With a Biographical Sketch of His Life*. Cincinnati: Day, 1837.

*The Statesmanship of Andrew Jackson as Told in his Writings and Speeches*. Edited by Francis Newton Thorpe. New York: Tandy-Thomas, 1909.

### Martin Van Buren

*The Autobiography of Martin Van Buren*. Edited by John C. Fitzpatrick. Washington, DC: U.S. Government Printing Office, 1920.

*Inquiry Into the Origin and Course of Political Parties in the United States*. Edited by his Sons. New York: Hurd and Houghton, 1867.

### John Tyler

*An Address Before the Two Literary Societies of Randolph-Macon College, June 19, 1838*. Richmond: J. C. Walker, 1838.

*An Address, Delivered Before the Literary Societies of the University of Virginia, on the Anniversary of the Declaration of Independence by the State of Virginia, June 29th, 1850*. Charlottesville: J. Alexander, 1850.

*Lecture Delivered Before the Maryland Institute for the Promotion of the Mechanic Arts, March 20, 1855*. Baltimore: J. Murphy, 1855.

*A Lecture Prepared at the Request of the Library Association of Petersburg, and Delivered on the 4th of May, 1854*. Petersburg, VA: Banks and Lewellen, 1854.

*The Letters and Times of the Tylers*. 3 vols. Richmond: Whittel and Shepperson, 1884– 1896.

## James K. Polk
*Correspondence of James K. Polk*. Edited by Herbert Weaver, et al. Nashville: Vanderbilt University Press, 1969–1979.

*The Diary of James K. Polk During His Presidency, 1845 to 1849. Now First Printed From the Original Manuscript in the Collections of the Chicago Historical Society*. 4 vols. Edited by Milo Milton Quaife. Chicago: McClurg, 1910.

*Polk; The Diary of a President, 1845–1849, Covering the Mexican War, the Acquisition of Oregon, and the Conquest of California and the Southwest*. Edited by Allan Nevins. New York: Longmans, Green, 1952.

## Millard Fillmore
*The Lady and the President: The Letters of Dorothea Dix and Millard Fillmore*. Edited by Charles M. Snyder. Lexington: University Press of Kentucky, 1975.

*Early Life of Millard Fillmore: A Personal Reminiscence*. Buffalo: Salisbury Club, 1958.

*An Examination of the Question, "Is It Right to Require Any Religious Test as a Qualification to be a Witness in a Court of Justice?"* Buffalo: C. Faxon, 1832.

*Millard Fillmore Papers*. 2 vols. Edited by Frank H. Severance. Buffalo: Buffalo Historical Society, 1907.

## James Buchanan
*Mr. Buchanan's Administration on the Eve of the Rebellion*. New York: Appleton, 1866.

*The Works of James Buchanan: Comprising His Speeches, State Papers, and Private Correspondence*. 12 vols. Edited by John Bassett Moore. Philadelphia: Lippincott, 1908–1911.

## Abraham Lincoln
*Abraham Lincoln: A Documentary Portrait Through His Speeches and Writings*. Edited by Don E. Fehrenbacher. New York: New American Library, 1964.

*Abraham Lincoln Chronology, 1809–1865*. Harry Edward Pratt. Springfield: Illinois State Historical Library, 1953.

*Abraham Lincoln, His Autobiographical Writings Now Brought Together for the First Time*. Edited by Paul M. Angle. New Brunswick, NJ: Rutgers University Press, 1948.

*Abraham Lincoln: His Speeches and Writings*. Edited by Roy P. Basler. Cleveland: World Pub. Co., 1946.

*Abraham Lincoln: Selected Speeches, Messages, and Letters*. Edited by Harry Williams. New York: Rinehart, 1957.

*Abraham Lincoln's Speech at Peoria, Illinois [16 Oct. 1854] in Reply to Senator Douglas: Seven Numbers of the Illinois Daily Journal, Springfield, Oct. 21, 23–28, 1854*. Peoria, IL: E. J. Jacob, 1952.

*Abraham Lincoln's Speeches*. Compiled by L. E. Chittenden. New York: Dodd, Mead, 1923.

*Abraham Lincoln's Speeches and Letters, 1832–1865*. Rev ed. Edited by Paul M. Angle. New York: Dutton, 1957.

*Anecdotes of Abraham Lincoln*. Edited by J. B. McClure. Chicago: Rhodes and McClure, 1889.

*An Autobiography of Abraham Lincoln, Consisting of the Personal Portions of His Letters, Speeches and Conversations*. Compiled by Nathaniel W. Stephenson. Indianapolis: Bobbs-Merrill, 1926.

*Collected Works*. 9 vols. Edited by Ray P. Basler. New Brunswick, NJ: Rutgers University Press, 1953–1955.

*Complete Works*. New and enlarged ed. Edited by John G. Nicolay and John Hay. New York: Tandy-Thomas Co., 1905.

*Conversations with Lincoln*. Edited by Charles M. Segal. New York: Putnam, 1961.

*Created Equal: The Complete Lincoln-Douglas Debates of 1858*. Edited by Paul M. Angle. Chicago: University of Chicago Press, 1958.

*The Illinois Political Campaign of 1858; A Facsimile of the Printer's Copy and his Debates with Senator Stephen Arnold Douglas*. Washington, DC: U.S. Library of Congress, 1958.

*In the Name of the People; Speeches and Writings of Lincoln and Douglas in the Ohio Campaign of 1859*. Edited by Harry V. Jaffa and Robert W. Johannsen. Columbus: Ohio State University Press, 1959.

*Letters and Addresses of Abraham Lincoln*. Edited by Mary McClean. New York: Unit Book Publishing Co., 1907.

*The Life and Writings of Abraham Lincoln*. Edited by Philip Van Doren Stern. New York: Modern Library, 1942.

*The Lincoln-Douglas Debates of 1858*. Edited by Robert W. Johannsen. New York: Oxford University Press, 1965.

*The Lincoln Encyclopedia; The Spoken and Written Words of A. Lincoln Arranged for Ready Reference.* Edited by Archer H. Shaw. New York: Macmillan, 1950.

*Lincoln Ideals, His Personality, and Principles as Reflected in His Own Words.* Washington, DC: Lincoln Sesquicentennial Commission, 1959.

*Lincoln Letters.* Norwood, MA: Plimpton Press, 1913.

*Lincoln Letters Hitherto Unpublished in the Library of Brown University and Other Providence Libraries.* Providence: Brown University Press, 1927.

*The Lincoln Papers: The Story of the Collection, With Selections to July 4, 1861.* 2 vols. David Chambers Mearns. Garden City, NY: Doubleday, 1948.

*Lincoln Speaks.* Chicago: Regnery, 1963.

*The Lincoln Treasury.* Compiled by Caroline Thomas Harnsberger. Chicago: Wilcox and Follett, 1950.

*Lincoln's Last Speech in Springfield.* Chicago: University of Chicago, 1925.

*The Literary Works of Abraham Lincoln.* Edited by Carl Van Doren. New York: Heritage Press, 1942.

*The Literary Works of Abraham Lincoln.* Edited by David D. Anderson. Columbus: Charles E. Merrill, 1970.

*The Living Lincoln: The Man, His Mind, His Times, and the War He Fought, Reconstructed from his own Writings.* Edited by Paul M. Angle and Earl Schenck Miers. New Brunswick, NJ: Rutgers University Press, 1955.

*The Living Words of Abraham Lincoln: Selected Writings of a Great President.* Edited by Edward Lewis and Jack Belck. Kansas City, MO: Hallmark Editions, 1967.

*New Letters and Papers of Lincoln.* Edited by Paul M. Angle. New York: Houghton Mifflin, 1930.

*The Philosophy of Abraham Lincoln In His Own Words.* Compiled by William E. Baringer. Indian Hills, CO: Falcon's Wing Press, 1959.

*Political Debates Between Abraham Lincoln and Stephen A. Douglas.* Cleveland: Burrows Bros, 1894.

*The Political Thought of Abraham Lincoln.* Edited by Richard N. Current. Indianapolis: Bobbs-Merrill, 1967.

*Quotations From Abraham Lincoln*. Edited by Ralph Y. McGinnis. Chicago: Nelson-Hall, 1977.

*A Strange Affair*. Edited by Roger W. Barrett. Peoria, IL: E. J. Jacob, 1933.

*Treasury of Lincoln Quotations*. Edited by F. Kerner. New York: Doubleday and Co., Inc., 1965.

*Uncollected Works of Abraham Lincoln*. Compiled by R. Rockwell Wilson. New York: Primavera Press, 1947.

*Wit and Wisdom of Abraham Lincoln*. Edited by H. J. Long. Cleveland: World, 1965.

*Words of Lincoln*. Compiled by O. H. Oldroyd. Washington, DC: O. H. Oldroyd, 1895.

*The Writings of Abraham Lincoln*. 8 vols. Edited by A. B. Lapsley. New York: Putnam, 1905–1906.

### Andrew Johnson
*Papers of Andrew Johnson*. Edited by Leroy P. Graf and Ralph W. Haskins. Knoxville: University of Tennessee Press, 1967.

*Speeches of Andrew Johnson, President of the United States*. Edited by Frank Moore. Boston: Little, Brown Co., 1865.

*Trial of Andrew Johnson, President of the United States, Before the Senate of the United States, On Impeachment by the House of Representatives for High Crimes and Misdemeanors*. 3 vols. Washington, DC: U.S. Government Printing Office, 1868.

### Ulysses S. Grant
*General Grant's Letters to a Friend [Elihu B. Washburne], 1861–1880*. New York: T. Y. Crowell, 1897.

*Letters of Ulysses S. Grant to his Father and His Younger Sister, 1857–1878*. Edited by Jesse Grant Cramer. New York: Putnam, 1912.

*Mr. Lincoln's General; U. S. Grant, an Illustrated Autobiography*. Edited by Roy Meredith. New York: Dutton, 1959.

*The Papers of Ulysses S. Grant*. Edited by John Y. Simon. 10 vols. Carbondale: Southern Illinois University Press, 1967– .

*Personal Memoirs*. Edited by Everette B. Long. Cleveland: World Pub. Co., 1952.

*Personal Memoirs of U. S. Grant*. 2 vols. New York: C. L. Webster, 1885–1886.

*Ulysses S. Grant: Conversations and Unpublished Letters*. Edited by M. J. Cramer. New York: Eaton and Mains, 1897.

### Rutherford B. Hayes

*Diary and Letters of Rutherford Birchard Hayes, Nineteenth President of the United States*. 5 vols. Edited by Charles Richard Williams. Columbus: Ohio State Archaeological and Historical Society, 1922–1926.

*Hayes: The Diary of a President 1875–1881*. Edited by T. Harry Williams. New York: McKay, 1964.

*The Hayes-Bryan Correspondence*. Edited by E. W. Winkler. Austin: Southwestern Historical Quarterly, 1921–1926.

*An Historical and Critical Study of the Speeches of Rutherford B. Hayes with an Appended Edition of His Addresses*. Upton Sinclair Palmer. Ph.D. diss. University of Michigan, 1950.

*Teach the Freeman: The Correspondence of Ruterford B. Hayes and the Slater Fund for Negro Education, 1881–1887*. 2 vols. Edited by Louis D. Rubin. Baton Rouge: Louisiana State University Press, 1959.

### James Garfield

*The Diary of James A. Garfield*. 4 vols. Edited by Harry James Brown and Frederick D. Williams. East Lansing: Michigan State University, 1967–1981.

*Discovery and Ownership of the Northwestern Territory*. Cleveland: Western Reserve and Northern Ohio Historical Society, 1881.

*Garfield-Hinsdale Letters: Correspondence Between James Abram Garfield and Burke Aaron Hinsdale*. Edited by Mary L. Hinsdale. Ann Arbor: University of Michigan Press, 1949.

*Politics and Patronage in the Guilded Age: The Correspondence of James A. Garfield and Charles E. Henry*. Edited by James D. Norris and Arthur H. Shaffer. Madison: State Historical Society of Wisconsin, 1970.

*Wild Life of the Army: Civil War Letters of James A. Garfield*. Edited by Frederick D. Williams. East Lansing: Michigan State University Press, 1964.

*Works of James Abram Garfield*. 2 vols. Edited by Burke A. Hinsdale. Boston: J. R. Osgood, 1882–1883.

## Grover Cleveland

*Addresses, State Papers and Letters*. Edited by Albert Ellery Bergh. New York: Sundial Classics Co., 1909.

*Fishing and Shooting Sketches*. New York: Outing Pub. Co., 1906.

*Good Citizenship*. Philadelphia: H. Altemus Co., 1908.

*The Independence of the Executive*. Princeton: Princeton University Press, 1913.

*Letters of Grover Cleveland, 1850–1908*. Edited by Allan Nevins. Boston: Houghton Mifflin, 1933.

*Presidential Problems*. New York: Century Co., 1904.

*Principles and Purposes of our Form of Government as Set Forth in Public Papers of Cleveland*. Compiled by Francis Gottsberger. New York: G. G. Peck, 1982.

*Public Papers of Grover Cleveland, Governor, 1883 [–1884]*. Albany: Argus Co., 1883–1884.

*The Self-Made Man in American Life*. New York: Crowell, 1897.

*Writings and Speeches*. Edited by George F. Parker. New York: Cassell, 1892.

## Benjamin Harrison

*The Correspondence Between Benjamin Harrison and James G. Blaine, 1882–1893*. Edited by Albert T. Volwiler. Philadelphia: American Philosophical Society, 1940.

*Speeches of Benjamin Harrison, Twenty-Third President of the United States; A Complete Collection of His Public Addresses From February, 1888, to February, 1892*. Compiled by Charles Hedges. New York: United States Book Co., 1892.

*This Country of Ours*. New York: Scribner's, 1897.

*Views of an Ex-President; Being His Addresses and Writings on Subjects of Public Interest Since the Close of His Administration as President of the United States*. Compiled by Mary Lord Harrison. Indianapolis: Bowen-Merrill, 1901.

## William McKinley

*Speeches and Addresses of William McKinley, From His Election to Congress to the Present Time*. New York: Appleton, 1893.

*Speeches and Addresses of William McKinley, From March 1, 1897 to May 30, 1900*. New York: Doubleday and McClure, 1900.

*The Tariff in the Days of Henry Clay, and Since; An Exhaustive Review of Our Tariff Legislation From 1812 to 1896*. New York: Henry Clay Pub. Co., 1896.

**Theodore Roosevelt**
*American Ideals and Other Essays, Social and Political*. New York: Putnam, 1897.

*Average Americans*. New York: Putnam, 1920.

*A Book-Lover's Holidays in the Open*. New York: Scribner's, 1916.

*A Compilation of the Messages and Speeches of Theodore Roosevelt, 1901–1905*. 2 vols. Edited by Alfred Henry Lewis. Washington, DC: Bureau of National Literature and Art, 1906.

*Conservation of Womanhood and Childhood*. New York: Funk and Wagnalls, 1912.

*The Deer Family (and Others)*. New York: Macmillan, 1903.

*Fear God and Take Your Own Part*. New York: Doran, 1916.

*The Foes of Our Own Household*. New York: Doran, 1917.

*The Free Citizen: A Summons to Service of the Democratic Ideal. Selections from His Writings and Stories From His Record*. Edited by Hermann Hagedorn. New York: Macmillan, 1956.

*Good Hunting: In Pursuit of Big Game in the West*. New York: Harper, 1907.

*Gouverneur Morris*. Boston: Houghton Mifflin Co., 1888.

*The Great Adventure: Present-Day Studies in American Nationalism*. New York: Scribner's, 1918.

*History as Literature, and Other Essays*. New York: Scribner's, 1913.

*The Hunting and Exploring Adventures of Theodore Roosevelt*. Edited by Donald Day. New York: Dial Press, 1955.

*Hunting Trips of a Ranchman; Sketches of Sport on the Northern Cattle Plains*. New York: Putnam, 1885.

*Hunting Trips on the Prairies and in the Mountains*. New York: Putnam, 1900.

*Letters from Theodore Roosevelt to Anna Roosevelt Cowles, 1870–1918.* New York: Scribner's, 1924.

*The Letters of Theodore Roosevelt.* Edited by Elting E. Morison. Cambridge: Harvard University Press, 1951–1954.

*Letters of Theodore Roosevelt, Civil Service Commissioner, 1889–1895.* Washington, DC: U.S. Civil Service Commission, 1958.

*Letters to Kermit from Theodore Roosevelt, 1902–1908.* Edited by William H. Irwin. New York: Scribner's, 1946.

*Life of Thomas Hart Benton.* Boston: Houghton Mifflin, 1887.

*Life-Histories of African Game Animals.* 2 vols. New York: Scribner's, 1914.

*National Strength and International Duty.* Princeton: Princeton University Press, 1917.

*The Naval Operations of the War Between Great Britain and the United States, 1812–1815.* Boston: Little, Brown, 1901.

*The Naval War of 1812; or, The History of the United States Navy During the Last War With Great Britain; To Which Is Appended an Account of the Battle of New Orleans.* 4th ed. New York: Haskell House, 1889.

*The New Nationalism.* New York: The Outlook Co., 1910.

*New York.* New ed. New York: Longmans, Green, 1895.

*Oliver Cromwell.* New York: Scribner's, 1900.

*Outdoor Pastimes of an American Hunter.* New and enlarged ed. New York: Scribner's, 1908.

*Presidential Addresses and State Papers.* 4 vols. New York: Collier, 1905.

*Public Papers of Theodore Roosevelt, Governor, 1899 [–1900].* 2 vols. Albany, NY: Brandow Print Co., 1899–1900.

*Ranch Life and the Hunting-Trail.* New York: Century Co., 1888.

*The Real Roosevelt, His Forceful and Fearless Utterances on Various Subjects.* Alan Warner. New York: Putnam, 1910.

*Realizable Ideals (the Earl Lectures).* San Francisco: Whittaker and Ray-Wiggin Co., 1912.

*Roosevelt in the Kansas City Star*. New York: Houghton Mifflin, 1921.

*Roosevelt's Writings*. Edited by M. G. Fulton. New York: Macmillan, 1920.

*The Rough Riders*. New York: Scribner's, 1899.

*Selections from the Correspondence of Theodore Roosevelt and Henry Cabot, 1884–1918*. 2 vols. New York: Scribner's, 1925.

*Theodore Roosevelt: An Autobiography*. New York: Scribner's, 1920.

*Theodore Roosevelt's America; Selections from the Writings of the Oyster Bay Naturalist*. Edited by Farida A. Wiley. New York: Devin-Adair, 1955.

*Theodore Roosevelt's Letters to His Children*. Edited by Joseph Bucklin Bishop. New York: Scribner's, 1919.

*The Strenuous Life; Essays and Addresses*. New York: Century Co., 1902.

*Theodore Roosevelt Cyclopedia*. Edited by Albert Bushnell Hart and Herbert Ronald Ferleger. New York: Roosevelt Memorial Association, 1941.

*Theodore Roosevelt on Race, Riots, Reds, Crime*. Compiled by Archibald B. Roosevelt. West Sayville, NY: Putnam, 1957.

*The Theodore Roosevelt Treasury: A Self-Portrait From His Writings*. Compiled by Hermann Hagedorn. New York: Putnam, 1957.

*Theodore Roosevelt's Diaries of Boyhood and Youth*. New York: Scribner's, 1928.

*Through the Brazilian Wilderness*. New York: Scribner's, 1914.

*The Wilderness Hunter; An Account of the Big Game of the United States and Its Chase with Horse, Hound, and Rifle*. New York: Putnam, 1893.

*The Winning of the West [1769–1807]*. 4 vols. New York: Putnam, 1889–1896.

*Works of Theodore Roosevelt*. 20 vols. New York: Scribner's, 1926.

*Writings of Theodore Roosevelt*. Edited by W. H. Harbough. Indianapolis: Bobbs-Merrill, 1966.

**William H. Taft**
*The Anti-Trust Act and the Supreme Court*. New York: Harper, 1914.

*Ethics in Service; Addresses Delivered in the Page Lecture Series, 1914, Before the Senior Class of the Sheffield Scientific School, Yale University*. New Haven: Yale University Press, 1915.

*Four Aspects of Civic Duty.* New York: Scribner's, 1906.

*Liberty Under Law, An Interpretation of the Principles of Our Constitutional Government.* New Haven: Yale University Press, 1922.

*Our Chief Magistrate and His Powers.* New York: Columbia University Press, 1916.

*Political Issues and Outlooks; Speeches Delivered Between August, 1908, and February, 1909.* New York: Doubleday, Page, 1909.

*Popular Government; Its Essence, Its Permanence and Its Perils.* New Haven: Yale University Press, 1913.

*Present Day Problems; A Collection of Addresses Delivered on Various Occasions.* New York: Dodd, Mead, 1908.

*The Presidency, Its Duties, Its Powers, Its Opportunities and Its Limitations; Three Lectures.* New York: Scribner's, 1916.

*The President and His Powers.* New York: Columbia University Press, 1967.

*Presidential Addresses and State Papers of William Howard Taft.* 2 vols. New York: Doubleday, Page, 1910.

*Representative Government in the United States; Being the Opening Lecture of the James Stokes Lectureship on Politics, at New York University.* New York: New York University Press, 1921.

*Taft Papers on League of Nations.* Edited by Theodore Marburg and Horace E. Flack. New York: Macmillan, 1920.

*The United States and Peace.* New York: Scribner's, 1914.

*World Peace; A Written Debate Between William Howard Taft and William Jennings Bryan.* New York: Doran, 1917.

### Woodrow Wilson
*Congressional Government: A Study in American Politics.* Boston: Houghton Mifflin, 1885.

*Constitutional Government in the United States.* New York: Columbia University Press, 1908.

*A Crossroads of Freedom, the 1912 Campaign Speeches.* Edited by John Wells Davidson. New Haven: Yale University Press, 1956.

*Day of Dedication: The Essential Writings and Speeches of Woodrow Wilson.* Compiled by A. Fried. New York: Macmillan Co., 1965.

*Division and Reunion, 1829–1889.* New York: Longmans, Green, 1893.

*George Washington.* New York: Harper, 1896.

*A History of the American People.* 5 vols. New York: Harper, 1902.

*John Wesley's Place in History.* New York: Abingdon Press, 1915.

*Leaders of Men.* Edited by T. H. Vail Motter. Princeton: Princeton University Press, 1952.

*Mere Literature, and Other Essays.* Boston: Houghton Mifflin, 1896.

*The New Freedom; A Call for the Emancipation of the Generous Energies of a People.* New York: Doubleday, Page, 1913.

*An Old Master, and Other Political Essays.* New York: Scribner's, 1893.

*The Papers of Woodrow Wilson.* 40 vols. Edited by Arthur S. Link. Princeton: Princeton University Press, 1966–1982.

*The Political Thought of Woodrow Wilson.* Edited by E. David Cronin. Indianapolis: Bobbs-Merrill, 1965.

*The Politics of Woodrow Wilson: Selections from His Speeches and Writings.* Edited by August Heckscher. New York: Harper, 1956.

*The Priceless Gift: The Love Letters of Woodrow Wilson and Ellen Axson Wilson.* Edited by Eleanor Wilson McAdoo. New York: McGraw-Hill, 1962.

*The Public Papers of Woodrow Wilson.* 6 vols. Edited by Ray Stannard Baker and William E. Dodd. New York: Harper and Brothers, 1925–1927.

*Robert E. Lee, An Interpretation.* Chapel Hill: University of North Carolina Press, 1924.

*The Road Away from Revolution.* New York: Atlantic Monthly, 1923.

*Selected Addresses and Public Papers.* Edited by A. B. Hart. New York: Boni and Liveright, 1918.

*The State; Elements of Historical and Practical Politics.* Rev ed. Boston: Heath, 1898.

*The Study of Public Administration.* Washington, DC: Public Affairs Press, 1955.

*War Addresses of Woodrow Wilson.* Boston: Ginn, 1918.

*When a Man Comes to Himself*. New York: Harper, 1901.

*The Wilson Reader*. Edited by Francis Farmer. New York: Oceana Publications, 1956.

### Warren G. Harding
*Our Common Country; Mutual Good Will in America*. Edited by Frederick E. Schortemeier. Indianapolis: Bobbs-Merrill, 1921.

*Rededicating America: Life and Recent Speeches of Warren G. Harding*. Edited by Frederick E. Schortemeier. Indianapolis: Bobbs-Merrill, 1920.

### Calvin Coolidge
*America's Need for Education, and Other Educational Addresses*. Boston: Houghton Mifflin, 1925.

*The Autobiography of Calvin Coolidge*. New York: Cosmopolitan Book Corp., 1929.

*Calvin Coolidge, His Ideals of Citizenship as Revealed Through His Speeches and Writings*. Edited by Edward Elwell Whiting. Boston: W. A. Wilde, 1924.

*Foundations of the Republic; Speeches and Addresses*. New York: Scribner's, 1926.

*Have Faith in Massachusetts; A Collection of Speeches and Messages*. Boston: Houghton Mifflin, 1919.

*The Price of Freedom; Speeches and Addresses*. New York: Scribner's 1924.

*The Talkative President: The Off-the-Record Press Conferences of Calvin Coolidge*. Edited by Howard H. Quint and Robert H. Ferrell. Amherst: University of Massachusetts Press, 1964.

*Your Son, Calvin Coolidge: A Selection of Letters from Calvin Coolidge to His Father*. Edited by Edward C. Lathem. Hanover, NH: University Press of New England, 1968.

### Herbert Hoover
*Addresses Upon the American Road, 1933–1938*. New York: Scribner's, 1938.

*Addresses Upon the American Road, 1940–1941*. New York, Scribner's, 1941.

*Addresses Upon the American Road, World War II, 1941–1945*. New York: Van Nostrand, 1946.

*Addresses Upon the American Road, 1945–1948*. New York: Van Nostrand, 1949.

*Addresses Upon the American Road, 1948–1950*. Stanford: Stanford University Press, 1951.

*Addresses Upon the American Road, 1950–1955*. Stanford: Stanford University Press, 1955.

*Addresses Upon the American Road, 1955–1960*. Caldwell, ID: Caxton Printers, 1961.

*An American Epic*. 4 vols. Chicago: Henry Regnery Co., 1959–1964.

*American Ideals Versus the New Deal*. New York: Scribner's, 1936.

*American Individualism*. Garden City, NY: Doubleday, Page, 1922.

*America's First Crusade*. New York: Scribner's, 1943.

*America's Way Forward*. New York: Scribner's, 1939.

*The Basis for Lasting Peace*. New York: Van Nostrand, 1945.

*A Boyhood in Iowa*. New York: Aventine Press, 1931.

*Campaign Speeches of 1932, by President Hoover and Ex-President Coolidge*. Garden City, NY: Doubleday, Doran, 1933.

*The Challenge to Liberty*. New York: Scribner's, 1934.

*A Cause to Win: Five Speeches by Herbert Hoover on American Foreign Policy in Relation to Soviet Russia*. Concord, NH: Rumford Press, 1951.

*Fishing for Fun—and Wash Your Soul*. New York: Random House, 1963.

*Forty Key Questions About Our Foreign Policy*. New York: Updegraff Press, 1952.

*Further Addresses Upon the American Road, 1938–1940*. New York: Scribner's, 1940.

*Herbert Hoover: Proclamations and Executive Orders, March 4, 1929 to March 4, 1933*. 2 vols. Washington, DC: Government Printing Office, 1974.

*Herbert Hoover's Challenge to America: His Life and Words*. Edited by Robert L. Polley. Wasksha, WI: Country Beautiful Foundation, 1965.

*Hoover After Dinner; Addresses Delivered Before the Gridiron Club of Washington, D.C., with Other Informal Speeches*. New York: Scribner's, 1933.

*The Hoover Commission Report on Organization of the Executive Branch of the Government*. New York: McGraw Hill, 1949.

*The Hoover-Wilson Wartime Correspondence, September 24, 1914 to November 11, 1918*. Edited by Francis W. O'Brien. Ames: Iowa State University Press, 1974.

*The Memoirs of Herbert Hoover*. 3 vols. New York: Macmillan, 1951–1952.

*The New Day; Campaign Speeches of Herbert Hoover, 1928*. Stanford: Stanford University Press, 1928.

*On Growing Up: Letters to American Boys and Girls Including the Uncommon Man, and Other Selections*. Edited by William Nichols. New York: Morrow, 1962.

*The Ordeal of Woodrow Wilson*. New York: McGraw Hill, 1958.

*Principles of Mining; Valuation, Organization and Administration; Copper, Gold, Lead, Silver, Tin and Zinc*. New York: Hill Pub. Co., 1909.

*The Problems of Lasting Peace*. Garden City, NY: Doubleday, Doran, 1943.

*The Reminiscences of Herbert Clark Hoover*. Glen Rock, NJ: Microfilming Corp. of America, 1975.

*The State Papers and Other Public Writings, 1929–33*. 2 vols. Edited by William Starr Myers. Garden City, NY: Doubleday, Doran, 1934.

*Two Peacemakers in Paris: The Hoover-Wilson Post-Armistice Letters, 1918–1920*. Edited by Francis W. O'Brien. College Station, TX: A & M University Press, 1978.

### Franklin Delano Roosevelt

*Ah That Voice: The Fireside Chats of Franklin Delano Roosevelt*. Compiled by Kenneth D. Yielding and Paul H. Carlson. Odessa, TX: John Ben Shepperd, Jr., Library of the Presidents, Presidential Museum, 1974.

*As FDR Said; A Treasury of his Speeches, Conversations and Writings*. Frank Kingdon. New York: Duell, Sloan and Pearce, 1950.

*Complete Presidential Press Conferences of Franklin D. Roosevelt, 1933–1945*. 12 vols. new York: Da Capr, 1972.

*F.D.R., Columnist; The Uncollected Columns of Franklin D. Roosevelt*. Edited by Donald Scott Carmichael. Chicago: Pellegrine and Cudahy, 1947.

*F.D.R.: His Personal Letters, 1905–1945.* 4 vols. Edited by Elliot Roosevelt and Joseph P. Lash. New York: Duell, Sloan and Pearce, 1947–1950.

*The FDR Memoirs.* Bernard Asbell. New York: Doubleday, 1973.

*For The President —Personal and Secret: Correspondence Between Franklin D. Roosevelt and William C. Bullitt.* Edited by Orville H. Bullitt. Boston: Houghton Mifflin, 1972.

*Franklin D. Roosevelt and Conservation, 1911–1945.* 2 vols. Edited by Edgar B. Nixon. Hyde Park, NY: National Archives and Records Service, General Services Administration, 1957.

*Franklin D. Roosevelt and Foreign Affairs.* Edited by Edgar B. Nixon. Cambridge: Harvard University Press, 1969.

*Franklin D. Roosevelt and Foreign Affairs, January 1937–August 1939.* Edited by Donald B. Schewe. New York: Garland, 1979–1980.

*Franklin D. Roosevelt's Own Story, Told in His Own Words From his Private and Public Papers as Selected by Donald Day.* Boston: Little, Brown, 1951.

*Government —Not Politics.* New York: Covici-Friede, 1932.

*The Happy Warrior, Alfred E. Smith: A Study of a Public Servant.* Boston: Houghton Mifflin, 1928.

*Index to the Complete Recorded Speeches of Franklin Delano Roosevelt: 278 Speeches Dating From 1920 to 1945.* North Hollywood: Center for Cassette Studies, 1974.

*Looking Forward.* New York: John Day, 1933.

*Memorable Quotations of Franklin D. Roosevelt.* Edited by E. Taylor Parks and Lois F. Parks. New York: Crowell, 1965.

*Nothing to Fear; The Selected Addresses of Franklin Delano Roosevelt, 1932–1945.* Edited by B. D. Zevin. Boston: Houghton Mifflin, 1946.

*The New Deal: A Documentary History.* Edited by W. E. Leuchtenburg. Columbia: University of South Carolina Press, 1968.

*On Our Way.* New York: Day, 1934.

*Public Papers of Franklin D. Roosevelt, Forty-Eighth Governor of the State of New York, Second Term, 1932.* Albany, NY: J. B. Lyon, 1939.

*The Public Papers and Addresses of Franklin D. Roosevelt, with a Special*

*Introduction and Explanatory Notes by President Roosevelt.* 13 vols. Compiled by Samuel I. Rosenman. New York: Russell and Russell, 1969.

*Records of the Town of Hyde Park, Dutchess County.* Hyde Park, NY: Dutchess County Historical Society, 1928.

*Rendezvous With Destiny: Addresses and Opinions of Franklin Delano Roosevelt.* Edited by J. B. S. Hardman. New York: Dryden, 1944.

*Roosevelt and Churchill: Their Secret Wartime Correspondence.* Edited by Frances L. Lowenheim, Harold D. Langley, and Manfred Jones. New York: Saturday Review Press, 1975.

*Roosevelt and Frankfurter: Their Correspondence, 1928–1945.* Edited by M. Freedman. Boston: Little, Brown, 1967.

### Harry S Truman
*Freedom and Equality, Addresses.* Edited by David S. Horton. Columbia, SC: University of Missouri Press, 1960.

*Letters from Father: The Truman Family's Personal Correspondence.* Edited by Margaret Truman. New York: Pinnacle Books, 1982.

*The Man from Missouri: The Memorable Words of the Thirty-Third President.* Edited by Ted Sheldon. Kansas City, MO: Hallmark Editions, 1970.

*Memoirs.* 2 vols. Garden City, NY: Doubleday, 1955–1956.

*Mr. Citizen.* New York: Bernard Geis Associates, 1960.

*Mr. President.* New York: Farrar, Straus, and Young, 1952.

*Public Papers of the Presidents: Harry S Truman, 1945–1953.* 8 vols. Washington, DC: U.S. Government Printing Office, 1961–1966.

*The Truman Program: Addresses and Messages.* Edited by M. B. Schnapper. Washington, DC: Public Affairs Press, 1949.

*Truman Speaks.* New York: Columbia University Press, 1960.

*The Truman Years: The Words and Times of Harry S Truman.* Edited by Robert L. Polley. Waukesha, WI: Country Beautiful, 1976.

### Dwight D. Eisenhower
*At Ease: Stories I Tell To Friends.* Garden City, NY: Doubleday, 1967.

*Crusade in Europe.* New York: Doubleday, 1948.

*The Eisenhower Diaries.* Edited by Robert H. Ferrell. New York: W. W. Norton, 1981.

*Eisenhower Speaks: Dwight D. Eisenhower in his Messages and Speeches.* Edited by Rudolph L. Treuenfels. New York: Farrar, Straus, 1948.

*General Dwight D. Eisenhower: Remarks at Freedoms Foundation at Valley Forge, 1948–1969.* Compiled by Edward Salt. Valley Forge, PA: Freedoms Foundations, 1969.

*In Review: Pictures I've Kept: A Concise Pictorial Autobiography.* Garden City, NY: Doubleday, 1969.

*Mandate for Change: The White House Years, 1953–56.* Garden City, NY: Doubleday, 1963.

*The Papers of Dwight David Eisenhower: The War Years.* 5 vols. Edited by Alfred D. Chandler. Baltimore: Johns Hopkins Press, 1970.

*Peace With Justice: Selected Addresses of Dwight D. Eisenhower.* New York: Columbia University Press, 1961.

*Public Papers of the Presidents of the United States, Dwight D. Eisenhower, 1953–61.* Washington, DC: U.S. Government Printing Office, 1958–1961.

*The Quotable Dwight D. Eisenhower.* Edited by Elsie Gallagher. Anderson, SC: Droke House, 1967.

*Selected Speeches of Dwight David Eisenhower, 34th President of the United States.* Washington, DC: U.S. Government Printing Office, 1970.

*Waging Peace, 1956–1961: The White House Years.* Garden City, NY: Doubleday, 1965.

### John F. Kennedy

"An Address to the United Nations, September 25, 1961." In *The United States and the United Nations.* Edited by Franz B. Gross, 227–288. Norman: University of Oklahoma Press, 1964.

*As We Remember Joe.* Cambridge, England: Cambridge University Press, 1945.

*The Burden and the Glory.* Edited by Allan Nevins. New York: Harper and Row, 1964.

*Creative America.* New York: Ridge Press, 1964.

*Every Citizen Holds Office*. Washington, DC: Citizenship Committee, National Education Association, 1964.

*The First Book Edition of John F. Kennedy's Inaugural Address*. New York: Watts, 1965.

*Good Fences Make Good Neighbors. Convocation (Address) October 8, 1957, the University of New Brunswick*. Frederiction: University of New Brunswick Press, 1960.

*A John F. Kennedy Memorial Miniature*. New York: Random House, 1966.

*John F. Kennedy on Education*. Edited by William T. O'Hara. New York: Teachers College Press, Columbia University, 1966.

*John F. Kennedy on Israel, Zionism, and Jewish Issues*. Compiled by Ernest E. Barbarash. New York: Herzl Press, 1965.

*John F. Kennedy Speaks: The Texts of Eleven Major Speeches by the Late President Together with a Selection of Photographs*. Manila: Regional Service Center, 1964.

*John Fitzgerald Kennedy: A Compilation of Statements and Speeches Made During His Service in the United States Senate and House of Representatives*. Washington, DC: U.S. Government Printing Office, 1964.

*Kennedy and the Press: The News Conferences*. Edited by Harold W. Chase and Allen H. Lerman. New York: Thomas Y. Crowell, 1965.

*The Kennedy Presidential Press Conferences*. New York: E. M. Coleman Enterprises, 1978.

*The Kennedy Reader*. Compiled by Jay David. Indianapolis: Bobbs-Merrill, 1967.

*Let the Lady Hold Up Her Head: Reflections on American Immigration Policy*. New York: American Jewish Committee, 1957.

*Moral Crisis: The Case for Civil Rights*. Minneapolis: Gilbert Pub. Co., 1964.

*A Nation of Immigrants*. New York: Anti-Defamation League of B'nai B'rith, 1959.

*President Kennedy Speaks*. Washington, DC: United States Information Agency, 1961.

*President Kennedy's Program*. Washington, DC: Congressional Quarterly Service, 1961.

*Profiles in Courage*. New York: Harper and Row, 1956.

*The Public Papers of the Presidents of the United States, John F. Kennedy*. Washington, DC: U.S. Government Printing Office, 1961– .

*Religious Views of President Kennedy*. Compiled by Nicholas A. Schneider. St. Louis: Herder, 1967.

*Sam Houston and the Senate*. Austin: Pemberton Press, 1970.

*A Selection of Speeches and Statements on the United Nations by President John F. Kennedy*. New York: American Association for the United Nations, 1963.

*The Strategy for Peace*. Edited by Allan Nevins. New York: Harper and Brothers, 1960.

*To Turn the Tide: A Selection from President Kennedy's Public Statements From His Election Through the 1961 Adjournment of Congress, Setting Forth the Goals of His First Legislative Year*. Edited by John W. Gardner. New York: Harper and Row, 1962.

*Why England Slept*. New York: Funk, 1940.

*Words to Remember*. Kansas City, MO: Hallmark Cards, 1967.

**Richard M. Nixon**
*The Challenge We Face*. New York: McGraw Hill, 1960.

*Education for the 1970's: Renewal and Reform; Messages to the Congress*. Washington, DC: U.S. Government Printing Office, 1970.

*Leaders*. New York: Warner Books, 1982.

*The Public Papers of the Presidents of the United States, Richard M. Nixon, 1969–74*. Washington, DC: U.S. Government Printing Office, 1971–1975.

*The Real War*. New York: Warner Books, 1980.

*RN: The Memoirs of Richard Nixon*. New York: Grosset and Dunlap, 1978.

*Setting the Course: The First Year*. New York: Funk and Wagnalls, 1970.

*Six Crises: With a New Preface*. New York: Pocket, 1968.

*United States Foreign Policy for the 1970's: Building for Peace: A Report by President Richard Nixon to the Congress, February 25, 1971*. New York: Harper and Row, 1971.

*The Young Nixon: An Oral Inquiry*. Edited by Renee K. Schule. Fullerton, CA: Oral History Program, California State University, Fullerton, 1978.

### Gerald R. Ford

*The Challenges That Face America*. New York: Encyclopedia Americana/CBS News Audio Resource Library, 1975. Sound recording.

*A Discussion with Gerald R. Ford: The American Presidency*. Washington, DC: American Enterprise Institute, 1977.

*Portrait of the Assassin*. With J. R. Stiles. New York: Simon and Schuster, 1965.

*Selected Speeches by Gerald R. Ford*. Edited by Michael V. Doyle. Arlington, VA: R. W. Beatty, 1973.

*Seminar in Economic Policy*. Washington, DC: American Enterprise Institute, 1978.

*A Time to Heal*. New York: Harper and Row/Reader's Digest Press, 1979.

*The War Powers Resolution: Striking a Balance Between the Executive and Legislative Branches*. Washington, DC: American Enterprise Institute, 1977.

### Jimmy Carter

*A Government as Good as the People*. New York: Simon and Schuster, 1977.

*I'll Never Lie to You: Jimmy Carter in His Own Words*. Compiled by Robert L. Turner. New York: Ballantine Books, 1976.

*Keeping Faith: Memories of a President*. New York: Bantam, 1982.

*Presidential Campaign 1976*. Washington, DC: U.S. Government Printing Office, 1976.

*Why Not the Best?* Nashville: Broadman Press, 1975.

### Ronald Reagan

*Creative Society: Some Comments on Problems Facing America*. 2nd rev ed. Old Greenwich, CT: Devin-Adair, 1981.

*Sincerely, Ronald Reagan*. Edited by Helene Von Damm. New York: Berkley Books, 1980.

*Where's the Rest of Me: The Autobiography of Ronald Reagan*. With Richard D. Hubler. New York: Karz Publishers, 1981.

## GUIDES TO PRESIDENTIAL PUBLICATIONS

We have described a variety of tools which contain different kinds of presidential documents and have annotated many different sources you can use to find information about presidential activities and publications. Many of the bibliographical tools we have cited are both an index to presidential actions and an index and compilation of the documents themselves; other tools only reprint selective documents and a few can only be used to identify presidential activities. Consequently, it is important to distinguish between the two.

### Sources of Published Papers

Appendix 14, p. 250, identifies which tools can be used to find the text of different kinds of presidential publications. The only category left out of the table is treaties and agreements, which we covered earlier. Each of the tools cited is indexed and can be used as a guide to presidential activities and texts.

### Sources of Information

Appendix 15, p. 252, lists additional reference tools for identifying presidential activities; these may also include a few selected texts or cite particular publications or texts. These tools are useful if you do not know the specific speech, message, or address you are looking for or if you are doing some preliminary research and want both background information and citations to documentary matter. We have followed this complete overview to the sources you can use to find the texts and activities of presidents with sections designed to illustrate the sources for speeches, messages, and executive orders and proclamations.

### Guides to Speeches

Appendix 16, p. 254, identifies the tools to facilitate locating presidential speeches and remarks. Some of the tools listed for finding current materials can also be used for retrospective searching, since many of them have been published for considerable periods of time.

### Guides to Messages

This guide emphasizes current research; consequently, we have not fully described tools useful only for historical research, especially those guides to documents of the eighteenth and nineteenth centuries. As Appendix 17, Sources of Presidential Messages, p. 255, indicates, for retrospective research prior to the turn-of-the-century, you must review the predecessors of the *Congressional Record* and document guides such as Poore's and Ames'. Anyone interested in learning more about those tools and how to use them should consult the research guides listed in the first chapter.

# Guides to Proclamations and Executive Orders

Appendix 18, p. 256, identifies sources for finding presidential proclamations and executive orders. We have already discussed all of the current sources. In addition to Richard's *Compilation of Messages and Papers* and the *Document Catalog*, there are several retrospective compilations and guides to proclamations and executive orders. We have listed these below in order of the years they cover.

| | |
|---|---|
| 1789–1873 | Beaman, Middleton G., and A. K. McNamara. *Index of Federal Statutes, 1789–1873*. Washington, DC: U.S. Government Printing Office, 1911. |
| 1789–1940 | Lord, Clifford L., ed. *List and Index of Presidential Executive Orders, Unnumbered Series*. Newark, NJ: Historical Records Survey, 1943. |
| 1845–1936 | *Presidential Executive Orders*. Dobbs Ferry, NY: Trans-Media Publishing Co., 1980. |
| 1862–1938 | Lord, Clifford L., ed. *Presidential Executive Orders, Numbered 1–8030*. New York: Books for Historical Record Survey, 1944. |
| 1874–1931 | McCenon, Walter H., and Wilfred C. Gibert. *Index to the Federal Statutes, 1874–1931*. Washington, DC: U.S. Government Printing Office, 1933. |
| 1961–1977 | U.S. Office of Federal Register. *Codification of Presidential Proclamations and Executive Orders*. Washington, DC: U.S. Government Printing Office, 1979. |

## SPECIAL COMPILATIONS

The following sections focus on special compilations of presidential documents and activities. Because they comprise discrete categories, we have separated these collections from our previous discussion of presidential papers.

## Documents

In 1980, University Publications of America began publishing a Presidential Documents Series under the editorial direction of Frank Freidel, Richard S. Kirkendal, and Dawn Van Ec. The series is on microfilm with an accompanying printed guide. The set includes minutes of cabinet meetings, daily diaries, and assorted collections containing a variety of presidential papers. Listed below are the sets that have been published to date:

1. *The Presidential Diaries of Henry Morganthau, Jr. (1938–1945)*. Frederick, MD: University Publications of America, 1980.
2. *Map Room Messages of President Roosevelt (1942–1945)*. Frederick, MD: University Publications of America, 1980. Microfilm.
3. *Map Room Messages of President Truman (1945–1946)*. Frederick, MD: University Publications of America, 1980. Microfilm.

4. *Potsdam Conference Documents*. Frederick, MD: University Publications of America, 1980. Microfilm.

5. *Official Conversations and Meetings of Dean Acheson (1949–1953)*. Frederick, MD: University Publications of America, 1980. Microfilm.

6. *Minutes and Documents of the Cabinet Meetings of President Eisenhower (1953–1961)*. Frederick, MD: University Publications of America, 1980. Microfilm.

7. *Minutes of Telephone Conversations of John Foster Dulles and of Christian Herter (1953–1961)*. Frederick, MD: University Publications of America, 1980. Microfilm.

8. *Appointment Book of President Kennedy (1961–1963)*. Frederick, MD: University Publications of America, 1980. Microfilm.

9. *President Kennedy and the Press*. Frederick, MD: University Publications of America, 1980. Microfilm.

10. *Daily Diary of President Johnson (1963–1969)*. Frederick, MD: University Publications of America, 1980. Microfilm.

11. *History of the Department of Justice (1963–1969)*. Frederick, MD: University Publications of America, 1980. Microfilm.

12. *History of the Federal Trade Commission (1963–1969)*. Frederick, MD: University Publications of America, 1980. Microfilm.

13. *Minutes and Documents of the Cabinet Meetings of President Johnson (1963–1969)*. Frederick, MD: University Publications of America, 1981. Microfilm.

14. *Israel: National Security Files*. Frederick, MD: University Publications of America, 1981. Microfilm.

15. *National Economy Under President Johnson: Administrative Histories*. Frederick, MD: University Publications of America, 1982. Microfilm.

16. *Crises in Panama and the Dominican Republic*. Frederick, MD: University Publications of America, 1981. Microfilm.

17. *Department of Health, Education and Welfare: (1963–1969): Official History and Documents*. Frederick, MD: University Publications of America, 1982. Microfilm.

## Speeches

The following items provide quick reference to inaugural addresses, State of the Union Addresses, and major campaign speeches.

*Inaugural Addresses of the Presidents of the United States from George Washington, 1789 to Richard Milhous Nixon, 1973*. Washington, DC: U.S. Government Printing Office, 1974.

Israel, Fred L., ed. *The State of the Union Messages of Presidents 1790–1966.* 3 vols. New York: Robert Hector Publishers, 1966.

Singer, Aaron, ed. *Campaign Speeches of American Presidential Candidates, 1928–1972.* New York: Frederick Ungar Publishing Co., 1976.

## Vetoes

There are three useful tools for researching vetoes.

*Presidential Vetoes: List of Bills Vetoed and Action Taken Thereon by the Senate and House of Representatives, 1789–1976.* Washington, DC: U.S. Government Printing Office, 1978.
   This guide lists all bills vetoed in chronological order arranged by congressional session and presidential administration. The vetoes are listed by bill number and provide the document number and pages of the *Congressional Record* where the message is printed.

U.S. Congress. Senate. *Veto Messages of the Presidents of the United States, with the Action of Congress Thereon.* Compiled by Ben Perley Poore. 49th Cong., 2nd Sess. S. Doc. 53, Washington, DC: U.S. Government Printing Office, 1883.

Jackson, Carlton. *Presidential Vetoes, 1792–1945.* Athens: University of Georgia Press, 1967.

## Quotations

The following books are collections of miscellaneous presidential anecdotes, quotations, and remarks. They can be useful for tracing famous quotations or witicisms.

Adler, William, ed. *Presidential Wit From Washington to Johnson.* New York: Trident Press, 1966.

Boller, Paul F. *Presidential Anecdotes.* New York: Oxford University Press, 1981.

Braymon, Harold. *The President Speaks Off-the-Record.* Princeton: Dow Jones Books, 1976.

Fell, Frederick V. *The Wit and Wisdom of the Presidents.* New York: F. Fell, 1966.

Filler, Louis. *The President Speaks: From William McKinley to Lyndon B. Johnson.* New York: Putnam, 1964.

Frank, Sidney. *The Presidents: Tidbits and Trivia.* Maplewood, NJ: Hammond, 1980.

Harnsberger, Caroline, ed. *Treasury of Presidential Quotations.* Chicago: Follet Publishing Co., 1964.

Standard dictionaries of quotations can be used to find a quotation made by a particular president, determine which president made a particular quotation, and can verify the wording. The best general books of quotations are *Bartlett's Familiar Quotations,* Brussell's *Dictionary of Quotable Definitions,* and Menchen's *New Dictionary of Quotations.* Since there are dozens of books of quotations, tracking down a quote may involve checking several compilations.

## PRESIDENTS AND THE PRESS

Press conferences and speeches are the primary methods of presidential communication to the public. In this section we identify some of the major reference tools for locating speeches and press conferences. In addition to the sources listed below, you should check newspaper indexes, *Reader's Guide to Periodical Literature, Magazine Index, CQ Weekly Report,* and *Facts on File* for information regarding press conferences and speeches.

*Vital Speeches of the Day.* New York: City News Publishing Co., 1934– .
This monthly journal prints important speeches of United States leaders verbatim. In addition to the speeches of presidents, you can find speeches by other members of the Executive Office, including members of the Council of Economic Advisors, the National Security Council, and policy advisors.

*White House Weekly.* Washington, DC: Feistritzer Publications, 1981– .
This publication offers a weekly analysis of the president. It focuses on the president's schedule, statements, speeches, and style and is indexed quarterly.

*U.S. President Press Conferences.* Washington, DC: Brookhaven Press, 1971.
This is a microfilm record of all of the press conferences of Woodrow Wilson, Calvin Coolidge, Herbert Hoover, Franklin D. Roosevelt, and Harry Truman (1913–1952). President Harding did not hold any press conferences, so he is not included.

*The Johnson Presidential Press Conferences.* Pine Plains, NY: Earl M. Coleman Enterprises, 1978.

*The Kennedy Presidential Press Conferences.* Pine Plains, NY: Earl M. Coleman Enterprises, 1978.

*The Nixon Presidential Press Conferences.* Pine Plains, NY: Earl M. Coleman Enterprises, 1978.

These volumes arrange the press conferences chronologically. They are indexed and cross-indexed by subject and public figure sections. In addition to these volumes, you can also use the *Weekly Compilation of Presidential Documents,* the *Public Papers of the Presidents,* and newspaper indexes to identify press conferences.

# TELEVISION COVERAGE

Television news coverage is available to the public through television news archives at various locations in the United States. Because newscasts devote a major portion of each program to governmental issues, they can be of considerable use to the presidential scholar.

## Archives

The following news archives are open for research, and materials in the various collections can be accessed by the news indexes in this section.

Vanderbilt University. Television News Archives. Nashville, TN.
The Television News Archives at Vanderbilt University is the most complete television news archives in the United States. Its holdings include a collection of evening newscasts and special news programs from the major networks since August 1968. The tapes of the news programs are available for a fee.

Public Broadcasting Service. Public Television Archives. Washington, DC.
This is a collection of PBS television materials.

U.S. Library of Congress. Motion Picture Broadcasting and Recorded Sound Division. Washington, DC.
Its holdings include a collection of television entertainment programs and tape copies of the programs in the Television News Archives at Vanderbilt University. You need to request these in advance because the library keeps these materials in storage.

U.S. National Archives and Record Service. Motion Picture Division on Audiovisual Archives Division. Washington, DC.
This collection of the CBS network evening news and news special programs (such as presidential speeches) may be borrowed through interlibrary loan. To gain access to these materials, use the *CBS News Index* or the *Television News Index.*

Additional information concerning various film and video collections in the Washington, D.C. area can be found in the following publication.

Rowan, Bonnie G. *Scholar's Guide to Washington, D.C. Film and Video Collections*. Washington, DC: Woodrow Wilson International Center for Scholars, Smithsonian Institution Press, 1980.

## Indexes

The following indexes are to television news programs.

*Television News Index: News and Abstracts*. Nashville: Vanderbilt University, Television News Archives, 1968– .
    This is a monthly index with abstracts. It provides an annual cumulative index. Terms used in the indexing are specific rather than general. The *Index* gives reference points to various subject matter on tapes, for the tapes have been dated and timed.

*CBS News Index*. New York: Columbia Broadcasting System, Inc., 1975– .
    The CBS News, other regular news programs, and news specials are indexed in this work. Subject headings are derived from newspapers and the entries are abstracted in a short descriptive phrase.

White House Motion Picture Reference Card Catalog.
    This card catalog notes the location of motion pictures and television tapes concerning the presidency, from 1897 to the present. Duplicate catalogs are located in the Library of Congress, Motion Picture Division and the National Archives and Records Service, Motion Picture Division, for public use.

The following paper provides further information on television archives and indexes.

Wilhoit, Frances G. "The Network News as History: Using Television Archives." *Proceedings of the American Historical Association, 59th annual meeting, Washington, DC December, 1980*. Ann Arbor, MI: University Microfilms, 1981.

# Archives and Manuscript Collections

In this section, we identify a variety of archives and special collections of presidential manuscripts. Because much of the material found in archives has been reproduced commercially, it is possible to find these materials in other libraries as well. Consequently, we provide information about the nature of the archives, such as their holdings, finding aids, and services. This information is essential for anyone interested in using an archive or special collection. Before planning a trip to an archive, you should write ahead to see if they have the kinds of materials you need.

## THE U.S. LIBRARY OF CONGRESS

The Library of Congress is the major archival center for presidential papers. Anyone researching the presidency or a particular president needs to determine what relevant materials are at the center. The Library of Congress has reproduced many of its holdings (e.g., Presidential Papers Program) and has made them available to other libraries. It is best to inquire ahead about materials that can only be used at the Library of Congress.

Manuscript Division
Washington, DC 20540

## Library Hours

*(Manuscript Reading Room)*
8:30 A.M.–5:00 P.M. Monday–Saturday
Closed Sundays and national holidays

The Manuscript Division of the Library of Congress has about 10,000 separate collections. There are nearly 40,000 million items dealing with American history and culture. There are 23 groups of presidential papers, from those of George Washington to those of Calvin Coolidge. For assistance, the researcher may consult reference librarians in the reading room or an area specialist in the division for more advanced service.

Papers of the following presidents are in the Library of Congress.

| | |
|---|---|
| George Washington | Ulysses S. Grant |
| Thomas Jefferson | James A. Garfield |
| James Madison | Chester A. Arthur |
| James Monroe | Grover Cleveland |
| Andrew Jackson | Benjamin Harrison |
| Martin Van Buren | William McKinley |
| William H. Harrison | Theodore Roosevelt |
| John Tyler | William H. Taft |
| James K. Polk | Woodrow Wilson |
| Zachary Taylor | Calvin Coolidge |
| Franklin Pierce | |
| Abraham Lincoln | |
| Andrew Johnson | |

## The Presidential Papers Program

On August 16, 1957, Public Law 85–147 gave the Library of Congress authority for the Presidential Papers Program in order to preserve and make accessible presidential papers. In 1958, the Manuscript Division began to organize and index over two million manuscripts. The project was completed in 1976. The Division also microfilmed the presidential papers. The 3,000 reels are available in many research libraries in the country and through interlibrary loan. Positive copies may be purchased from the Chief, Photoduplication Service, Library of Congress, Washington, DC 20540. The Indexes to the Presidential Papers are distributed by the Government Printing Office.

# THE PRESIDENTIAL LIBRARIES

The National Archives and Records Services administer seven presidential libraries throughout the country. The responsibility for providing buildings for the libraries belongs to the president, to nonfederal governmental agencies, or to private nonprofit corporations. These libraries contain the papers and files of the presidents as well as correspondence of the presidents and their associates. The libraries' holdings vary somewhat, but presidential papers and White House files are found in each of these libraries. Two works, available in most college, university, and public libraries, identify what materials are in the presidential libraries.

*National Union Catalog of Manuscript Collections.* Washington, DC: U.S. Library of Congress, 1959– .

*Prologue, The Journal of the National Archives.* Washington, DC: National Archives and Records Service, 1969– .
  When new holdings are added to presidential libraries, and when restricted materials are opened, notices are placed in *Prologue.*

Each library also provides guides to their holdings; these are available at college and university libraries and many public libraries. Some of the collections are closed by government regulations or by stipulation of the donor. Some of these can be used with donor permission. The guides will note which materials are restricted. Each library prints finding aids to its open collections; these are available through interlibrary loan.

## Restricted Documents

Researchers wanting to use restricted or not yet processed materials should write to the Director of the Library involved. If an item has been classified because of national security for more than ten years, a researcher may request a mandatory review by the government department which restricted it. The Director of the Library will supply a standard mandatory declassification review request form. After you return it, the Director will send it to the appropriate government agency. The agency reviews the document and advises the researcher of its decision. If the documents are declassified, copies with a bill for reproduction are sent to the researcher. If the agency does not declassify the document, you can then appeal the decision directly to the agency concerned.

## Reference Service by Mail

Sometimes a specific document can be furnished by mail. You must have an adequate citation in order to request a document. The citation should include: type of document (example, letter), name of sender and recipient, date, file number, book of material in which it is filed, and library. Charges for reproduced materials vary from library to library.

## Grants-in-Aid

Each presidential library offers a limited number of grants to researchers. These range from grants for travel to and living expenses while at the library to awards for scholars doing long term projects. Information about grants can be obtained by writing the library's director.

## Visiting a Presidential Library

The first step for the researcher planning to visit a presidential library is to request an application from the library. The application asks the researcher to supply information on his or her research topic. The staff can then determine which materials would be useful before the researcher arrives. Presidential libraries offer photocopy and microfilm reproduction services for a fee. Typewriters and tape recorders may be used for taking notes. You can inquire about available services (including mail reference service) before you arrive. Each presidential library provides an orientation session with an archivist who explains the procedures of that library. The researcher then checks the various finding aids to identify those materials he or she needs. For additional information on presidential libraries, see the bibliography, which lists materials on presidential libraries, papers and records.

## THE HERBERT HOOVER PRESIDENTIAL LIBRARY

Parkside Drive
West Branch, IA 52358
Phone: (319) 643-5301
Director: Mr. Thomas T. Thalken

## Library Hours

9:00 A.M. to 4:45 P.M. Monday–Friday
Closed national holidays

## Holdings

Collections of personal papers of friends and associates of President Hoover. The Hoover Papers are organized into the following periods:
  Pre-Commerce Period, 1895–1921 (until he became Secretary of Commerce).
  Commerce Period, 1921–1928.
  Campaign and Transition Period, 1928–1929.
  Presidential Period, 1929–1933.
  Post Presidential Period, 1933–1964.
  Special Collections, 1853–1964.
Oral Histories (Beginning with early family years).
Still Photographs (20,000).

Motion Picture Film (127,800 ft.).

Sound Recordings (240).

Microfilm of Manuscripts in Other Archives (2,000 reels).

The Hoover Institution on War, Revolution and Peace at Stanford houses the Hoover papers on the Commission for Relief in Belgium, 1914–1919, the U.S. Food Administration, 1917–1919, and the American Relief Administration, 1919–1924. Copies of most of these papers are found in the Herbert Hoover Presidential Library.

## Identifying Materials in the Library

The following guide is most helpful for identifying what materials are in the Hoover Library. The information for an item includes title; description of the item; identification of the individual; type of finding aid available; the NUCMC number; dates; and any use restrictions.

*Historical Materials in the Herbert Hoover Presidential Library.* West Branch, IO: National Archives and Records Service, 1983.

## Finding Aids

The Hoover Library provides finding aids for the Hoover papers and related collections in the library. There are two types, Registers and Container Lists. The Registers are the more complete. The Container Lists less detailed indicate box by box and folder by folder the organization of a particular collection.

## THE FRANKLIN D. ROOSEVELT LIBRARY

Albany Post Road
Hyde Park, NY 12538
Phone: (914) 229-8114
Director: Dr. William R. Emerson

## Library Hours

9:00 A.M. to 4:45 P.M. Monday–Friday
Between Memorial Day and Labor Day, the Search Room opens at 8:00 A.M.
During July and August, it is also open 9:00 A.M. to 4:45 P.M. on Saturdays, for use of materials requested on Friday.
Closed on National holidays

## Holdings

FDR's papers
    Records of his administration
    Personal records
    Family papers

Separate collections of his associates (150)
Includes the papers of Eleanor Roosevelt

Audiovisual collection

Still pictures (109,000)

Motion pictures (700 reels)
Professional picture film
Newsreels
Government movies
TV filmclips

Sound recordings (4,000)
Government agency productions
News programs

FDR's personal library (15,000 books and pamphlets)

Basic reference works and monographs on the era of FDR

## Identifying Materials in the Library

Brief descriptions of all of the collections found in the FDR Library are found in the following guide:

*Historical Materials in the Franklin D. Roosevelt Library.* Washington, DC: National Archives and Records Service, General Services Administration, 1982.

Each entry in this guide is listed alphabetically and gives the title, dates of contents, and size in linear feet. It provides information on restrictions placed on the materials. It also notes if the collection has not been processed by the library yet.

## Finding Aids

There are more detailed finding aids in the library's Search Room. Each collection is described in its own finding aid. A Registration Book provides basic information about each collection: biographical material on the individual who collected the data, a brief description of the papers in the collection, restrictions on access, and information on the literary property rights. The Shelf List indicates the organization of the papers by folder or box and is used for large and heavily used collections like the President's Official File. It is alphabetically indexed. Some collections have card indexes for individual documents.

## THE HARRY S TRUMAN LIBRARY

U.S. Highway 24 and Delaware Street
Independence, MO 64050
Phone: (816) 833-1400
Director: Dr. Benedict K. Zobrist

## Library Hours

8:45 A.M.–4:45 P.M. Monday–Friday
8:45 A.M.–4:45 P.M. Saturday with advance arrangement

## Holdings

Manuscripts (6,600 linear feet)
Presidential papers
It includes office files of members of the White House Staff and files maintained by White House Staff Offices.

President's Secretary's Files (PSF)
These files include official and personal correspondence; diaries; telegrams; memoranda; reports; President's appointment files; speech files; political files; legislative files; president's conference transcripts; and press releases. National security matters and CIA and NSC reports are also here.

White House Central Files
These served as central files for the entire White House Staff.
Official File (OF)
It contains official or semi-official materials such as: Correspondence (public opinion mail), Reports, Memoranda, Notes, Speech files, and other types of materials.

President's Personal File (PPF)
It contains personal correspondence, holiday greetings, autograph requests, and other materials of a personal nature.

General File (GF)
It contains material not important enough to classify by subject and is arranged alphabetically by the name of the correspondent.

Confidential File
Arranged alphabetically by name or subject, this contains security-classified and other sensitive materials.

Permanent File
It contains materials that future administrations might want to use. It is arranged by name or subject.

Senate Files

Post Presidential Papers
These are collections of individuals who were associates or officials.

Microfilm
Primary source materials in other depositories
Copies of papers of Truman administration officials
Records of Federal agencies in the Truman administration
Copies of papers of other presidential libraries
Copies of newspapers, periodicals, and other secondary sources on the Truman period

Oral History Interviews
   The emphasis is on presenatorial career, the work of the White House Staff,
   and U.S. foreign policy, 1945–1952.
Printed materials
   Books, periodicals, pamphlets, dissertations, and other printed items.
Audiovisual materials
   Still pictures (74,446)
   Sound recordings (2,625)
   Motion picture collection
      Film from newsreel, television (commercial and private donors)

## Identifying Materials in the Library

Brief descriptions of the collections of materials that are included in the Truman
Library are listed in the following guide. The size, composition, and use
restrictions of the collections are noted.

*Historical Materials in the Harry S Truman Library.* Independence, MO:
National Archives and Records Service, 1982.

## Finding Aids

Finding aids, available in the Library Research Room, describe the contents of
the collections and facilitate their use. A registration sheet describes the
contents and notes restrictions of many of the manuscript collections. Subject,
name, and numerical indexes are available for the White House Files. For the
other presidential papers and all other manuscript collections, shelf lists are
provided. They are guides to the folder titles in the document containers. The
Library has a card catalog for its book collection, and a master card index to
most of the oral history interviews. There are chronological and subject indexes
to the audiovisual collections.

## THE DWIGHT D. EISENHOWER LIBRARY

Southeast Fourth Street
Abilene, KS 67410
Phone: (913) 263-4571
Director: Dr. John E. Wickman

## Library Hours

9:00 A.M. to 4:45 P.M. Monday–Friday
Special arrangements can be made to do research on Saturdays
Closed on legal holidays

# Holdings

Manuscripts
  Papers (prepresidential, 1916–1952)
  Papers as president
  Post president
  Collections of associates
Microfilm
Oral History
Audiovisual Collection
  These materials documenting the times of President Eisenhower have been
    donated by individuals, organizations, and government agencies.
  Still photos (108,000)
  Motion picture films (75 35mm, 497 16mm, and 8 5mm)
  Videotapes (29)
  Audio tapes and discs (2,000)
Book Collection
  It includes about 21,000 titles relating to the life and times of President
    Eisenhower. Periodicals, theses and dissertations are included.

## Identifying Materials in the Library

The following guide provides an introduction to the Library's resources. It lists
the manuscripts, microfilm, and oral history materials found there. A brief
description is given for items in manuscript or microfilm form. The oral history
materials are alphabetically listed by the person interviewed.

*Historical Materials in the Dwight D. Eisenhower Library.* Abilene, KS:
  National Archives and Records Service, 1981.

## Finding Aids

There are several types of finding aids in the Library. The preliminary inventory
("PI") gives the most detailed description. The shelf list is less detailed, and
gives a box-by-box and folder-by-folder organization of the collections. Many
of the library's finding aids are available through interlibrary loan.

# THE JOHN F. KENNEDY LIBRARY

Morrissey Boulevard
Columbia Point
Boston, MA 02125
Phone: (617) 929-4500
Director: Mr. Dan H. Fenn, Jr.

# Library Hours

8:30 A.M.–4:30 P.M. Monday–Friday
Closed Thanksgiving, Christmas, and New Years

# Holdings

Archives and manuscripts
Papers of President Kennedy
Personal papers
Harvard records and notebooks
Correspondence 1943–1952
Boston office 1940–1956
Athenia records
Manuscripts
Senator's notes
Doodles

Prepresidential papers
House of Representatives files (1947–1952)
Campaign files
Senate files (1953–1960)
Transition files

Presidential papers
Presidential office files
National security files
White House central files
Bureau of the Budget bill reports
White House social files
Miscellaneous files

White House staff files
Papers of the post assassination period (1963–1974)
Collections of personal or organizational papers
Records of government agencies

Audiovisual Material
White House photographs
Sound recordings
Motion picture film

Printed materials
Includes books, government publications, periodicals, and microforms on
the life and career of JFK. *The Kennedy Collection: A Subject Guide* is a
catalog of materials in the Library.

Oral History Interviews

# Identifying Materials in the Library

The following guide describes the various collections and notes which collections are open for research.

*Historical Materials in the John Fitzgerald Kennedy Library.* Boston: National Archives and Records Service, 1981.

Other guides available from the Library are "Guide to the Use of Historical Materials in the John F. Kennedy Library," "The John F. Kennedy Library Audiovisual Collection," "John F. Kennedy: A Reading List," and "The John F. Kennedy Library Oral History Program and the Use of Oral History Interviews."

## Finding Aids

Registers and finding aids for the collections are available in the Research Room.

## THE LYNDON B. JOHNSON LIBRARY

2313 Red River Street
Austin, TX 78705
Phone: (512) 397-5137

## Library Hours

9:00 A.M.–5:00 P.M. Monday–Friday
9:00 A.M.–1:00 P.M. Saturday by appointment
Closed national holidays

## Holdings

Manuscripts and archives
  Papers of LBJ
    House of Representative papers 1937–1949
    Senate papers 1949–1961
    Vice presidential papers 1961–1963
    Presidential papers 1963–1969
    White House central files (WHCF)
    President's staff files
    National security files
    Appointments file
    Statements of Lyndon B. Johnson
    Administrative histories
    Scrapbooks
    White House social files
  Post Presidential Papers 1969–1973
Collections of Personal and Organizational Papers
Federal Records
Microfilm Records from Government Agencies

Audiovisual Materials
  Motion pictures
  Sound recording tapes
  Video tapes
  Still pictures
Oral History Interviews
Book Collection
  A collection of books, theses, dissertations, and a clipping file covering President Johnson, his associates, his administration, and issues of his times.

## Identifying Materials in the Library

The holdings of the Library are described in the following guide.

*Historical Materials in the Lyndon B. Johnson Library.* Austin: National Archives and Records Service, 1981.

## Finding Aids

The Library provides finding aids to most of President Johnson's papers and to many of the manuscript collections and government records. Many of the oral histories are indexed and have brief summaries. The audiovisual materials are indexed.

## THE GERALD R. FORD LIBRARY

1000 Beal Avenue
Ann Arbor, MI 48109
Phone: (313) 668-2218
Director: Mr. Don Wilson

## Library Hours

8:45 A.M.–4:45 P.M. Monday–Friday
Closed national holidays

## Holdings

Archives and Manuscript Collections
  Papers as congressman 1948–1973
  Papers as vice-president 1973–1974
  Papers as president 1974–1977
    White House central files
    White House staff files
    Miscellaneous files
  Personal Papers 1926–
  Postpresidential Papers, 1977–

Oral History Interviews
Interviews concerning Mr. Ford's early associations in Grand Rapids.

Printed Materials
Includes selected memoirs, reference books, list of holdings for other presidential libraries, studies, and government publications. A vertical file is maintained and microfilm copies of newspapers and news magazines are available.

Audiovisual Materials
Audio tape (2,600 tapes)
Video tape (765 tapes)
Still photographs (283,000 negatives)
Motion picture film (710,000 feet of 16mm film)

## Identifying Materials in the Library

The following guide supplies information on the materials available in the Library. It indicates which materials are open to research, the size of the collections, and the creator of the collections.

*Historical Materials in the Gerald R. Ford Library.* Compiled by David A. Horrocks and William H. McNitt. Ann Arbor: Gerald R. Ford Library, 1982.

## Finding Aids

Finding aids, available in the research room, describe the collections by giving date, quantity, scope, arrangement scheme, administrative or biographical history of creator of materials, and restrictions on access. A Folder Title List is available with the finding aids. A summary of contents is available for each of the file categories open in the White House Central Files, Subject Series. Finding aids are also available through interlibrary loan.

# Manuscript Collections

In addition the following libraries have collections of presidential materials.

## BUFFALO AND ERIE COUNTY HISTORICAL SOCIETY

25 Nottingham Court
Buffalo, NY 14216

## Hours

10:00 A.M.–5:00 P.M. Monday–Friday
12:00–5:00 P.M. Saturdays
Millard Fillmore was the first president of this Society which collects manuscripts concerning the history of Western New York from the eighteenth century to the present. The Society possesses the major collection of President Fillmore's papers. *A Guide to the Microfilm Edition of the Millard Fillmore*

*Papers* (1975) is available from the Society for $4.00. In 1907, the Society published the *Millard Fillmore Papers*, compiled by Frank H. Severance as volumes 10 and 11 of its publications. It is a reproduction of the documents of President Fillmore that the Society possesses.

# HOOVER INSTITUTION ON WAR, REVOLUTION AND PEACE

Stanford University
Stanford, CA 94305

## Hours

8:15 A.M.–4:45 P.M. Monday–Friday
Closed Saturdays, Sundays and national holidays
   The Hoover Institution holdings include the president's papers covering the Commission for Relief in Belgium, 1914–1919, the U.S. Food Administration, 1917–1919, and the American Relief Administration, 1919–1924. The following work gives a detailed inventory of the Herbert Hoover Papers in the Hoover Institution Archives.

*Herbert Hoover: A Register of his Papers in the Hoover Institution Archives.* Compiled by Elena S. Danielson and Charles G. Palm. Stanford: Hoover Institution Press, 1982.

   Another reference work lists all of the archival and manuscript material accessioned through 1978 at the Hoover Institution.

*Guide to the Hoover Institution Archives.* Compiled by Charles G. Palm and Dale Reed. Stanford: Hoover Institution Press, 1980.

## MASSACHUSETTS HISTORICAL SOCIETY

1154 Boylston Street
Boston, MA 02215

## Hours

9:00 A.M.–4:45 P.M. Monday–Friday
Closed national holidays and some local holidays
   The Adams Papers—the diaries, correspondence and many official papers of John, John Quincy and Charles Francis—were donated to the Society by their families. These papers are on microfilm, and available at many libraries throughout the country.

*Microfilms of the Adams Papers.* 608 reels. Boston: Massachusetts Historical Society, 1954–1959.
   A guide to the microfilm indicates which reels contains what materials, but there is no index for the papers. The original papers are not open to scholars

for research. They are being edited for book publication, and twenty-eight volumes have been published.

*The Adams Papers.* Cambridge: Harvard University Press, 1961– .
The Society has a chronological file containing copies of all Adams materials known to them, but it is not open to researchers. They can give a researcher specific information about letters written to or from the Adamses and the location of the letter. The Society also has some Adams material that is not part of the Adams Papers. This material can be used at the Society.

## THE HISTORICAL SOCIETY OF PENNSYLVANIA

1300 Locust Street
Philadelphia, PA 19107

### Hours

1:00 P.M.–9:00 P.M. Tuesday–Friday
Fee: $1.00 per day to nonmembers
The Buchanan Papers, about 25,000 items, are located in the Manuscript Department of the Historical Society of Pennsylvania and are open for research to qualified scholars. They are on microfilm and are available through interlibrary loan, 3 reels at a time. The Society also publishes *A Guide to the Buchanan Papers,* which can be purchased for $3.00 plus postage.

## THE OHIO HISTORICAL SOCIETY

The Manuscripts Department
I71 and 17th Avenue
Columbus, OH 43211

### Hours

9:00 A.M.–5:00 P.M. Tuesdays–Saturday
The Society holds the papers of Warren G. Harding. Most of the papers have been microfilmed and are available on interlibrary loan. The following guide also may be purchased from the Society.

*The Warren G. Harding Papers, An Inventory to the Microfilm Edition.* Columbus: Ohio Historical Society, 1970.

## THE RUTHERFORD B. HAYES PRESIDENTIAL CENTER

Spiegel Grove
Fremont, OH 43420–2796
Phone: (419) 332-2081

## Hours

1:30 P.M.–5:00 P.M. Monday
9:00 A.M.–5:00 P.M. Tuesday–Saturday
Closed Sundays and national holidays
   The Center holds the papers and presidential library of Rutherford B. Hayes and papers of many of his contempories. *The Rutherford B. Hayes Papers* include: Hayes and Webb Family Genealogies, diaries, commonplace books, law notebooks, campaign notebooks, incoming correspondence 1829–1893, White House records, Civil War records, business papers, speeches and messages, and miscellaneous items. The *Papers* are open to all researchers. The Center's reading room has an index to the *Hayes Papers*. There is a separate index to President Hayes' speeches and indexes to the personal papers of other members of the Hayes family. The *Hayes Papers* are available on microfilm. A guide booklet to the microfilm edition is also available.

*The Rutherford B. Hayes Papers*. 304 reels. Fremont, OH: The Rutherford B. Hayes Presidential Center, 1982.

   For additional information on archival materials, see the following guide to over 1,300 depositories and 20,000 collections of personal papers.

Hammer, Philip M., ed. *Guide to Archives and Manuscripts in the United States*. New Haven: Yale University Press, 1961.

# Other Research Centers

A variety of research centers, both federal and private, disseminate information about the presidency and the federal government. There are several directories useful not only for finding addresses, telephone numbers, etc., but for determining what an organization or agency does and what kinds of services it provides. In the course of research on the president, you often run across the name of a particular institution that is advocating a change in policy or seeking reform or merely publishing information about federal activities as a public service. In order to find out more about an organization or institution, you can consult a directory.

## Directories

The following is a descriptive list of the major directories. At the end of the description list are the citations to a number of secondary directories.

*Washington Information Directory*. Washington, DC: Congressional Quarterly, 1975– .
   This is a thoroughly indexed guide to over 5,000 information sources in Congress, the executive branch, and nongovernmental organizations. This annual directory helps the researcher make some sense out of the maze of agencies, institutes, associations, and foundations in the Washington area. In

addition to the standard organizational information, a concise statement spells out the committee's, organization's, or agency's activities. Besides identifying all of the major divisions within the Executive Office, the directory also discusses hundreds of organizations and public interest groups, like Ralph Nader's Public Citizen Inc., Americans for Democratic Action, and the National Committee for an Effective Congress. These organizations seek to change government procedures and regulations, monitor legislative proposals, and assess and evaluate federal programs. Many public interest groups distribute newsletters and other materials free of charge or for a nominal fee. It is certainly worthwhile to write to organizations asking about their activities and what publications are available to the public. The *Directory* is indexed by subject and agencies.

Kruzas, Anthony T., and Kay Gill, eds. *Government Research Centers Directory.* 2nd ed. Detroit: Gale Research Co., 1981.

The directory identifies and describes all research facilities funded by the federal government. It provides a wealth of information about research centers, bureaus, and institutes, both in regard to the kinds of analysis they conduct and the collection of data. The directory has a name index, subject keyword index, agency index, and geographical index.

Thomas, Robert C., and James A. Ruffner, eds. *Research Centers Directory.* 7th ed. Detroit: Gale Research Co., 1982.

This directory is the best guide for finding out information about university related and other nonprofit research organizations throughout the U.S. and Canada. The directory is arranged in sixteen broad catagories, listing research institutes, centers, foundations, laboratories, and bureaus. It is easy to use and includes a subject index, alphabetical index, and institutional index. The directory is updated periodically by the supplement, *New Research Centers,* also published by Gale. This supplement lists new research centers as well as those being formed.

Jennings, Margaret, comp. *Library and Reference Facilities in the Area of the District of Columbia.* 11th ed. White Plains, NY: Knowledge Industry Publications, 1983.

This directory includes profiles on more than 450 libraries and reference centers in the District of Columbia area. It includes federal, public, academic, and special libraries. It is useful for identifying smaller reading rooms and information and referral centers. Each entry provides information on the services, collections, hours and any restrictions on use. The address, telephone number and name of the individual in charge are also listed. This directory is especially useful for anyone doing research in Washington. You can save time by knowing in advance which libraries have certain resources, what services they provide, and whether you can use the library.

*Inventory of Information Resources and Services Available to the U.S. House of Representatives, Parts I-IV.* Westport, CT: Greenwood Press, 1977.

This is an excellent guide to internal sources of congressional information on the legislative process, managing of congressional offices, and the organization and operation of Congress. It also describes the resources of the Congressional Budget Office, General Accounting Office, Government Printing Office, Library of Congress, and Office of Technology Assessment. The last two parts of the compendium discuss executive branch information resources and private organization information services. These last two sections are most useful in regard to the presidency and the executive branch.

### Additional Directories:

*A Directory of Information Sources in the United States: Social Sciences.* Rev ed. Washington, DC: Library of Congress, 1973.

*Federal Regulatory Directory.* Washington, DC: Congressional Quarterly, 1979– .

Nagel, Stuart, and Marian Neef. *Policy Research Centers Directory.* Urbana, IL: Policy Studies Organization, 1978.

Nagel, Stuart, and Marian Neef. *The Political Science Utilization Directory.* Urbana, IL: Policy Studies Organization, 1975.

*A Researcher's Guide to Washington.* Coral Springs, FL: B. Klein Publications, 1979.

*Washington Pocket Directory: A Citizen's Guide to Major Government Offices and Information Services.* Washington, DC: Want Publishing Co., 1983.

## Selected Centers

A number of research centers, foundations, and private institutions study presidential activities. The following list represents the major institutions whose work includes the presidency. Below are the addresses for the agencies or organizations whose publications we have referred to throughout the book.

American Enterprise Institute for Public Policy Research
1150 17th St., N.W.
Washington, DC 20036
Tel: (202) 296-5616

American Institute for Political Communication
402 Prudential Building
Washington, DC 20005
Tel: (202) 783-6373

American Institute of Public Opinion
53 Bank Street
Princeton, NJ 08541
Tel: (609) 924-9600

Americans for Democratic Action
1424 16th St., N.W.
Washington, DC 20036
Tel: (202) 265-5771

Bill Status Office
2401A Rayburn House Office Building
Washington, DC 20515
Tel: (202) 225-1772

The Brookings Institution
1775 Massachusetts Ave., N.W.
Washington, DC 20036
Tel: (202) 483-8919

Center for Congressional and Presidential Studies
College of Public and International Affairs, American University
Massachusetts and Nebraska Avenues, N.W.
Washington, DC 20016
Tel: (202) 686-2378

Center for Public Financing of Elections
201 Massachusetts Ave., N.W.
Washington, DC 20002
Tel: (202) 546-5511

Center for the Study of the Presidency
208 East 75th Street
New York, NY 10021
Tel: (212) 249-1200

Citizen's Research Foundation
245 Nassau St.
Princeton, NJ 08540
Tel: (609) 924-0246

Clerk of the House of Representatives
H-105 Capitol Building
Washington, DC 20515
Tel: (202) 225-7000

Commerce Department
Census Bureau
Population Division
Washington, DC 20233
Tel: (202) 763-5161

Common Cause
2030 M St., N.W.
Washington, DC 20036
Tel: (202) 833-1200

Congressional Budget Office
Second and D Street, S.W.

Washington, DC 20515
Tel: (202) 225-4416

Congressional Information Service
7101 Wisconsin Ave.
Washington, DC 20014
Tel: (301) 654-1550

Congressional Quarterly Inc.
1414 22nd Street, N.W.
Washington, DC 20037
Tel: (202) 296-6800

Congressional Record Office
H–112 Capitol Building
Washington, DC 20515
Tel: (202) 225-2100

Democratic National Committee
1625 Massachusetts Ave., N.W.
Washington, DC 20036
Tel: (202) 797-5900

Eagleton Institute of Politics
Rutgers University
Wood Lawn, Neilson Campus
New Brunswick, NJ 08903
Tel: (201) 828-2210

Elections Research Center
1619 Massachusetts Ave., N.W.
Washington, DC 20036
Tel: (202) 387-6066

Fair Campaign Practices Committee
613 Pennsylvania Ave., S.E.
Washington, DC 20003
Tel: (202) 544-5656

Federal Communications Commission
1919 M St., N.W.
Washington, DC 20554
Tel: (202) 655-4000

Federal Election Commission
1325 K Street, N.W.
Washington, DC
Tel: (202) 382-5162

Free Congress and Education Foundation
721 2nd Street, N.E.
Washington, DC 20002
Tel: (202) 546-3004

Friends Committee on National Legislation
245 2nd Street, N.E.
Washington, DC 20002
Tel: (202) 547-4343

General Accounting Office
441 G Street, N.W.
Washington, DC 20548
Tel: (202) 386-4949

Government Printing Office
Congressional Desk
North Capitol and H Streets, N.W.
Washington, DC 20401
Tel: (202) 376-2030

Governmental Affairs Institute
1776 Massachusetts Ave., N.W.
Washington, DC 20036
Tel: (202) 833-2500

Harvard Legislative Research Bureau
Harvard Law School
Hasting Hall
Cambridge, MA 02138
Tel: (617) 495-4400

Heritage Foundation
513 C Street, N.E.
Washington, DC 20002
Tel: (202) 546-4400

Hudson Institute
Quaker Ridge Road
Croton-on-Hudson, NY 10520
Tel: (914) 762-0700

Institute for Contemporary Studies
260 California Street
Suite 811
San Francisco, CA 94111
Tel: (415) 398-3010

Institute of Election Administration
American University
Washington, DC 20016
Tel: (202) 676-2350

Inter-University Consortium for Political and Social Research
P.O. Box 1248
Ann Arbor, MI 48106
Tel: (313) 764-2570

Joint Center for Political Studies
1426 H Street, N.W.
Washington, DC 20005
Tel: (202) 638-4477

Laboratory for Political Research
Regional Social Science Data Archive
University of Iowa
321A Schaeffer Hall
Iowa City, IA 52240
Tel: (319) 353-3945

Library of Congress
Congressional Research Service
10 1st Street, S.E.
Washington, DC 20554
Tel: (202) 426-5770

Louis Harris and Associates
1270 Avenue of the Americas
New York, NY 10020
Tel: (212) 245-7414

National Committee for an Effective Congress
201 Massachusetts Ave., N.E.
Washington, DC 20002
Tel: (202) 833-4000

National Opinion Research Center
University of Chicago
6036 South Ellis Ave.
Chicago, IL 60637
Tel: (312) 752-6444

Public Citizen, Inc.
1346 Connecticut Ave.
Washington, DC 20036
Tel: (202) 293-9142

Robert Maynard Hutchins Center for the Study
of Democratic Institutions
Box 4068
Santa Barbara, CA 93103
Tel: (805) 961-2611

Roper Public Opinion Research Center
Williams College
Williamstown, MA 01267
Tel: (413) 458-7131

Republican National Committee
310 1st Street, S.E.

Washington, DC 20003
Tel: (202) 484-6500

Secretary of the Senate
S-221 Capitol Building
Washington, DC 20501
Tel: (202) 224-2115

Twentieth Century Fund
41 East 70th Street
New York, NY 10021
Tel: (212) 535-4441

Senate Historical Office
United States Senate
Washington, DC 20510
Tel: (202) 224-6900

White Burkett Miller Center of Public Affairs
University of Virginia
Box 5707
Charlottsville, VA 22905
Tel: (804) 924-7236

For information concerning current activities of these organizations, write directly to the organization. Most of these organizations are listed in one of the above mentioned directories.

## CHAPTER 4

# Secondary Sources on the Presidents

There are many different sources for finding biographical data about presidents. Some are more comprehensive than others. We have listed all the major references. While not all libraries will have all of these works, they will have most of them. This list is by no means exhaustive, since there are literally hundreds of compendiums about presidents that give brief biographies of each president. These works are easy to find by looking under the subject heading "Presidents" in any library's card catalog. Some of the works below were included because they provide biographical data and information on the federal government in general.

## FACTBOOKS

### PRESIDENTS

### General

Kane, Joseph N. *Facts About the Presidents: A Compilation of Biographical and Historical Data.* 4th ed. New York: H. W. Wilson, 1981.
　　This reference work contains short biographies of the presidents from Washington to Reagan. The biographical sketches include information concerning their social and family background. There is also a short description of elections, including the candidates of all the parties contending for the office as well as the electoral results. A profile of the administration is included with each biography. Data includes the following: the composition of the Cabinet, Supreme Court appointments, the party leadership within the House and Senate for each Congress, and important dates and events that occurred during the administration. The work also contains a section of comparative data, divided into two areas. The first focuses on the presidents

and includes a wide range of information, such as cultural and vocational background, religious information, and books written by the presidents. The second examines the presidency, giving information on the electoral process and the scope of the office.

Wilson, Vincent. *The Book of the Presidents*. 6th ed. Brookeville, MD: American History Research, 1981.
    This book is a compendium of facts and lore about the presidents from Washington to Nixon. Separate chapters are devoted to each of the presidents. Each chapter includes the following sections: (1) biographical data, including familial and social background; (2) early years; (3) significant public achievements prior to election; (4) presidential administration(s); and (5) the period following presidential years. There are short subsections covering elections, conventions, inaugurations, vice-presidents, cabinets, and the Supreme Court. The work has several appendices (1) a chronological key to the Congresses, Administrations and Constitutional Amendments; (2) Major Acts and Treaties; and (3) a Statistical Summary. It is a valuable general source for basic dates, names, and events. It does not, however, provide detailed historical coverage, and the information provided is uneven in terms of its value and usefulness.

Two more general factbooks are:

*The Presidents: From the Inauguration of George Washington to the Inauguration of Jimmy Carter*. Rev ed. Washington, DC: U.S. Department of Interior, 1977.

*World Book of America's Presidents*. 2 vols. Chicago: World Book Encyclopedia, 1982.

## Genealogy

The first annotated entry is the single best volume on presidential genealogy. The other books are of a more specialized nature.

*Burke's Presidential Families of the United States of America*. London: Burke's Peerage, 1975.
    This unique and highly specialized volume may not be of great interest to scholars of presidential elections, but it makes for fascinating reading. Each chapter (there is one for each president) gives a very short biography, portrait, and chronology of important events. The writings of each president are also given. The bulk of each chapter is devoted to a tracing of the president's family. There are detailed sections on lineage, descendants, and brothers and sisters.

Laird, Archibald. *Monuments Marking the Graves of the Presidents*. North Quincy, MA: Christopher Publishing House, 1971.

Perling, Joseph J. *President's Sons: The Prestige of Name in a Democracy.* New York: Odyssey, 1947.

Tucker, Robert W. *The Descendants of the Presidents.* Charlotte, NC: Delmar Printing Co., 1975.

*Wills of the U.S. Presidents.* New York: Communication Channels, 1976.

## Miscellaneous

The following three categories of factbooks are not essential research tools, but they are unique collections of information you might spend hours looking for had someone not already compiled them.

### General

Cooke, Donald E. *Atlas of the Presidents.* Rev ed. Maplewood, NJ: Hammond, 1977.

Lange, H. Jack, comp. *Letters of the Presidents.* Los Angeles: Los Angeles Times Syndicate, 1964.

Miller, Carl, comp. *Marches of the Presidents, 1789–1909: Authentic Marches and Campaign Songs.* New York: Chappell, 1968.

Seuling, Barbara. *The Last Cow on the White House Lawn and Other Little Known Facts About the Presidency.* Garden City, NY: Doubleday, 1978.

Smith, Don. *Peculiarities of the Presidents.* 4th ed. Van Wert, OH: Wilkinson Printing Co., 1946.

Taylor, John M. *From the White House Inkwell: American Presidential Autographs.* Rutland, VT: C. E. Tuttle Co., 1968.

### Pictures and Photographs

*American Heritage Pictorial History of the Presidents of the United States.* New York: Simon and Schuster, 1968.

Bassett, Margaret B. *Profiles and Portraits of American Presidents.* New York: McKay, 1976.

Blaisdell, Thomas C., and Peter Selz. *The American Presidency in Political Cartoons, 1776–1976.* Salt Lake City, UT: Peregine Smith, 1976.

Durrant, John, and Alice Durrant. *Pictorial History of American Presidents.* New York: Castle Books, 1975.

Lorant, Stefan. *The Glorious Burden: The History of the Presidency and Presidential Elections from George Washington to James Earl Carter.* Lenox, MA: Authors Edition, 1976.

Milhollen, Hirst D., and Milton Kaplan. *Presidents on Parade*. New York: Macmillan, 1948.

Post, Robert C. *Every Four Years*. Washington, DC: Smithsonian Exposition Books, 1980.

Whitney, David C. *The Graphic Story of the American Presidents*. Chicago: J. G. Ferguson Publishing Co., 1975.

### Inaugurations

Cable, Mary. *The Avenue of the Presidents*. Boston: Houghton Mifflin, 1969.

Durbin, Louise. *Inaugural Cavalcade*. New York: Dodd, Mead, 1971.

Dusterburg, Richard B. *Official Inaugural Medals of the Presidents of the United States*. 2nd ed. Cincinnati: Medallion Press, 1976.

Kitter, Glen D. *Hail to the Chief! Inauguration Days of our Presidents*. Philadelphia: Chilton Books, 1965.

U.S. National Archives. *List of Motion Pictures and Sound Recordings Relating to Presidential Inaugurations*. Washington, DC: National Archives, 1960.

## ADMINISTRATIONS

*Political Profile Series*. New York: Facts on File, 1976– .
    Each volume in this series covers a presidential administration and provides political profiles of influential men and women during that specific time period. In addition to being a biographical directory, the series is a guide to dates, events, places, and offices held. Besides the five volumes listed below, a volume is planned for *The Carter Years*.

*The Truman Years*. New York: Facts on File Publications, 1982.

*The Eisenhower Years*. New York: Facts on File Publications, 1977.

*The Kennedy Years*. New York: Facts on File Publications, 1976.

*The Johnson Years*. New York: Facts on File Publications, 1976.

*The Nixon/Ford Years*. New York: Facts on File Publications, 1979.

    Another tool, cited earlier, useful for researching a presidential administration is the CQ series *Congress and the Nation*. Each volume covers an administration and, as such, is a good overview of a presidential term. If you are studying a particular administration, it is easy to acquire additional information for that time period by using a variety of indexes, such as the *Social Sciences Index, Public Affairs Information Service Bulletin,* and *Reader's Guide to Periodical Literature*.

# BIOGRAPHICAL SOURCES

## Directories and Collections

Biographical collections and directories can direct you to information about presidents, cabinet members, presidential advisors, or important people in the Executive Office or the executive branch. Consequently, they can be useful for finding information about anyone within the president's circle of advisors. Most directories and collections provide information about an individual's family, educational background, achievements, as well as standard biographical data (such as birth and death dates).

Sources for biographies fall into two categories—biographical indexes and biographical collections and directories. In this section, we will cover collections and directories; we will cover indexes in a following section. The first sources are directories focusing on the executive branch; following those are directories focusing on Congress and a section on general political directories and collections. In addition to the sources listed here, most general encyclopedias, yearbooks, and even some almanacs are good sources for short biographical sketches.

### Executive Branch

Sobel, Robert. *Biographical Directory of the United States Executive Branch 1774–1972.* 2nd ed. Westport, CT: Greenwood, 1977.

This is a biographical dictionary of executive branch officials. Each short sketch includes birth date, educational, social, political, and career information. The directory is well-indexed. The eight types of indexes are (1) a listing of Presidential Administrations; (2) Heads of State and Cabinet Officials; (3) other Federal Government Service; (4) State, County, and Municipal Government Service; (5) Military Service by Branch; (6) Education; (7) Place of Birth; and (8) Marital Information. There are over 600 biographies of individuals who have served in the executive branch.

Brownstein, Ronald, and Nina Easton. *Reagan's Ruling Class: Portraits of the President's Top 100 Officials.* Washington, DC: Presidential Accountability Group, 1982.

This collection is based on interviews with top officials and administrators, colleagues, and experts, as well as reviews of testimony speeches, articles, and books. The profiles of the leaders include a description of the office and its responsibilities, the political and financial background of the individual, and current activities and key issues related to the office.

### Congress

*Biographical Directory of the American Congress, 1774–1971.* Rev ed. U.S. Congress. Washington, DC: U.S. Government Printing Office, 1972.

This directory provides short biographies, arranged alphabetically, of senators and representatives who served in Congress from 1774–1971. It also includes a chronological list of executive officers of administrations from 1789–1971, a listing of delegates to the Continental Congress, and a listing of Congresses by date and session.

Ehrenhalt, Alan, ed. *Politics in America: Members of Congress in Washington and at Home.* Washington, DC: Congressional Quarterly, 1980– .
This directory provides a description of each member's performance, legislative influence, political power, personal style, election data and campaign finances, voting records, and interest group rating. It also provides profiles and maps of each congressional district and the results of the most recent presidential primaries and election returns. The directory is issued every two years.

*Congressional Directory.* U.S. Congress. Washington, DC: U.S. Government Printing Office, 1809– .
Published annually, this directory contains biographical, organizational, and statistical information about members and administrative units of the government. The *Directory* is a who's who of the Congress and all government departments. It includes (1) biographical sketches of congressmen; (2) state delegations; (3) terms of service; (4) committees; (5) congressional sessions; (6) governors of states; (7) votes cast for congressmen; (8) biographical sketches of Cabinet members and Supreme Court Justices; (9) officials of independent agencies, (10) press galleries; (11) maps of congressional districts; and (12) an index by individuals. Material about individual members is submitted by the members themselves. In 1978, a supplement to the *Directory* was issued for the first time. Since this time, supplements are published between printings of the complete *Directory.*

*Congressional Staff Directory.* Edited by Charles B. Brownson. Alexandria, VA: Congressional Staff Directory, 1959– .
This yearly publication, a companion to the official *Congressional Directory,* lists the staffs of all congressmen, the committees and subcommittees of both houses, and short biographical sketches of key staff personnel. Included are the committee and subcommittee assignments, key federal officials and their liaison staffs, and an index of personal names. An alphabetical listing of cities, with a population of over 1,500, provides the latest census figures, number of the congressional district, and the names of the congressmen. Prior to its publication every April, a *C. S. D. Advance Locator* is issued at the beginning of the year. This helps to fill the information gap until the complete *Directory* is published. In September, before each congressional election, an advance *C. S. D. Election Index* is published, previewing candidates, providing past election statistics, and listing the cities and towns in each district.

*The Almanac of American Politics: The Senators, the Representatives—Their Records, States and Districts.* Michael Barone, Grant Ujifusa, and Douglas Matthews. Washington, DC: National Journal, 1972– .
This extensive guide to legislators and their districts provides invaluable background material. The work is arranged alphabetically by state and contains an introductory description of the state's political background. This is followed by a section covering legislators, giving a sketch of their background, ideology, and record. More importantly, it provides a short outline of their careers, the committees they serve on, their record on key votes, and

their electoral history. It includes ratings of congressmen by interest groups like the AFL-CIO's Committee on Political Education (which rates members of Congress on their voting related to labor issues). Finally, there is a profile of each district within the state, the political background of the district, census data, federal outlays, tax burdens, and characteristics of the voters. The work is biennially revised and updated.

## General Political Directories

The following directories can be used to find information on politicians, both at the federal level and the state and local level. They also include party leaders and other important political leaders. Since governors, state legislators, and party leaders across the country often play a role in presidential elections and politics, these directories can be quite useful. Following the annotated entries is a list of other directories, some of which are more specialized or historical in nature. Depending on a researcher's need, they can be an invaluable reference tool.

*Who's Who in American Politics: A Biographical Directory of United States Political Leaders.* New York: R. R. Bowker Co., 1967– .
 This directory presents biographical data for about 12,500 political figures from presidents down to the local levels, including federal government employees, national party leaders, state legislators, local officials of large cities, county chairmen of party and minority party leaders. The information given includes address, party affiliation, education, family data, political and business background, and achievements. The directory is revised biennially.

*Who's Who in Government.* Indianapolis: Marquis Who's Who, 1972– .
 This directory provides biographical information on political leaders on the federal and state level. This work presents the same information as the above directory; its value lies in the format of its indexes. One index arranges political figures according to office within the government structure. A second arranges politicians according to type of responsibilities.

*National Roster of Black Elected Officials.* Washington, DC: Joint Center for Political Studies, 1969– .
 This annual work lists black elected officials at all levels of government, providing the mailing address and office held. There is an analysis of changes by region, state, and level of office. The Joint Center also publishes the monthly newsletter *Focus* which regularly prints articles concerning congressional affairs affecting blacks.

*Taylor's Encyclopedia of Government Officials; Federal and State.* Dallas: Political Research, 1969– .
 This work is not really an encyclopedia at all, but a directory of members of the federal and state government departments and agencies. While no biographical information is given for officials, the value of this series is that it has quarterly supplements, listing changes, additions, and corrections. Thus this series would record changes far in advance of the annual directories.

*Who Was Who in American Politics. A Biographical Dictionary of Over 4,000 Men and Women who Contributed to the United States Political Scene from the Colonial Days up to and Including the Immediate Past.* Edited by Dan Morris and Inez Morris. New York: Hawthorn Books, 1974.

*The American Bench: Judges of the Nation.* 2nd ed. Edited by Mary Reincke and Nancy Lichterman. Minneapolis: Reginald Bishop Forster and Associates, Inc., 1979.

*American Biographies.* Wheeler Preston. New York: Harper and Brothers, 1940.

*Appleton's Cyclopaedia of American Biography.* 6 vols. Edited by James Grant Wilson and John Fiske. New York: D. Appleton and Co., 1888–1889.

*Appleton's Cyclopaedia of American Biography.* 2 vols. Edited by James Grant Wilson. New York: D. Appleton and Co., 1901.

*A Supplement to Appleton's Cyclopaedia of American Biography.* 6 vols. Edited by L. E. Dearborn. New York: Press Association Compilers, Inc., 1918–1931.

*Biographical Dictionary of the Federal Judiciary.* Compiled by Harold Chase, Samuel Krislov, Keith O. Boyum, and Jerry N. Clark. Detroit: Gale Research Co., 1976.

*Biographical Directory of the Governors of the United States 1789–1978.* 4 vols. Edited by Robert Sobel and John Raimo. Westport, CT: Microfilm Review, Inc., Meckler Books, 1978.

*Current Biography Yearbook.* New York: H. W. Wilson Co., 1940–1980.

*Dictionary of American Biography.* 26 vols. Edited under the auspices of the American Council of Learned Societies. New York: Scribner's, 1928–1936, 1944, 1958, 1973, 1974, 1977, 1980.

*Dictionary of American Diplomatic History.* John E. Finding. Westport, CT: Greenwood Press, 1980.

*Encyclopedia of American Biography.* Edited by John A. Garraty. New York: Harper and Row, 1974.

*The National Cyclopaedia of American Biography.* 57 vols. New York: James T. White and Co., 1892–1977.

*The Twentieth Century Biographical Dictionary of Notable Americans.* 10 vols. Edited by Rossiter Johnson. Boston: The Biographical Society, 1904.

*Webster's American Biographies.* Edited by Charles Van Doren. Springfield, MA: G and C Merriam Co., 1974.

*Who Was Who in America, Historical Volume, 1607–1896: A Companion Volume of Who's Who in American History.* Rev ed. Chicago: Marquis Who's Who, Inc., 1967.

*Who Was Who in America, Volume One, 1897–1942: A Companion Volume of Who's Who in American History.* Chicago: Marquis Co., 1943.

*Who Was Who in America, Volume Two, 1943–1950: A Companion Biographical Reference Work to Who's Who in America.* Chicago: Marquis Co., 1963.

## Biographical Indexes

Biographical indexes provide references to more complete information in periodicals, books or biographical encyclopedias. While it is possible to identify biographical information through newspapers and general indexes, it is time-consuming and haphazard. Often, you need to find information about an emerging politician, such as a new cabinet member or an appointee to a presidential council or advisory body. Biographical indexes can be especially useful in such cases.

*Biography Index.* New York: H. W. Wilson, 1946– .
This quarterly index identifies biographical materials in books and magazines. It includes references to obituaries, diaries, collections of letters, and memoirs. The entries are arranged by the name of the biographee, and the profession/occupation index makes it possible to identify various kinds of political figures. There is also a *Current Biography Cumulated Index, 1940–1979* published by Wilson in 1973.

*Biographical Dictionaries Master Index.* Detroit: Gale Research Co., 1975–1976.
Along with its 1979 and 1980 supplements, this is a guide to biographical listings in over fifty current *Who's Who*. It is a valuable tool for finding information about recent political actors.

*Biography and Geneology Master Index.* 8 vols. Detroit: Gale Research Co., 1980.
This guide provides citations to information in all of the major biographical dictionaries in political science and history. By using this guide to identify information about political figures, both living and dead, you can find several—sometimes dozens—of references about a single person. In 1982, a three-volume supplement to the *Index* was published.

*Bio-Base.* 2nd ed. Detroit: Gale Research Co., 1981– . Microfiche.
This reference service provides citations to biographical sketches in more

than 375 biographical indexes. In part, some of the citations come from the
hardcover editions of the above two Gale indexes. But because it includes
thousands of other citations, it is the most complete single index to biographical materials.

## Databases

There is essentially not only one on-line biographical database, BIOGRAPHY
MASTER INDEX, produced by Gale Research Co. An expanded on-line
version of *Bio-Base*, it is an index to biographical information contained in
more than 600 source publications, including Who's Who, dictionaries, handbooks, and encyclopedias. Records include the name of the individual, birth
and death dates, and the names and dates of biographical sources.

   You can use a variety of other databases to identify information about
political figures and materials written by them. Since most databases can be
searched by author and key words in the title, it is possible to search a database
to see what a particular president, cabinet member, or member of the Council of
Economic Advisors has written. You can also search the titles of entries to
gather citations about individuals. This strategy could be used to advantage
using a number of databases, including AMERICA: HISTORY AND LIFE;
PSYCINFO; SOCIOLOGICAL ABSTRACTS; PAIS INTERNATIONAL;
UNITED STATES POLITICAL SCIENCE DOCUMENTS; SOCIAL SCI-
SEARCH; and COMPREHENSIVE DISSERTATION INDEX. Because polit-
ical biographies have long been a traditional line of research for dissertations
written in the fields of history and political science, a subject search for
dissertations written about a president can yield hundreds of citations.

## RESOURCE COLLECTIONS

In this section, we identify two categories of materials that merit special
mention. The first is the series of chronologies published by Oceana Publications for each of the presidents. These are the best guides for a date-by-date
history of a president's term in office and are especially useful for identifying
the sequence of events related to a particular issue or time (See Appendix 19,
p. 257, for a list of the terms of presidents by year and congress.) The second set
focuses on identifying sources of secondary materials for the vice-presidents and
cabinet members.

## Chronologies

*Presidential Chronologies Series*. Dobbs Ferry, NY: Oceana Publications,
1967– .

   This series of thirty-five volumes covers the presidents from Washington
to Ford. Each volume has a detailed chronological section outlining the
private and public lives of the president. This is followed by a documents
section including public speeches, legislation, private letters, and excerpts
from diaries and memoirs. The series also contains a selected bibliography
on each president. This volume supplies key dates in the lives of the

presidents, a personal name and subject index, a general bibliography on the presidency, and additional documentation. The titles are as follows:

*John Adams, 1735–1826.* H. F. Bremer, 1967.

*John Q. Adams, 1767–1848.* K. V. Jones, 1970.

*James Buchanan, 1791–1868.* I. J. Sloan, 1968.

*Martin Van Buren, 1782–1862.* I. J. Sloan, 1969.

*Grover Cleveland, 1837–1908.* R. I. Vexler, 1968.

*Calvin Coolidge, 1872–1933.* P. R. Moran, 1970.

*Dwight David Eisenhower, 1890–1969.* R. I. Vexler, 1970.

*Gerald Ford, 1913– .* G. Lankevich, 1977.

*James A. Garfield, 1831–1881/Chester A. Arthur, 1830–1886.* H. B. Furer, 1970.

*Ulysses S. Grant, 1822–1885.* P. R. Moran, 1968.

*Warren G. Harding, 1865–1923.* P. R. Moran, 1970.

*Benjamin Harrison, 1833–1901.* H. J. Sievers, 1969.

*William Henry Harrison, 1773–1841/John Tyler, 1790–1862.* D. A. Durfee, 1970.

*Rutherford B. Hayes, 1822–1893.* A. Bishop, 1969.

*Herbert Hoover, 1874–1964.* A. S. Rice, 1971.

*Andrew Jackson, 1767–1845.* R. Shaw, 1969.

*Thomas Jefferson, 1743–1826.* A. Bishop, 1971.

*Andrew Johnson, 1808–1875.* J. N. Dickinson, 1970.

*Lyndon B. Johnson, 1908– .* H. B. Furer, 1971.

*John F. Kennedy, 1917–1963.* R. A. Stone, 1971.

*Abraham Lincoln, 1809–1865.* I. Elliot, 1970.

*James Madison, 1751–1836.* I. Elliot, 1969.

*William McKinley, 1843–1901.* H. J. Sievers, 1970.

*James Monroe, 1758–1831.* I. Elliot, 1969.

*Richard M. Nixon, 1913– .* H. F. Bremer, 1975.

*Franklin Pierce, 1804–1869.* I. J. Sloan, 1968.

*James Polk, 1795–1849.* J. J. Farrell, 1970.

*Franklin D. Roosevelt, 1882–1945.* H. F. Bremer, 1971.

*Theodore Roosevelt, 1858–1919.* G. J. Black, 1969.

*William H. Taft, 1857–1930.* G. J. Black, 1970.

*Zachary Taylor, 1784–1850/Millard Fillmore, 1800–1874.* J. J. Farrell, 1971.

*Harry S Truman, 1884–* H. B. Furer, 1970.

*George Washington, 1732–1799.* H. F. Bremer, 1967.

*Woodrow Wilson, 1856–1924.* R. I. Vexler, 1969.

*Name and Subject Index to the Presidential Chronology Series, From George Washington to Gerald R. Ford.* R. Gibson, 1977.

## Vice-Presidents and Cabinet

Vexler, Robert I. *The Vice-President: Biographical Sketches of the Vice-Presidents and Cabinet Members.* 2 vols. Dobbs Ferry, NY: Oceana, 1975.

This dictionary gives rather short biographical sketches, useful for identifying which particular cabinet members were in a certain administration. Once having identified a figure, the researcher can proceed to seek more in-depth studies.

Bell, Christopher, comp. *Vice Presidents of the United States, 1789–1961.* Washington, DC: Library of Congress, Legislative Reference Service, 1962.

Extremely brief biographical notes on vice-presidents are given. Again, this guide is best suited for fast identification of vice-presidents and highlights of their careers.

For biographical data on vice-presidents and cabinet members, you can also use Sobol's *Biographical Directory of the United States Executive Branch* and the tools described in the section on Biographical Resources. Because many vice-presidents and cabinet members have also served as presidents, you can find citations about them in almost all of the bibliographies mentioned throughout this volume.

## BIBLIOGRAPHIES

In this section, we list several general bibliographies dealing with presidents. Following the general bibliographies is a comprehensive list of bibliographies on each president. In addition to all of these, you should also check the bibliographies by Davison and Greenstein mentioned earlier. The Presidential Chronology series also contains bibliographies in each of the volumes on the presidents. You can also identify bibliographies from books and journal articles by using the *Bibliographic Index.* As the following list shows, there are numerous bibliographies on various topics of the presidency and individual presidents. Working with these, as well as indexes and other tools, a student or researcher can easily compile a bibliography to suit his research interests.

## General

Bates, Dorothy M., comp. *Presidential Inability: Proposals Introduced in the Congress, 1920–1962.* Washington, DC: Library of Congress, Legislative Reference Service, 1962.

This is an excellent historical guide to all the proposals put before Congress regarding presidential inability. This is especially useful for an analysis of the development of the Twenty-Fifth Amendment to the Constitution.

Bates, Dorothy M., comp. *Presidential Succession and Inability: Selected References, 1951–1967*. Washington, DC: Library of Congress, Legislative Reference Service, 1962.

This concise bibliography focuses on succession and inability. These topics were much discussed in the literature at the time, and this bibliography is one of the best on the subject.

Holloway, O. Willard. *The American Presidency: A List of Selected Reading*. Fort Sill, OK: Artillery and Guide Missile School Library, 1956.

This bibliography is very selective and now out-of-date, but it serves as a very basic reading list.

Kingsley, Thomas C. *The Federal Impeachment Process: A Bibliographic Guide*. Ithaca: Cornell University Libraries, 1974.

This is the most complete guide to the impeachment process. As impeachment is a very narrow topic, most other bibliographies on the presidency contain only a very few citations.

Library of Congress. General Reference and Bibliography Division. *Presidential Inaugurations: A List of Selected References*. Rev ed. Washington, DC: U.S. Government Printing Office, 1960.

This extensive bibliography contains citations to books, articles, and newspapers all focusing specifically on presidential inaugurations, including the activities, speeches, balls and other topics.

Library of Congress. General Reference and Bibliography Division. *The Presidents of the United States, 1789–1962: A Selected List of References*. Compiled by D. H. Mugridge. Washington, DC: U.S. Government Printing Office, 1966.

This selected bibliography covers the office of the presidency, presidential elections, the White House (i.e., the physical building and the domestic lives of the presidents), and the office of the vice-president. Also included are citations to collective biographies, biographies of individual presidents, and the writings of individual presidents. Most of the entries are for monographs, but there are articles and essays included from periodicals and symposia. Each section and sub-section is arranged chronologically. The annotations vary in length. Some entries are not annotated; others have several lines devoted to them. There is a useful preface, a subject index, and an index of authors, editors, and titles.

Shull, Steven A. "Presidential Interactions: An Annotated Bibliography." *Presidential Studies Quarterly* 8 (Winter 1975): 79–95.

This short bibliography is an excellent guide to the literature of institutional interaction as it relates to the presidency.

Sutton, Ottie K., ed. *Choosing the President*. Colorado Springs: The Air Force Academy, 1974.

This short, unannotated bibliography covers all aspects of the selection of a president, from the conventions to voting behavior. It is comprised of books and articles. While not especially extensive in its coverage of the literature, it does cite numerous important federal documents such as hearings, committee prints, etc.

Tompkins, Dorothy Campbell, comp. *The Office of Vice President: A Selected Bibliography.* Berkeley: Bureau of Public Administration, University of California, 1957.
This is a brief bibliography focusing on the office and role of the vice-president. The bibliography also includes short sections on (1) disability and succession; (2) compensation of the vice-president; and (3) proposals to change the office of vice-president.

Tompkins, Dorothy Campbell, comp. *Presidential Succession—A Bibliography.* Rev ed. Berkeley: Institute of Governmental Studies, University of California, 1965.
This concise bibliography provides important guides to the topics of presidential succession, presidential mobility, and the Twenty-Fifth Amendment. The bibliography is especially good in tracing the history of the major Congressional hearings and bills concerning those subjects. Numerous references to works in professional journals, including academic and law periodicals, are also cited.

Tompkins, Dorothy Campbell, comp. *Selection of the Vice President.* Berkeley: Institute of Government Studies, University of California, 1974.
This short but useful bibliography focuses on the issues surrounding the selection of a vice-president. It includes sections on the selection of four recent vice-presidential candidates: Johnson, Humphrey, Agnew, and Eagleton. An important section treats the special case of the nomination of Gerald R. Ford. A third section relates to works on the Twenty-Fifth Amendment to the Constitution. A final section covers proposals that concern new methods for selection of the vice-president.

## Individual Presidents

In this section, we list all the bibliographies we have found on each individual president. In addition to these, you can review the presidential factbooks, bibliographies on the presidency, and presidential chronologies series described earlier. To supplement or compile a bibliography of your own on a particular president, you can go through the indexes and abstracting services listed earlier in the guide.

### George Washington
*Bibliotheca Washington: A Descriptive List of Biographies and Biographical Sketches of George Washington.* Detroit: Gale Research Co., 1967.

### Thomas Jefferson
*Thomas Jefferson, Annotated Bibliography of Writings About Him (1836–1980).* New York: Garland Publishing, 1983.

## Andrew Jackson

*Jacksonian Democracy and the Historians.* Gainesville: University of Florida Press, 1964.

*Jacksonian Democracy.* Washington, DC: American Historical Association, 1958.

## Abraham Lincoln

Angle, Paul McClellan. *A Shelf of Lincoln Books: A Critical, Selective Bibliography of Lincolniana.* New Brunswick, NY: Rutgers University Press, 1946.

Baker, Monty R. "Abraham Lincoln in Theses and Dissertations." *Lincoln Herald* 74 (Summer 1972): 107–111.

Basler, Roy P. *The Lincoln Legend: A Study in Changing Conceptions.* Boston: Houghton Mifflin, 1935.

Gunderson, Robert G. "Another Shelf of Lincoln Books." *Quarterly Journal of Speech* 48 (October 1962): 308–313.

Searcher, Victor. *Lincoln Today: An Introduction to Modern Lincolniana.* New York: T. Yoseloff, 1969.

## Theodore Roosevelt

Grantham, Dewey W. "Theodore Roosevelt in American Historical Writing, 1945–1960." *Mid-America* 43 (January 1961): 3–35.

## Woodrow Wilson

Turnbull, Laura Shearer. *Woodrow Wilson, A Selected Bibliography of his Published Writings, Addresses and Public Papers.* Princeton: Princeton University Press, 1948.

## Herbert Hoover

Tracey, Kathleen, comp. *Herbert Hoover—A Bibliography: His Writings and Addresses.* Stanford: Hoover Institution Press, 1977.

## Franklin Delano Roosevelt

Chambers, Clarke A. "FDR, Pragmatist-Idealist: An Essay in Historiography." *Pacific Northwest Quarterly* 52 (April 1961): 50–55.

Rosen, Elliot A. "Roosevelt and the Brains Trust: An Historiographical Overview." *Political Science Quarterly* 87 (December 1972): 531–557.

Stewart, William James, comp. *Era of Franklin D. Roosevelt: A Selected Bibliography of Periodical, Essay, and Dissertation Literature, 1945–1971.* 2nd ed. Hyde Park, NY: National Archives and Records Services, General Services Administration, 1974.

Watson, Richard L. "Franklin D. Roosevelt in Historical Writing, 1950–1957." *South Atlantic Quarterly* 57 (Winter 1958): 104–126.

### Harry S Truman
Kirkendall, Richard S., ed. *The Truman Period as a Research Field, A Reappraisal, 1972.* Columbia: University of Missouri Press, 1974.

Stapleton, Margaret L. *The Truman and Eisenhower Years: 1945–1960: A Selective Bibliography.* Metuchen, NJ: Scarecrow Press, 1973.

### Dwight D. Eisenhower
Alexander, Charles C. *Holding the Line: The Eisenhower Era, 1952–1961.* Bloomington: Indiana University Press, 1975.

Bohanan, Robert D., comp. *Dwight D. Eisenhower: A Selected Bibliography of Periodical and Dissertation Literature.* Washington, DC: National Archives and Records Service, 1981.

Stapleton, Margaret L. *The Truman and Eisenhower Years, 1945–1960: A Selective Bibliography.* Metuchen, NJ: Scarecrow Press, 1973.

### John F. Kennedy
Crown, James Tracy. *The Kennedy Literature: A Bibliographical Essay on John F. Kennedy.* New York: New York University Press, 1968.

Library of Congress. *John Fitzgerald Kennedy, 1917–1963; A Chronological List of References.* Washington, DC: General Reference and Bibliography Division, Reference Department, 1964.

Newcomb, Joan I. *John F. Kennedy: An Annotated Bibliography.* Metuchen, NJ: Scarecrow Press, 1977.

Thompson, William Clifton. *A Bibliography of Literature Relating to the Assassination of President John F. Kennedy.* San Antonio, TX: Copy Distributing Co., 1968.

### Richard M. Nixon
Bellush, Jewel, and A. Walling. "Watergate: A Preliminary Bibliography." *National Civil Review* 63 (February 1974): 110–114.

Halpern, Paul J., ed. *Why Watergate?* Pacific Palisades, CA: Palisades Publishers, 1975.

Rosenberg, Kenyon C., and J. K. Rosenberg, eds. *Watergate: An Annotated Bibliography.* Littleton, CO: Libraries Unlimited, 1975.

# PART III

# Running For Office

# CHAPTER 5

# Campaigns and Elections

Campaigning and elections have long been an area of intensive research for political scientists and historians. In the last thirty years, the amount of data has increased significantly. There is now information available on almost every aspect of campaigning and elections, including public opinion polls, election returns and studies, and finance. The tools cited here are not only a source for data, but can be used for generating your own. We have included a table of presidential election returns in Appendix 20, p. 262, for reference.

This field of research is also a rapidly changing one. There are now more primaries than ever before and the cost of campaigning is constantly increasing. Campaigns now start much earlier than they did before, and the role of political action committees has changed the way candidates raise funds and even their campaign strategies. In addition to the resources discussed, it is important to remember that many of the tools described in previous sections can be used for researching campaigns and elections. Almanacs, newspapers, newsmagazines, and indexes are vital research tools. Many of the bibliographies and resources, such as the publications of Congressional Quarterly, also contain a considerable amount of material relevant to this subfield.

## CAMPAIGNS

### Finances

One area of election statistics that has been badly neglected is campaign contributions. It is only within the last twenty years that a systematic collection of data on campaign contributions has been undertaken. As the issue of money in elections has always been important, the massive volumes of campaign contribution statistics should lead to many new and fascinating studies. In accordance with the Federal Election Campaign Act of 1971 (Public Law 92–225), the General Accounting Office, Clerk of the House, and the Secretary

167

of the Senate were responsible for making public statistics on contributions to presidential and congressional candidates. Unfortunately, the act was amended by P. L. 93–443, and the data is not required to be made public.

Even so, it is now possible to do extensive research on campaign expenditures. The materials issued by Common Cause and the federal government provide financial data on campaign spending. By using both sources of information, you can examine campaign spending according to (1) candidate; (2) party; (3) contest; (4) committee; (5) type of contribution; (6) size of contribution; and (7) state. The amount of statistics now published provide researchers with considerable material for extended analyses. With the continuation of those publications, the researcher will also have the opportunity to conduct time-series research.

*CRF Listing of Contributors of National Level Political Committees to Incumbents and Candidates for Public Office.* Edited by Herbert E. Alexander and Caroline D. Jones. Princeton: Citizens' Research Foundation, 1968–1970.

This work provides data on contributions given to candidates by national-level political committees of the Republican and Democratic parties, as well as committees representing labor, business and professional interests.

*CRF Listing of Political Contributors of $500 or More.* Edited by Herbert E. Alexander and Caroline D. Jones. Princeton: Citizen's Research Foundation, 1968–1972.

This provides a listing of contributors, arranged alphabetically, who gave to candidates both at the national and state level. It gives the address of the contributor, the amount of the contribution, and the candidate and party he contributed to.

*CRF Listing of Contributors and Lenders of $10,000 or More in 1972.* Edited by Barbara D. Paul, Mary Jo Long, Elizabeth C. Burns, Herbert E. Alexander. Princeton: Citizens' Research Foundation, 1975.

This work compiles campaign contributions to presidential, congressional, state and local committees, and candidates. More than 1,300 contributors, arranged alphabetically, are included. Their home and business addresses, profession and business affiliation are also given. CRF has also gathered data on individuals who made contributions of more than $10,000 in presidential election years since 1960. This data has been published in Herbert E. Alexander's quadrennial series, *Financing the . . . Election.* Six volumes in all have been published, covering the 1960, 1964, 1968, 1972, 1976, and 1980 elections.

*Studies in Political Finance.* Princeton: Citizens' Research Foundation, No. 1, 1960– .

These studies tend to be very specific, usually examining a single state or election contest. As research studies, they serve as examples of what directions an analysis of political contributions can take. The first twenty-one studies have also been published in a three-volume series by CRF, *Studies in Money in Politics,* edited by Herbert E. Alexander.

Common Cause. The Campaign Finance Monitoring Project. *1972 Federal Campaign Finances*. 10 vols. Washington, DC: Common Cause, 1974.

This work provides a summary of the campaign finances of every major candidate for Congress in the 1972 general election. The study is organized into ten volumes, divided by regional area (1) New England States; (2) Mid-Atlantic States; (3) Border States; (4) Southeastern States; (5) Southern States; (6) Southwestern States; (7) West Coast States; (8) Mountain States; (9) Plains States; and (10) Great Lake States. Each volume contains data on three areas of a candidate's campaign finances (1) a summary of campaign financial data; (2) a listing of registered special interest and national political party committees and their contributions; and (3) a list of large contributions from individuals. A five-volume set of the *1974 Congressional Campaign Finances* has also been published by Common Cause.

Common Cause. The Campaign Finance Monitoring Project. *1972 Federal Campaign Finances: Interest Groups and Political Parties*. 3 vols. Washington, DC: Common Cause, 1974.

This work provides the finances of all nationally registered political committees which contributed $5,000 or more to federal candidates in 1972. The lists have been arranged into three volumes (1) Business, Agriculture and Dairy, and Health; (2) Labor; and (3) Miscellaneous, Democratic, and Republican. Each volume contains (1) a detailed table of contents, covering the interest groups for that volume; (2) a financial summary for each interest committee, including a brief description of the group or interest that the committee represents and its activities in the 1972 elections; (3) a complete listing of every individual and group that received contributions from the committee and the amount received; and (4) an index listing the name and affiliation of all political committees registered during 1972.

The Federal Election Commission, using information based on financial disclosure provisions of the 1977 House and Senate ethics codes, has initiated a new series, the *FEC Disclosure Series*. Congressional Quarterly and the *National Journal* also publish studies based on Common Cause and Federal data, as well as research conducted by their own staff. In addition to these sources, a looseleaf service is now available to all aspects of campaign finance.

Schwarz, Thomas J., and Alan G. Straus. *Federal Regulation of Campaign Finance and Political Activity*. Albany: Matthew Bender, 1981– .

This two-volume set will be updated with periodic looseleaf additions and an annual supplement. It provides a detailed description of the history and development of laws governing campaign finance and lobbying and includes the amended statutes and regulations of the Federal Election Campaign Act, Presidential Primary Matching Account Act, Lobbying Act, Hatch Act, and Federal Communications Act. The two volumes provide a discussion of what constitutes contributions and expenditures, as well as what parties, corporations, labor unions and other groups must do to comply with the law. There are also sections covering the statutes regulating lobbying and broadcasting activities. Though this guide is designed as a sourcebook for candidates, accountants, lawyers, and party officials involved in campaigns, it is an excellent reference source for students and researchers.

# Interest Groups

In this section, we discuss some directories that identify and provide information on lobbyists, political action committees, and other associations and organizations involved in the political process. While the directories listed below will provide a considerable amount of information about interest groups, some of the sources cited earlier are also useful. Both *Congressional Quarterly Weekly Report* and *National Journal* give extensive coverage to interest groups. *CQ Weekly Report* regularly lists new lobbyists and publishes the ratings of congressmen by various interest groups, such as the AFL-CIO Committee on Political Education. The newsletters cited earlier are an invaluable source for learning about the activities of interest groups. Newspaper and magazine literature supply important information, for their coverage goes behind the scene to detail the efforts of political groups. Trade, industrial, and professional journals have regular columns or sections on national politics. Consult these indexes for guidance: *Business Periodicals Index, Applied Science and Technology Index,* and *Public Affairs Information Service Bulletin.* One particularly useful newsletter is *Political Finance/Lobby Reporter.* This newsletter, published 48 times a year by Amward Publications, provides short stories on current issues and developments in regard to financing as well as new lobby registrations.

## LOBBYISTS

*Directory of Washington Representatives of American Associations and Industry.* Washington, DC: Columbia Books, 1977– .

This directory includes lobbyists, legal advisors, information collectors and consultants representing public interest groups, corporations, labor unions, trade and professional associations, state and local governments, Political Action Committees, and foreign governments. The information is gathered from the lobby registration filed with the Clerk of the House of Representatives, the Foreign Agent Registrations of the Department of Justice, dockets of regulatory agencies, commissions and departments, and other federal records. The information is arranged in two alphabetically cross-referenced lists. The first is a list of representatives by name, address, and date of registration. The second lists organizations by the address, name and title of their representatives, and a brief description of their activities. There are also subject and country indexes.

*Directory of Registered Lobbyists and Lobbyist Legislation.* 2nd ed. Chicago: Marquis Academic Media, 1976.

This is a comprehensive sourcebook of all registered lobbyists in Washington and the forty-eight states requiring registration. The directory is arranged by state, with lobbyists listed alphabetically. The name, address, phone

number, and organizational ties are given for each lobbyist. For easy reference use, there is a lobbyist index and organizational index. The complete
texts of all federal and state laws relating to lobbying are reprinted.

*The Washington Lobbyist/Lawyers Directory*. 5th ed. Edited by Ed Zuckerman.
Washington, DC: Amward Publications, 1982.
This directory lists lobbyists in an alphabetical name index. They are then
cross-indexed according to their business or organizational affiliation. A
third part of the guide indexes the political action committees of corporations, unions, and professional associations.

Close, Arthur C., ed. *Washington Representatives*. 8th ed. Washington, DC:
Columbia Books, 1984.
This annual directory is organized much like the prior two volumes. It
contains a list of representatives, a list of organizations, a subject index, and
a country index. This directory includes a list of the congressional committees and their membership and regulatory agencies that are the focus of
lobbying efforts.

## POLITICAL ACTION COMMITTEES

Fraser, Edith, ed. *The PAC Handbook*. Cambridge: Ballinger Publishing Co.,
1982.
The volume, intended more as a handbook for groups forming PACs or
already established PACs, nevertheless contains much useful information
relevant to researching the organization, funding, and business management
of PACs.

*Political Action Register*. Orlando, FL: Interstate Bureau of Regulations,
1982– .
This looseleaf service is the best comprehensive authority on the laws and
regulations governing the organization of PACs. It details the rights, responsibilities, and legal requirements of PACs as well as how the states handle the
reporting requirements, responsibilities, and penalties relating to PACs. It
also includes information regarding the role of PACs in campaign fund
raising.

The following directories to PACs provide a listing of PACs and their
interests. As the number of PACs grows with each election, keeping up with the
number and affiliation of PACs is difficult. Consequently, for current research
you should always be sure to use *CQ Weekly Report* and the *National Journal*.

Roeder, Edward. *PACs Americana: A Directory of Political Action Committees
and Their Interests*. Washington, DC: Sunshine Services Corporation, 1982.

Schapsmeier, Edward L., and Frederick H. Schapsmeier. *Political Parties and
Civic Action Groups*. Westport, CT: Greenwood Press, 1981.

*Tyke's Register of Political Action Committees.* Washington, DC: Tyke Research
Associates, 1978.

## OTHER DIRECTORIES

The directories listed below were not designed to identify lobbyists and
interest groups per se, but if you want to acquire additional information about a
particular association, organization, or group represented by a registered lobbyist, these directories will give you more detailed information.

*Encyclopedia of Associations.* Detroit: Gale Research Co., 1956– .

*Greenwood Encyclopedia of American Institutions.* Westport, CT: Greenwood
Press, 1977– .

*National Directory of Corporate Public Affairs.* Washington, DC: Columbia
Books, 1983.

*National Trade and Professional Association of the United States and Canada.*
Washington, DC: Columbia Books, 1975– .

*Research Service Directory.* 2nd ed. Detroit: Gale Research Co., 1982.

# Communications

In the age of the electronic media, the role of image-makers is perhaps
becoming more important than the candidates themselves. Sophisticated public
relations firms work extremely hard to package and sell their candidates.
Without a doubt, there is an obvious connection between a candidate's financial
funds and his ability to maximize radio and television exposure. While there is
not an abundance of statistical information on communications, there are some
important sources of data.

Federal Communications Commission. *Survey of Political Broadcasting.*
Washington, DC: 1960– .
     This series contains data on primary and general elections obtained
through questionnaires sent to broadcast stations, including AM and FM
radio stations and TV stations. The information covers several major areas of
interest (1) overall political broadcast activity; (2) charges for political
broadcasts; (3) political broadcast activity with respect to specified offices;
and (4) editorializing. The 1970 edition of the *Survey of Political Broadcasting* is in the following hearings: U.S. Senate, Committee on Commerce, *The
Federal Election Campaign Act of 1971.* Hearings before a Subcommittee on
Communication of the Committee of Commerce, Senate, on S.1, S.382, and
S.956, 92nd Congress, 1st Sess., 1971. For additional information regarding
rulings by the FCC on political broadcasting, check the following: *Decisions
and Reports, 1st series, 1934–1965,* and *Decisions and Reports, 2nd series,*
1965– .

U.S. Department of Commerce, comp. *Decisions Interpreting the Communications Act of 1934.* 2 vols. Washington, DC: U.S. Government Printing Office, 1978.

This volume contains reports, decisions, memoranda, orders, and policy statements regarding the regulation of political broadcasting. The *Federal Communications Law Journal* contains numerous articles relating to political communication.

Rosenbloom, David, ed. *The Political Marketplace.* New York: Quadrangle Books, Campaign Communications Institute for Politics, 1972.

This directory, intended as a guide to campaign information for political candidates, also serves as an excellent reference work. Even though it was written solely for the 1972 elections, it continues to be a valuable source of information. The book is a large compendium of campaign services. It includes a directory to (1) campaign management and consulting firms; (2) political advertising and public relations firms; (3) computer-list and direct mail houses; (4) television and radio time buyers; (5) media outlets and film producers; (6) telephone consultants; (7) demographic and audience research firms; and (8) other aspects of campaign management.

Kaid, Lynda Lee, Keith R. Sanders, and Robert O. Hirsch. *Political Campaign Communication: A Bibliography and Guide to the Literature.* Metuchen, NJ: Scarecrow Press, 1974.

A general bibliography on the communication process in political campaigns, this book contains over 1,500 entries, the majority of which are unannotated. It covers from 1950 to 1972. This bibliography includes books, articles, government documents, pamphlets, and dissertations and has a subject index. The scope of the citations covers: analytical and evaluative articles, public opinion polling, media use and expenditures, and all aspects of the communication process.

Hansen, Donald A., and J. Herschel Parsons. *Mass Communications: A Research Bibliography.* Berkeley: Glendessary Press, 1968.

This bibliography identifies almost 3,000 books and articles on mass communication. While the scope of this bibliography is much broader than just the political aspects of mass communication, it does contain many relevant citations. It is also useful for finding theoretical and empirical studies of a general nature which can be applied to research on the presidency.

Another source of information on political communication is the literature in the fields of communication and journalism. Journals such as *Political Communication and Persuasion, Journalism Quarterly, Quarterly Journal of Speech, Public Opinion Quarterly, Columbia Journalism Quarterly,* and *Journal of Communication* are a rich source for information dealing with politics and the media. The best way to identify materials in this area is to use *Communication Abstracts* and *Journalism Abstracts.*

You can use these two tools to research other topics, such as the role of the media in covering campaigns, elections, and presidential politics, or the use of public relations techniques employed in campaigning or by a president in office. In general, you can rely on these abstracting services to research any aspect of the presidency related to the media or mass communication.

# Conventions

Long before an election takes place, candidates must undergo the tedious and enduring campaign trail leading to their national nominating conventions. They must compete in preference primaries and contend with state political caucuses. In essence this process is the fight for convention delegates. In this section, we provide an introduction to the basic works for you to use to become familiar with the entire nominating process. The first set of sources focuses on the nomination of presidential candidates and the manner in which delegates to the national conventions are chosen. The following document collections are guides to the platforms. The last two tools are guides to the voting records on conventions.

## PROCEDURES

U.S. Congress. Senate. *Nomination and Election of the President and Vice President of the United States including the Manner of Selecting Delegates to National Political Conventions*. Washington, DC: U.S. Government Printing Office, 1956– .
    This series analyzes the procedure of the nomination and election of the president and vice-president. It examines the rules of the major political parties, federal and state laws, and constitutional clauses governing the procedure. The document describes the manner in which delegates to the national conventions are selected, the number of delegates to be selected, and the dates on which the selection are made. It lists the states in which presidential preference primaries are held, the dates of such primaries, and the filing deadlines for candidates or delegates. Some statistical data is also included, such as the popular and electoral vote of presidential elections, campaign costs, and expenditures for political broadcasts.

National Municipal League. *Presidential Nominating Procedures: A Compendium of Election Practices in 1972*. 2 vols. New York: National Municipal League, 1973.
    This compendium is a comprehensive state-by-state guide to nominating procedures. The introduction provides an excellent history of the presidential nominating procedure and includes a detailed classification of preference primaries, delegate selection procedures, and state conventions. The individual state sections give the following information: (1) general statement on the delegate selection process and number of delegates for each party; (2) preference primaries; (3) delegate selection primaries; (4) convention system; (5) state-level committees; (6) national delegate caucus; and (7) a bibliography of state statutes and party rules and regulations.

*Third Party Presidential Nominating Conventions, Proceedings, Records, etc.*
8 reels. LaCrosse, WI: Northern Micrographics, 1974.

With the sparse coverage of third-party conventions, this microfilm collection is extremely useful, for it brings together various sources of information on the conventions—official proceedings, newspaper reports, parties' campaign books, and miscellaneous reports, minutes, and statements. Over fifteen minor parties are contained in the collection, including the following parties:

American Party 1856, 1888

Anti-Masonic Party 1830–1836

Constitutional Union Party 1860

Free Soil Party 1848–1852

Greenback Party 1840–1852

Liberal Party 1840–1852

Populist Party 1892–1900

Progressive Party (Roosevelt) 1912–1916

Progressive Party (La Follette) 1924

Progressive Party (Wallace) 1948–1968

Prohibition Party 1872–1924, 1936–1968

Socialist Labor Party 1877–1968

Socialist Party of America 1900–1968

Union Labor Party 1888

A softbound index provides easy access to the various publications in the collection.

Both the Democratic and Republican parties publish a written record of their convention proceedings. The *Republican Party, National Convention, Official Report of the Proceedings* is usually published within a year of the event, while the *Democratic Party, National Convention, Proceedings* are usually published several years after the convention. The Republican National Committee distributes the *Proceedings* free of charge to a large number of academic libraries. On the other hand, academic libraries must purchase the *Proceedings of the Democratic Convention*. Consequently, you may find better coverage of recent Republican Conventions in libraries. The Library of Congress has microfilmed the convention proceedings of both parties (Republican, 1856–1952, Democratic, 1832–1952), and many libraries have purchased these microfilms. One last source of the party platforms is the quadrennial publication issued by the Clerk of the House of Representatives, *Platforms of the Democratic Party and the Republican Party.*

## PLATFORMS

Johnson, Donald Bruce. *National Party Platforms.* 2 vols. 6th rev ed. Champaign: University of Illinois Press, 1978.

*National Party Platforms of 1980.* Champaign: University of Illinois Press, 1982.

This standard reference work is a comprehensive collection of party platforms for all major and minor parties competing at the national level. It presents authenticated copies of platforms for all major and principal minor parties. It includes the names of all presidential and vice-presidential candidates, as well as the distribution of popular and electoral votes. The material is arranged in chronological order, and there is a comprehensive index to the platforms.

In addition to the volumes by Johnson, two similar volumes contain platforms and secondary analysis and information.

Chester, Edward W. *A Guide to Political Platforms.* Hamden, CT: Shoe String Press, 1977.

McKee, Thomas H. *The National Conventions and Platforms of all Political Parties, 1789–1905: Convention, Popular, and Electoral Vote.* 3rd ed. St. Clair Shore, MI: Scholarly Press, 1970.

# VOTING

Bain, Richard C., and Judith H. Parris. *Convention Decisions and Voting Records.* 2nd ed. Washington, DC: Brookings Institution, 1973.

This provides a narrative account of the convention proceedings of the two major parties between 1832 and 1972. Each convention is prefaced by a brief summary of the political situation. The Appendices list the nominees of the major parties, convention officers, and voting records, arranged chronologically within each convention, giving roll-call votes of important motions. This is undoubtedly the best source for convention roll-call votes. To update this volume, the researcher should consult the *Congressional Quarterly Weekly Report,* the *National Journal,* or *The New York Times.*

*National Party Conventions, 1831–1980.* Washington, DC: Congressional Quarterly, 1982.

This concise reference work is the best ready reference guide to conventions. While it does not reprint platforms in their entirety, it does include excerpts and provides a chronology of all the nominating conventions and breakdowns on state-by-state delegation voting on ballots and other decisions.

Naturally, newspapers are an invaluable resource for anyone interested in researching national conventions. They are useful not only for the reporting of the proceeding, but as a record of journalists' perceptions of the convention, issues, and public interest. *The New York Times,* the *Washington Post,* and other major newspapers cover conventions extensively; you should also remember to check the newspapers of the city and state where the conventions were held. Even if those newspapers are not indexed, you can use indexes for the *Times* and *Post* to pinpoint specific days and events.

*Time, Newsweek,* and others cited in the section on magazines will also give extensive coverage to national conventions. To find information about conventions, it is wise to check *Reader's Guide to Periodical Literature, Public Affairs Information Service Bulletin,* the *Magazine Index,* and even *Business Periodicals Index.*

# Secondary Sources

This category includes a variety of miscellaneous materials relevant to the study of campaigns. Some of the items cited have only been published once, while others are part of a series. Though there are not as many bibliographies on campaigns as there are on other aspects of the presidency, the few that exist are useful.

## RESOURCE MATERIALS

During each presidential campaign, various reference services appear designed specifically for that campaign or intended to be issued on a short-term basis. Students and researchers studying a campaign in progress should take the time to investigate such services. The first item below is an example of this kind of research tool.

*The 1980 Presidential Campaign News Digest Service.* New York: Arno Press, 1980.
     This looseleaf service was based on the abstracting and indexing service of the *Information Bank of The New York Times.* The *Information Bank* includes abstracts of newspapers and magazine articles from over fifty publications, but most of the information comes from *The New York Times, The Wall Street Journal,* the *Washington Post,* and *Business Week.* This service includes a fully indexed background report of over 1,500 abstracts from January 1979 to November 1979. In addition to the background report, twelve monthly update reports and indexes were issued for the time period of February 1980 through January 1981. This service provided a current research service as the campaign progressed.

*Campaign '76: A CBS Reference Book.* New York: Arno Press, 1977.

*Campaign '78: A CBS Reference Book.* New York: Arno Press, 1979.
     These two volumes contain various kinds of information on elections, congressional districts, and campaigning in general taken from published government sources. While these volumes do not supply much new information, they are good compendia for these specific campaigns.

U.S. National Portrait Gallery, Smithsonian Institution. *'If Elected . . .': Unsuccessful Candidates for the Presidency, 1796–1968.* Washington, DC: Smithsonian Institution, 1972.
     A valuable history of unsuccessful candidates for the presidency, this work includes major-party as well as third-party candidates. There is a short study of each candidate, focusing on his life and philosophy. The work

includes a selected bibliography for the unsuccessful candidates. Election statistics, including the electoral and popular votes from 1789 to 1968, are also included. The data also include information on third-party candidates.

## BIBLIOGRAPHIES

The bibliographies listed below focus on campaigning and the activities of political parties. Most of the bibliographies cited in other sections of this guide also have sections on campaigning, especially the volumes by Greenstein and Davison.

Agranoff, Robert. *Political Campaigns: A Bibliography.* De Kalb: Center for Governmental Studies, Northern Illinois University, 1972.
    This bibliography provides about two hundred unannotated citations. It focuses on three areas (1) campaign strategies, electioneering, and party activities; (2) campaign techniques, media advertising, polls; and (3) campaigns and election finance.

Szekely, Kalman S., comp. *Electoral College: A Selected Annotated Bibliography.* Littleton, CO: Libraries Unlimited, 1970.
    While this bibliography is selective, it is the most comprehensive compilation on the subject. It contains 794 items covering periodicals, books, pamphlets, and unpublished dissertations. The sources span the time from the Constitutional Convention to 1970. The work is arranged according to a subject outline in the following categories: (1) Historical Background and Organization; (2) Arguments in Favor of Retaining Present System; (3) Arguments Against Present System; (4) Proposals to Reform Present System; (5) Popular Interest in Reform; and (6) Reapportionment of Electoral System. Unfortunately, the only subject access to entries is through the table of contents, since the work lacks a subject index. There are no cross-references for items from section to section; consequently, items are listed under only one section. For the most part, annotations are far too brief and do not give an indication of the contents of the entries. The listing of state statutes governing presidential electors is incomplete, with no entries appearing for California, Connecticut, District of Columbia, and Ohio.

*The Democratic and Republican Parties in America: A Historical Bibliography.* Santa Barbara, CA: ABC-Clio, 1983.
    This bibliography includes over 1,000 abstracts summarizing journal articles published between 1973 and 1982. The bibliography covers such topics as the origin and growth of parties, candidates and campaigns, platforms and lobbying. The entries are arranged by chapter, and there is a detailed multiterm subject index.

Goehlert, Robert. *Political Parties in the United States: A Bibliography.* Monticello, IL: Vance Bibliographies, 1982.
    This unannotated bibliography includes over 300 citations to journal literature and books published during the past decade. The citations are primarily from journals in political science and policy studies.

Miles, William. *The Image Makers: A Bibliography of American Presidential Campaign Biographies.* Metuchen, NJ: Scarecrow Press, 1979.
This bibliography includes books, pamphlets, magazines, almanacs, speeches, and miscellaneous political compendia on candidates of official parties. It includes citations to both successful and unsuccessful candidates and many vice-presidential contenders. The materials cited include both favorable and unfavorable accounts. Many of the citations in this bibliography are to publications not widely owned by most libraries, such as pamphlets and party documents. More than 500 of the titles in the bibliography have been published as a microfiche collection by University Microfilms International, the *Presidential Election Campaign Biographies.*

# ELECTIONS

In this section, we focus on presidential elections. While we have limited this section to only a single aspect of the electoral system, we feel that the primacy of the office and the amount of material on the subject requires a lengthy section on presidential elections. Since many sources include statistics on congressional elections, it is useful to indicate the scope of each book. Consequently, we describe in full sources that simultaneously cover other federal elections. Our main consideration is to identify major sources of statistics available for a study of the presidential elections. In order to assist the reader in finding more obscure sources of data, we have listed all the major reference works giving statistical sources. We have included, too, any significant bibliography relating to presidential elections. In evaluating each source, we have indicated the extent, usefulness, and content of the data. This section will direct the researcher towards additional information centers and materials.

## Electoral Systems

As the laws regulating campaigning finances and electoral procedures have an impact on party competition and the nature of the electoral process, it is important to know where to find information on legislation governing elections and party activities. The three Senate publications listed below provide an introduction and analysis to the statutes governing elections.

*Factual Campaign Information.* Compiled by the Senate Library. Washington, DC: U.S. Government Printing Office, 1939– .
This series is compiled to serve Senators in their campaigns and is the best source for information of the American electoral system. Although emphasizing senatorial elections, it includes information about minor parties and presidential and congressional primaries. There is a lengthy section on the major statutory provisions governing federal elections and other miscellaneous laws and a section dealing with party organizations, both Republican and Democratic. Members of national committees, senatorial campaign committees, national congressional committees, and chairmen of state committees are listed.

U.S. Congress. Senate. Select Committee on Presidential Activities. *Election Reform: Basic References.* 93rd Congress, 1st Sess. Washington, DC: U.S. Government Printing Office, 1973.

This work is a collection of eighteen essays and reports on the issue of campaign spending. The articles have been well chosen and provide a good discussion on the issue. The work includes a short history of the major events in the movement for federal campaign reform. There is an annotated bibliography of selected references on financing political campaigns. The bibliography covers the period from 1967 to 1973. The text of the Federal Election Campaign Act of 1971 is reprinted.

U.S. Federal Election Commission. *Federal Election Campaign Laws.* Washington, DC: U.S. Government Printing Office, 1984.

This is a compilation of all federal laws affecting federal elections and campaign practices. Included are the Federal Election Campaign Act of 1971, the Federal Election Act Amendments of 1974, and the Hatch Act. These laws, as well as commentaries on them, have been reprinted in various Congressional Quarterly publications.

Several excellent reference guides contain information on the electoral system and political parties of the United States, as well as other countries. These tools give concise information about the American electoral and party system. Since cross-national research is especially prevalent in the areas of election and campaign research, these tools are useful for comparative research as well. They can be used as factbooks to find information, as a source of data, and a tool for generating data.

Day, Alan J., and Henry W. Degenhardt. *Political Parties of the World: A Keesing's Reference Publication.* Detroit: Gale Research Co., 1980.

Delury, George. *World Encyclopedia of Political Systems and Parties.* New York: Facts on File, 1983.

*Political Handbook and Atlas of the World.* New York: Harper and Row, 1927– .

*Statesman's Yearbook.* New York: St. Martin's Press, 1864– .

*Worldmark Encyclopedia of the Nations.* New York: Worldmark Press, 1976.

# Voting and Ecological Data

## STATISTICAL INDEXES

In addition to voting and election returns data, researchers often are interested in finding data on government expenditures, the number of employees in the executive department, or some economic or social trend. Because there are almost 8,000 federal publications containing statistical data, it is important to know how to identify and locate the information you need. Fortunately, there are several indexes and guides to use.

Andriot, John L. *Guide to U.S. Government Statistics.* Arlington, VA: Documents Index, 1973.
This guide to federal statistics lists publications on departments and agencies. The guide also includes a subject index identifying the types of data published. It is useful for identifying broad categories of data and for determining what information departments and agencies disseminate.

U.S. Bureau of the Census. *Catalog of United States Census Publications, 1790–1972.* Washington, DC: U.S. Government Printing Office, 1974.
This catalog indexes and describes all decennial census publications, as well as all other census data on government—population, business, manufacturing, etc. For publications since 1972, review the monthly *Catalog of U.S. Census Publications* and the annual publications. The monthly catalogs also include information on machine-readable data, reports, and tabulations. Since more and more census data are being made available in this format, this is an important section for anyone using data in machine-readable form.

*American Statistics Index.* Washington, DC: Congressional Information Service, 1973– .
The *Statistics Index* is issued in looseleaf format and cumulated yearly. The 1974 edition, a special volume, indexes federal statistical publications issued between 1960 and 1973. Indexing data produced by the federal government, this service includes more than 400 departments and agencies. The index provides access to data by subject, title, author, agency report, report number, and category breakdown. The twenty category breakdowns enable a user to find data by census division, industry, sex, income, commodity, race etc. Each entry has an accession number that directs you to the abstract. The abstract provides complete bibliographical information on the publication. A descriptive synopsis of the data includes its coverage, time span, arrangement, and any other specific details. In addition to indexing and abstracting the publications, CIS also makes all of the publications available for purchase on microfilm. This is the place to start when you want to identify federal data. When researching the presidency, you can use it to identify not only data about the office, but statistical publications of the Executive Office and the executive branch as well.

*Statistical Reference Index.* Washington, DC: Congressional Information Service, 1980– .
This reference guide is published in the same format as its companion, the *American Statistics Index,* but they differ in content. This index provides access to data published by the private sector, by foundations, research centers, institutes, industrial and commercial organizations, etc. While not particularly useful for researching the presidency directly, it can lead you to data about interest groups, lobbying groups, or industries affected by legislation or regulation. You will find statistical data for any sector of society affected by the actions of the president, either as a legislator or executive.

## DATA COMPILATIONS

In an elections study, it is crucial to know something about the voters themselves. Factors such as age, sex, race, education, and income can help explain why the electorate voted a certain way. This information is generally available only from public opinion surveys. The U.S. Bureau of Census is the largest producer of aggregate data; you can draw political, economic, and social variables from census data. Hundreds of subject categories are broken down geographically by congressional districts, counties, standard metropolitan statistical areas, unincorporated places, and city blocks. With some patience, the researcher can find the information he or she needs.

U.S. Bureau of the Census. *Congressional District Data Book; A Statistical Abstract Supplement.* Washington, DC: U.S. Government Printing Office, 1963– .

The *Congressional District Data Book* presents a wide range of data from census and recent election statistics for congressional districts. It reports socioeconomic data—population, sex, residency, race, age, households and families, marital status, industry, occupation, migration, and housing. Maps for each state show counties and congressional districts. Appendices give data on apportionment, redistricting, and the population of the districts. Since the material is based on the decennial census, new editions and supplements are irregularly issued. The Census Bureau also publishes maps of congressional districts in its *Congressional District Atlas.* Congressional Quarterly has published *Districts in the 1980's,* which contains the essential demographic and political information on all 435 congressional districts. This is the most up-to-date guide, providing data and maps for the new districts. Although the Congressional Quarterly volume does not provide as much information as the Census series, it is easier to use.

U.S. Bureau of the Census. *County and City Data Book; A Statistical Abstract Supplement.* Washington, DC: U.S. Government Printing Office, 1949– .

This work presents a wide range of statistical information for counties, standard metropolitan statistical areas, cities, urbanized areas and unincorporated places. It includes statistics on agriculture; bank deposits; birth and deathrates; business firms; crime; education; employment; government revenue and expenditures; housing; income; migration; public assistance; savings; social security; and presidential voting. The data presented is taken from various censuses, including the census of governments, census of business, manufactures and mineral industries, and the census of population and housing.

Two series within Current Population Reports provide information on the voting population. The *Population Estimates, P–25 Series* includes regular reports on the estimates and projections of the voting age population. The *Population Characteristics, P–20 Series* provides information about the characteristics of the voting population and their degree of participation in general elections. Those reports, as well as others published by the Census Bureau, are indexed in the *Bureau of the Census Catalog* and the *American*

*Statistics Index: A Comprehensive Index to the Statistical Publications of the U.S. Government.* The *American Statistics Index,* as noted earlier, is the most inclusive index to statistics published by the federal government, for it provides abstracts of the documents it indexes and covers the publications of all major statistical agencies and the statistics reported in committee hearings and prints. It would be impossible to systematically search for statistics published in hearings and prints without this index. The American Political Science Association has published two guides to census data in its Instructional Monograph Series: *U.S. Census Data for Political & Social Research: A Manual for Students* and *A Resource Guide* (1976). Both were prepared by Phyllis G. Carter, formerly Chief, Census History Staff, Data User Services Division in the Bureau of the Census.

Listed below are all the P–20 and P–25 *Current Population Reports* that focus on voting and registration. Some of the P–20 series, the *Voting Participation in Elections,* are available from the Census Bureau in machine-readable form. They are also in the archival holdings of the Inter-University Consortium for Political and Social Research (see the section on Data Archives). The *County and City Data Books* and the *Congressional District Data Books* are also available from the Census Bureau in machine-readable form and are in the archival holdings of the ICPSR.

*P–20 Series, Population Characteristics.*

No. 143, Oct. 1965. *Voter Participation in the National Election, Nov. 1964.*

No. 172, May 1968. *Characteristics of Persons of Voting Age, 1964–1968.*

No. 174, Aug. 1968. *Voting and Registration in the Election of Nov. 1966.*

No. 177, Dec. 1968. *Voter Participation in Nov. 1968.*

No. 192, Dec. 1969. *Voting and Registration in the Election of Nov. 1968.*

No. 208, Dec. 1970. *Voter Participation in Nov. 1970.*

No. 230, Dec. 1971. *Characteristics of New Voters: 1972.*

No. 244, Dec. 1972. *Voter Participation in Nov. 1972.*

No. 253, Oct. 1973. *Voting and Registration in the Election of Nov. 1972.*

No. 275, Jan. 1975. *Voter Participation in Nov. 1974.*

No. 293, April 1976. *Voting and Registration in the Election of Nov. 1974.*

No. 304, Dec. 1976. *Voter Participation in November 1976.*

No. 322, March 1978. *Voting and Registration in the Election of Nov. 1976.*

No. 332, Dec. 1978. *Voting and Registration in the Election of Nov. 1978.*

No. 344, Sept. 1979. *Voting and Registration in the Election of Nov. 1978.*

No. 359, Jan. 1981. *Voting and Registration in the Election of Nov. 1980.*

No. 370, April 1982. *Voting and Registration in the Election of Nov. 1980.*

*P–25 Series, Population Estimates.*

No. 15, Oct. 1948. *Estimates of the Population of Voting Age, by States: 1948.*

No. 90, March 1954. *Estimates of the Population of the United States and Components of Population Change: 1950–1954.*

No. 143, Oct. 1956. *Estimates of the Civilian Population of Voting Age, for States: Nov. 1952 and 1956.*

No. 185, Oct. 1960. *Estimates of the Civilian Population of Voting Age, for States: Nov. 1958.*

No. 221, Oct. 1960. *Estimates of the Civilian Population of Voting Age, for States: Nov. 1960.*

No. 225, Oct. 1962. *Estimates of the Civilian Population of Voting Age, for States: Nov. 1962.*

No. 315, Aug. 1965. *Estimates of the Population of Voting in General Elections, 1920–1964.*

No. 325, Jan. 1966. *Projections of the Population of Voting Age: Nov. 1966 and 1968.*

No. 342, June 1966. *Projections of the Population of Voting Age, for States: Nov. 1966 and 1968.*

No. 406, Oct. 1968. *Estimates of the Population of Voting Age, for States: Nov. 1968.*

No. 479, March 1972. *Projections of the Population of Voting Age, for States: Nov. 1972.*

No. 526, Sept. 1974. *Projections of the Population of Voting Age, for States: Nov. 1974.*

No. 626, May 1976. *Projections of the Population of Voting Age, for States: Nov. 1976.*

No. 627, June 1976. *Language Minority, Illiteracy, and Voting Data Used in Making Determinations for the Voting Rights Act Amendments of 1975 (Public Law 94–73).*

No. 732, Sept. 1978. *Projections of the Population of Voting Age for States: Nov. 1978.*

No. 879, March 1980. *Projections of the Population of Voting Age for States: Nov. 1980.*

No. 916, July 1982. *Projections of the Population of Voting Age for States: Nov. 1982.*

# District Data

Two special volumes are useful for finding specific data on congressional districts. While the *Congressional District Data Books* are the standard volumes for finding social, economic, and political data about districts, the following two works are best for finding data about industries and roll-call votes.

*Congressional District Business Patterns.* 2 vols. New York: Economic Information Systems, 1981.

This directory identifies industries and businesses within congressional districts. It reports the number of establishments within an industry, the number of employees, the volume of sales, and the industry's share of state and national employment and sales volume. The two-volume set provides a cross-reference table of industrial activity within districts. Consequently, you can use this guide to determine the economic basis, employment, and sales for any district and to make comparisons with other districts. It enables you to identify which districts have a particular industry and to determine which districts would be affected by legislation, regulatory actions, and administrative law. Thus, if you are interested in how legislation proposed by the president or executive action would affect districts, you would be able to map out the relevant areas.

Martis, Kenneth C. *The Historical Atlas of United States Congressional Districts 1789–1983.* New York: Free Press, 1983.

Only this atlas illustrates all congressional districts for the 97 Congresses. It identifies all representatives, locates their districts on maps, and includes a complete legal history of redistricting for every state. Thus the atlas provides an easy way to illustrate voting data and map voting patterns. By mapping the geographical patterns of any roll-call vote, you can quickly analyze regional and sectional politics. If you map the geographical distribution of committee memberships, party membership, and the margin of electoral victory, you can study presidential elections and illustrate geographical roll-call voting patterns. For example, you could map how Congress voted on bills vetoed by the president or on pieces and programs of legislation sponsored by the president.

If you need general information about a district, you can turn to two of the almanacs cited earlier as ready reference guides. Both the *Almanac of American Politics* and *Politics in America: Members of Congress in Washington and at Home* include data and information for congressional districts. They both provide short profiles of districts, including their social and economic structure, political history, and constituent concerns.

# Election Returns

The collection and distribution of statistics is a meticulous and time-consuming activity. Census data and social indicators are the first form of statistical measures governments systematically collect. The need for gathering election statistics is a recent phenomenon. In the United States the evolution of systematically recording election statistics is intertwined with the political process itself. The availability of such data makes it theoretically possible for every citizen to scrutinize and question campaign practices and outcomes. Election statistics are important to the citizen or scholar interested in analyzing the ideological or philosophical justifications of the federal system. This kind of investigation requires data collected over long periods of time. Two factors allow for a more convenient examination of election statistics. The greater the breakdown of tabulations, the more useful the data will be to the researcher. Secondly, to engage in a rigorous study of elections the scholar needs to check his data against several sources. The following guides are the best sources for election returns. The type of elections covered in the following sources are summarized for quick identification in Appendix 21, p. 268.

## UNITED STATES DATA

*Congressional Quarterly's Guide to U.S. Elections.* Washington, DC: Congressional Quarterly, 1975.

The most definitive source of statistical data on national elections, this work includes the complete voting records of elections for the presidency, Congress, and governorships. It provides extensive background material on the history of political parties, convention ballots and platforms, preference primaries, demographic data, the electorial college, and redistricting. A topical bibliography accompanies each major section. The format makes it an especially useful reference work. There are three ways to locate information. A detailed table of contents provides an overall view of the scope and coverage of the work. There are Candidate Indexes for presidential, gubernatorial, Senate, and House candidates. This allows the reader to pinpoint voting returns for over 60,000 candidates. Finally, a General Index covers all subjects discussed in the work. This guide is the single most useful source for researchers interested in presidential elections. Congressional Quarterly has published a supplement, *Guide to 1976 Elections.*

Congressional Quarterly. *Presidential Elections Since 1789.* 3rd ed. Washington, DC: Congressional Quarterly, 1983.

The concise reference volume gives the popular returns for elections through 1980. It supplies information on the Electoral College, primaries, minor-party nominations, and biographical data on presidential candidates. Concise and succinct in its coverage, it is a ready reference guide to presidential elections.

Congressional Quarterly also publishes the presidential and congressional election results in the *CQ Weekly Reports.* Listed below are some special *Congressional Quarterly Weekly Reports* on presidential election year results.

*CQ Weekly Report, No. 10, March 10, 1961. Complete Returns of the 1960 Elections by Congressional District.*

*CQ Weekly Report, No. 13, March 26, 1965. Complete Returns of the
1964 Elections by Congressional District.*

*CQ Weekly Report Supplement, Nov. 23, June 6, 1969. Complete
Returns of the 1968 Elections.*

*CQ Weekly Report, No. 8, Feb. 23, 1974. Complete 1972 Vote by
State, Congressional Districts.*

*CQ Weekly Report, No. 45, Nov. 6, 1976. Election Results.*

*CQ Weekly Report, No. 45, Nov. 8, 1980. Republican Rule.*

The *National Journal* also publishes the elections in a special issue a week or
two following an election. Both journals also publish several pre-election issues
on the candidates and campaign developments. For a week-by-week analysis of
a campaign and election, *CQ Weekly Report* and *National Journal* are indispensable. *The New York Times* and the *Washington Post,* as well as most major
newspapers, publish the unofficial election results the day after an election. You
may find it useful to check local newspapers for returns and for an analysis of
voting within a state and its major cities.

Government Affairs Institute, Washington, DC. *America Votes: A Handbook of
Contemporary American Election Statistics.* Compiled by Richard M.
Scammon. Washington, DC: Congressional Quarterly, 1955– .
    This biennial work includes presidential, congressional, and gubernatorial
returns. It records the total vote (Republican and Democratic), pluralities,
and percentages per county and congressional district. Sections on each of
the states include the following: (1) a profile of the state, giving the population, electoral vote, incumbent senators, representatives and governors, and
composition of the state legislature by party, and the postwar vote for
governor and Senator; (2) a map of the state, depicting counties and congressional districts; (3) a geographical breakdown by county and districts for
presidential, senatorial, and gubernatorial returns; and (4) tables of the
congressional returns. Every volume is virtually an almanac for each election
year.

Petersen, Svend. *A Statistical History of the American Presidential Elections.*
New York: Ungar, 1963.
    Next to *Congressional Quarterly's Guide to U.S. Elections,* this work is the
most complete compilation of presidential election statistics. It contains the
complete statistics for all presidential elections up to 1960. This publication
includes 133 statistical compilations, with tables indicating votes and percentages. The tables are organized according to election, states, and the 11
historical parties examined. It provides an analysis for each election where a
switch of less than 1% of the major party vote would have changed the
outcome. There are also many miscellaneous tables of specific interest (the
number of times parties carried states, high votes for winners and losers of
states, closest Democratic-Republican races in each state, tables for candidates who ran several times, identification of other votes, and many more).

The work is especially useful for information concerning minor parties and candidates. While comprehensive in coverage, its awkward design and layout make it somewhat difficult to use.

Robinson, Edgar Eugene. *The Presidential Vote, 1896–1932*. Stanford: Stanford University Press, 1934.

_____. *The Presidential Vote 1936: Supplementing the Presidential Vote, 1896–1932*. Stanford: Stanford University Press, 1940.

_____. *They Voted for Roosevelt: The Presidential Vote, 1932–1944*. Stanford: Stanford University Press, 1947.

This series is the first publication of election returns by states and counties for the thirteen presidential elections between 1896 and 1944. The works are arranged to facilitate study of all counties for any election or any county for all elections. Tables indicate the distribution of the presidential vote by sections of the country, states, and counties and the distribution of party control by section, state, and county. Vote categories include Democratic, Republican, and other. The "other vote" is explained in some detail in the appendices. Maps and other specific tables are used to illustrate additional dimensions of the election results. The narrative essays provide a good analysis and interpretation of the data. In the Roosevelt volume, a short introductory essay examines the meaning of Roosevelt's electoral base vis-a-vis his style of government. The three volumes by Robinson and the work by Burham mentioned earlier will be of particular interest to the researcher in need of election returns by county. These volumes provide the only source for county breakdowns for elections between 1836 and 1944.

Government Affairs Institute, Elections Research Center. *America at the Polls: A Handbook of American Presidential Election Statistics, 1920–1962*. Pittsburgh: University of Pittsburgh Press, 1965.

This work provides statistics for twelve elections from Harding through Johnson. The data are organized along two lines: National presidential voting figures by state and a detailed county-by-county breakdown of the data for each state. Both the state and county data include total vote, Republican-Democratic and other breakdown, and pluralities. The work is distinguished by the inclusion of percentages of the total vote and the major vote for Republican and Democratic candidates. Tables relating to national data are followed by notes listing candidates, their national vote, and any special characteristics in the state vote. Every state data section is followed by notes providing the composition of the "other" vote and any special characteristics of the state vote. The layout makes this volume easy to use and enjoyable to read.

Burnham, Walter Dean. *Presidential Ballots, 1836–1892*. Baltimore: Johns Hopkins Press, 1955.

This work is a compilation of voting returns for states and counties for presidential elections between 1836 and 1892. It is a backward extension of the series compiled by Edgar E. Robinson. The structure parallels Robinson's series, using the county as the smallest unit. Tables give county, state, regional, and national returns, broken down into Democratic, Republican, and other categories.

Runyon, John H., Jennifer Verdini, and Sally S. Runyon, eds. *Source Book of American Presidential Campaign and Election Statistics, 1948–1968.* New York: Frederick Unger, 1971.

This is a comprehensive source of presidential campaigns statistics. It is divided into the following subject areas: (1) Presidential Preference Primaries; (2) National Party Conventions; (3) Presidential Campaign Staff; (4) Campaign Itineraries; (5) The Cost of Presidential Campaigns; (6) Presidential Campaign Media Exposure; (7) Public Opinion Polls; (8) Voting Participation in Presidential Elections; and (9) Minor Party Voting. Each section includes references to data sources. A selected bibliography on presidential campaigns and elections is included. The book is well designed, allowing easy access to data. The sections on campaign media exposure demonstrate how creativity can be used in compiling and constructing special types of presidential election statistics. The variety of statistics is useful to the student or researcher with new ideas of how to correlate and combine different categories of statistics.

Republican Party National Committee. *Election Reports.* Washington, DC: The Republican Party, 1962– .

This series was begun in 1938. Since 1962, it has been published on a regular basis. The series analyzes America's biennial elections, pointing out how areas and groups voted, and highlighting notable aspects of the elections. Covering presidential, congressional, and gubernatorial elections, it provides the total vote, plurality, and the Republican percentage of the total vote. Beginning with the 1966 election report, it supplies a detailed examination of the elections (of registration, voter turnout, ticket-splitting, marginal races, voting group behavior, etc.). Statistical tables provide historical information by comparing current elections with past performances. Unlike *America Votes,* this work includes data on voter registration and voting population. While the statistics in this series can be found in other sources, the interpretive narrative is unique.

*Statistical Abstract of the United States.* Washington, DC: U.S. Bureau of Census, 1878– .

This annual document is the basic statistical abstract for social, economic and political affairs in the United States. First published in 1878, its coverage on elections changed considerably over the years. Recent volumes include information on votes cast for presidential, congressional, and gubernatorial elections, voter registration and participation, voting-age population, and campaign expenditures. The work is useful for locating other sources of data through its bibliographic citations. As an abstract, the series includes a wealth of additional background information to use in conjunction with the study of elections. There are statistics on education, employment, income, housing, communications, etc. The series is recognized by scholars as a standard source of statistical data on almost every aspect of society. For retrospective coverage of colonial times, volumes of the *Statistical Abstracts* should be used in conjunction with the *Historical Statistics of the United States, Colonial Times to 1970, Bicentennial Edition.* Washington, DC: U.S. Bureau of Census, 1975.

U.S. Congress. House. Clerk of the House of Representatives. *Statistics of the Presidential and Congressional Elections.* Washington, DC: U.S. Government Printing Office, 1920– .
    This official account of election returns for congressional and presidential elections began with the November 2, 1920 election. The series does not include any geographical breakdown of election returns. It has no real reference value, but is of interest as the official government record.

There are individual compilations of congressional election statistics for almost every state, published by state historical societies, legislative research bureaus, and university institutes. An example of such publications is *Minnesota Votes: Election Returns by County for Presidents, Senators, Congressmen, and Governors, 1857–1977.* (St. Paul: Minnesota Historical Society, 1977).
    If you are simply looking for general summaries of election statistics, consult the *World Almanac and Book of Facts, Information Please Almanac* and *Official Associated Press Almanac.* While each of the almanacs uses a different format, they all contain essentially the same information. Election returns since 1789 are given on a national basis, including the electoral vote, popular vote, and sometimes percentages or pluralities. For the most recent elections, the election results are broken down by state. These almanacs often vary from year to year in regard to the data given. Usually almanacs published following an election year will include somewhat more detailed statistics, such as election results by county. Beneficial for quick and easy checking, these sources should only be regarded as the initial step in more scholarly research.

## CROSS-NATIONAL ELECTORAL DATA

Students of presidential elections often compare election statistics with similar data of other countries. While this kind of comparison seems only natural, it must be conducted carefully and with an awareness of the limitations involved in such a study. There are several important distinctions to be kept in mind when making cross-national analyses. You must pay special attention to the difference in the political systems, including party structure, nominating procedures, and forms of elections.

Mackie, Thomas T., and Richard Rose. *The International Almanac of Electoral History.* 2nd ed. New York: Facts on File, 1982.

The work provides election results from twenty-four countries, all of which are classified as industrial societies conducting regular competitive elections. The election results for each country begin with the first competitive national election, i.e., the first election in which the majority of seats for the national government were contested by candidates from political parties. The organization for each country follows a standard pattern (1) evolution of the electoral system and franchise laws; (2) a list of political parties, both in English and the national language; and (3) election returns. The election returns are reported in a standard format of four tables (1) total number of votes for each party; (2) percentage of votes for each party; (3) number of seats each party wins; and (4) percentage of seats each party wins. Election returns are provided for each party that secured at least one percent of the vote. The chapter on the United States is an exception: because of the primacy of the presidential elections, only returns for those elections are given. The total vote, percentage of votes, number of electoral votes, and percentage of electoral votes are given for each political party. The value of this book is that it provides a standard format for comparative analysis.

Rokkan, Stein, and Jean Meyriait, eds. *International Guide to Election Statistics*. The Hague: Mouton, 1959.
  This was the first international guide to election statistics. It covers fifteen multiparty regimes of Western Europe. This volume does not include the United States. Like the previous handbook, this guide follows a standard list of contents for each country. The first section of each country's chapter begins with a chronology of the electoral system, including franchise qualifications, electoral procedures and registration procedures. The next section provides a description of sources of data for each period. Exact bibliographic citations to official and other statistical publications are given. Descriptions include the organization of the data, specifications of territorial units, contents of major tabulations, and language or languages of the tables. The third section is a review of period analyses of the data. The reviews are a representative selection of analyses conducted by national statistical agencies, academic research organizations, parties, or individual scholars. These analyses cover such areas as turnout variations, variations in party strength, and recruitment of candidates or electors. Most chapters include a fourth section, a summary table for the national results of elections or referenda. The summary table includes the number of registered voters, number of votes cast, and votes for each party in percent of votes cast and/or in percent of total electorate. While this book may be more difficult to use than the other handbook, it is especially useful for identifying obscure and little known election analyses.

Two other handbooks contain comparative information and data on electoral behavior. While they do not include election results, they do contain valuable data on election participation and behavior.

Rose, Richard. *Electoral Behavior: A Comparative Handbook*. New York: Free Press, 1974.

Rose, Richard. *Electoral Participation: A Comparative Analysis.* Beverly Hills: Sage Publications, 1980.

Several bibliographies include citations to articles and books about elections on a comparative basis.

Bloomfield, Valarie. *Commonwealth Elections, 1945–1970.* Westport, CT: Greenwood Press, 1977.

Inter-Parliamentary Union. *World-wide Bibliography on Parliaments.* 2 vols. Geneva: International Center for Parliamentary Documentation, 1978–1980.

The American Enterprise Institute for Public Policy Research publishes monographs on foreign elections. This series is useful for gathering data to compare with statistics on the United States. One of the volumes is a compendium of comparative data.

Butler, David, Howard R. Penniman, and Austin Ranney. *Democracy at the Polls: A Comparative Study of Competitive National Elections.* Washington, DC: American Enterprise Institute, 1981.

# Party Strength

Voting returns do not convey the entire story of an election. Students can learn considerably more about elections by developing their own statistical measures. Today, political scientists employ statistical data in highly sophisticated ways. By using data in different configurations, the researcher can bring to light new perspectives on elections. The following works examine concepts of party strength, competitiveness, and voting behavior.

Cox, Edward Franklin. *State and National Voting in Federal Elections, 1910–1970.* Hamden, CT: Archon Books, 1972.
This work uses the national elective format as the organization for the data. Tables are by nation and state and include the total vote and percentages of all votes for presidential and congressional elections. Data on the election of Representatives, compiled on a state wide aggregate basis, is not broken down by congressional district, which is a serious drawback. The national elective format provides a useful method for comparing the vote of the three national elective positions. With this kind of format, it is simple to measure the voting strength of each party for president, senators, and representatives in each election. The poor layout makes interpretation of the tables difficult and tedious.

Cox, Edward Franklin. *Voting in Postwar Federal Elections: A Statistical Analysis of Party Strengths Since 1945.* Rev ed. Dayton: Wright State University, 1968.

As an interpretation of the significance of American voting in federal elections from 1946 to 1966, the book presents measures of party performance, strength, competitiveness, and individual candidate performance. Geographical analyses are by district and state. The author delineates major trends and future directions for party competition and includes two chapters on methodological issues related to the statistical analyses employed in the study. The analyses of the eleven federal elections examined are presented in 251 tables. One failing is the lack of an index.

Cox, Edward Franklin. *The Representative Vote in the Twentieth Century.* Bloomington: Institute of Public Administration, Department of Political Science, Indiana University, 1981.

This volume extends and complements the two previously cited works by the author. It provides data for congressional elections, regular as well as special, from 1900 to 1972. What makes the statistical compendium special is that it provides complete data for all candidates and parties for elections to the House of Representatives. *Congressional Quarterly's Guide to U.S. Elections* only provides data for leading candidates, i.e., those with percentages in excess of five percent. Consequently, this volume is an important statistical compendium for anyone researching minor parties and party performance. It can also be used as a companion work to the other data sources on election returns.

Cummings, Milton C. *Congressmen and the Electorate: Elections for the U.S. House and President, 1920–1964.* New York: The Free Press, 1966.

This work provides an extensive analysis of the interrelationships between the vote for congressmen and president in presidential election years. It examines the degree of similarities and differences between presidential and congressional support polled by the major parties. Other issues covered in the book are ticket-splitting, party strength, the role of minor parties, and the impact of the electoral system on presidential and congressional elections. The work includes 51 statistical tables relating to the topics discussed.

David, Paul T. *Party Strength in the United States, 1872–1970.* Charlottesville: University Press of Virginia, 1972.

The aim of this book is to provide index numbers for party strength from 1872–1970. The study contains the percentages of the vote won by Democratic, Republican, and other parties and candidates in presidential, gubernatorial, and congressional elections. The text provides the statistical and technical background to the formulation of the index numbers. Additional data covering the later elections can be found in:

"Party Strength in the United States: Changes in 1972." *Journal of Politics* 36 (August 1974): 785–796.

"Party Strength in the United States: Some Corrections." *Journal of Politics* 37 (May 1975): 641–642.

"Party Strength in the United States: Changes in 1976." *Journal of Politics* 40 (August 1978): 770–780.

Janda, Kenneth. *Political Parties: A Cross-National Survey.* New York: Free Press, 1982.
   This is the most systematic and comprehensive empirical study of political parties thoughout the world. Included in the volume are surveys of 153 parties in 58 countries from 1950 to 1978. The first section describes the conceptual framework, using twelve basic concepts (1) institutionalization; (2) government status; (3) social attraction, concentration, and reflection; (4) issue orientation; (5) goal orientation; (6) autonomy; (7) degree of organization; (8) centralization of power; (9) coherence; (10) involvement; (11) electoral data; and (12) validating the framework. The concepts are measured by clusters of more than 100 variables to illustrate party characteristics. The second section provides the findings for each country, chapter-by-chapter. A party history and electoral trends are included with the data and analysis for each country. The volume is useful for studying not only American political parties, but for comparing parties cross-nationally. In addition to providing data on party strength, it is an unmatched compendium of data on party characteristics. The data is also available as a file from the ICPSR.

# Public Opinion

The public opinion survey is a rather recent development in social science research. There are several ways to find information about polls focusing on the presidency and presidential elections.

## POLLS

Gallup, George Horace. *The Gallup Poll; Public Opinion, 1935–1971.* 3 vols. New York: Random House, 1972.
   This is a complete collection of the Gallup Polls from 1935 to 1971. An index in the third volume provides easy subject access to the polls. Volume I includes three essays by Paul Terry on election survey methods in general and the Gallup Poll election survey techniques in particular:

"Election Survey Procedures of the Gallup Poll," pp. xi–xxii.
"Gallup Poll Election Survey Experience, 1950–1960," pp. xxiii–xxx.
"Election Survey Methods," pp. xxxi–xliv.

Supplementary volumes have also been published:

   *The Gallup Poll: Public Opinion, 1972–1977.* Wilmington, DE: Scholarly Resources, 1978.

   *The Gallup Poll: Public Opinion, 1978.* Wilmington, DE: Scholarly Resources, 1979.

   *The Gallup Poll: Public Opinion, 1979.* Wilmington, DE: Scholarly Resources, 1980.

*The Gallup Poll: Public Opinion, 1980.* Wilmington, DE: Scholarly Resources, 1981.

*The Gallup Poll: Public Opinion, 1981.* Wilmington, DE: Scholarly Resources, 1982.

*The Gallup Poll: Public Opinion, 1982.* Wilmington, DE: Scholarly Books, 1983.

*Gallup Opinion Index Report; Political, Social and Economic Trends.* Princeton: Gallup International, 1965– .

This series publishes data generated by the American Institute of Public Opinion and Gallup affiliates. The *Report* is published monthly, with special issues occurring from time to time. The surveys are based on a population of at least 1,500 scientifically chosen respondents. The surveys include findings on presidential popularity, presidential performance, and a variety of campaign and election issues.

*Current Opinion: A Monthly Digest of the Public's Views on Contemporary Issues.* Williamstown, MA: Roper Public Opinion Research Center, Williams College, 1973–1977.

This digest provides the results of surveys conducted by numerous opinion organizations, including the Canadian Institute of Public Opinion, the Harris Survey, and the Gallup Poll. In all, over 100 survey research organizations provided data for the journal.

*Public Opinion.* Washington, DC: American Enterprise Institute for Public Policy Research, 1978– .

This bimonthly journal supersedes *Current Opinion.* Like its predecessor, it provides the results of surveys conducted by public opinion research organizations throughout the country. The journal also publishes several research articles on the results of surveys and public opinion studies in each issue.

*The Harris Survey Yearbook of Public Opinion.* New York: Louis Harris and Associates, 1970– .

Each annual volume contains the Harris Polls for that year. Since some Harris polls have been conducted for the *Washington Post* syndicate and *Newsweek,* it is also possible to track down Harris polls through indexes. The *Washington Post* is indexed by *Newspaper Index,* and *Newsweek* is indexed in *Reader's Guide to Periodical Literature.* The results of surveys conducted for publication, as well as reprints, are available from Louis Harris and Associates.

## BIBLIOGRAPHIES

Bibliographies on public opinion and communication can be used to identify books, articles, research reports, and dissertations on all aspects of public opinion, including political attitudes toward the presidency, use of polls in campaigns, analysis of media surveys on candidates, and political imagery and symbols. These bibliographies also include citations to materials on the role of the media in politics and how the president communicates to the public.

*Bibliography of Publications, 1941–1960: Supplement, 1961–December 1971.* Chicago: National Opinion Research Center, 1972.

Cutlip, Scott M. *A Public Relations Bibliography.* Madison: University of Wisconsin Press, 1965.

Gilbertson, Norma L. *Cumulative Index to the Public Opinion Quarterly.* Irving on Hudson, NY: Columbia University Press, 1972.

Mowlana, Hamid. *International Communications.* Dubuque, IA: Kendall Hunt Publishing Co., 1971.

Price, Warren C. *The Literature of Journalism: An Annotated Bibliography.* Minneapolis: University of Minnesota Press, 1959.

Price, Warren C., and Calder M. Pickett. *An Annotated Journalism Bibliography: 1958–1968.* Minneapolis: University of Minnesota Press, 1970.

# GUIDES TO SURVEY RESEARCH

For students or researchers unfamiliar with the use of public opinion polls in the literature, a number of handbooks and guides provide definitions, descriptions of concepts, and techniques used in conducting surveys. These describe the theoretical concepts used in survey research and how polls are used in research. Journals relating to public opinion and political behavior frequently publish articles on mass communication and findings based on survey research. These include *Public Opinion Quarterly* (the primary research journal in the field of public opinion), *Political Behavior, Political Psychology, Political Communication and Persuasion, Micropolitics,* and *Journalism Quarterly.*

Altschuler, Bruce E. *Keeping a Finger on the Public Pulse: Private Polling and Presidential Elections.* Westport, CT: Greenwood Press, 1982.

Backstrom, Charles H., and Gerald Hursh-Ceaser. *Survey Research.* 2nd ed. New York: Wiley, 1981.

Bennet, W. Lance. *The Political Mind and the Political Environment: An Investigation of Public Opinion and Political Consciousness.* Lexington, MA: Lexington Books, 1975.

Bogart, Leo. *Silent Politics: Polls and the Awareness of Public Opinion.* New York: Wiley-Interscience, 1972.

Cantril, Albert H., ed. *Polling on the Issues*. Cabin John, MD: Seven Locks Press, 1980.

Chandler, Robert. *Public Opinion; Changing Attitudes on Contemporary Political and Social Issues*. New York: Bowker, 1972.

Childs, Harwood. *A Reference Guide to the Study of Public Opinion*. Ann Arbor, MI: Gryphon Books, 1971.

Gallup, George H. *The Sophisticated Poll Watcher's Guide*. Princeton: Princeton Opinion Press, 1972.

Luttbeg, Norman R. *Public Opinion and Public Policy: Models of Political Linkage*. Homewood, IL: Dorsey Press, 1974.

Nimmo, Dan D., and Charles M. Bonjean. *Political Attitudes and Public Opinion*. New York: McKay, 1972.

Nimmo, Dan D., and Keith R. Sanders, eds. *Handbook of Political Communication*. Beverly Hills: Sage, 1981.

Renshon, Stanley Allen. *Handbook of Political Socialization: Theory and Research*. New York: The Free Press, 1977.

Robinson, John P., Jerrold G. Rusk, and Kendra B. Head. *Measures of Political Attitudes*. Ann Arbor: Institute for Social Research, Survey Research Center, 1968.

Roll, Charles W., and Albert H. Cantril. *Polls: Their Use and Misuse in Politics*. New York: Basic Books, 1972.

Smith, Bruce Lannes, and Chitra M. Smith. *International Communication and Political Opinion, A Guide to the Literature*. Princeton: Princeton University Press, 1956.

Smith, Bruce Lannes, Harold D. Lasswell, and Ralph D. Casey. *Propaganda, Communication, and Public Opinion; a Comprehensive Reference Guide*. Princeton: Princeton University Press, 1946.

Sonquist, John A., and William C. Dunkelburg. *Survey and Opinion Research: Procedures for Processing and Analysis*. Englewood Cliffs, NJ: Prentice-Hall, 1977.

Strouse, James C. *The Mass Media, Public Opinion and Public Policy Analysis: Linkage Explorations*. Columbus: C. E. Merrill Pub. Co., 1975.

Finally, many of the ABC/*Washington Post,* CBS/*New York Times* and Harris surveys are available as a data set. The Inter-University Consortium for

Political and Social Research has many of these in its archival holdings. See the
following section on Data Archives for a listing of what is available.

# Data Archives

## ICPSR RESOURCES

Data archives throughout the country have quantitative data on presidential
elections. The major social science data archive is the Inter-University Consortium for Political and Social Research at the University of Michigan. One
among many of the major files of data available from the Consortium is the
*Historical Elections Returns, 1824–1972*. This collection of election data
contains county-level returns for presidential, gubernatorial, and congressional
elections. For more information about the archive's holdings, consult the
Consortium's *Guide to Resources and Services, 1983–1984* (Ann Arbor: University of Michigan, 1983).

The ICPSR also holds other data files of interest to presidential elections.
There are some files on specific preference primaries and elections in particular
states. Many of the statistical sources mentioned throughout this guide, such as
Census Bureau publications and public opinion polls, are available on tape. For
example, the *Congressional District Data Book* and *County and City Data Books*
are available, as well as CBC/*New York Times* and ABC/*Washington Post Polls*.

The *Guide to Resources and Services* includes information about ICPSR
training programs, classes, remote access computer assistance, and servicing
information on how to obtain data and codebooks from the Consortium. The
listing of archival holding provides the name of the data collector, the title and
detailed description of the data file and publications that have used the data.
Listed below are a selected number of data files dealing with presidential
primaries, conventions, candidates, elections, ecological data, and public
opinion polls. At the end of the list are datasets on the Congress (such as roll-
call voting). These are useful for studying the presidency, especially in regard
to legislative programs and decision making.

## Primaries, Conventions, and Candidates

Audits and Surveys, Inc.: *New Hampshire Primary Study, 1968*.

CBS News/The New York Times: *CBS News/New York Times Election Surveys,
1978*.

CBS News/The New York Times: *CBS News/New York Times Election Surveys,
1980*.

The Detroit News: *Michigan Survey of Voter Attitudes, October 1980*.

The Detroit News: *National Survey of Voter Attitudes, June 1980*.

Mayer, Philip: *Florida Primary Study, 1972*.

Miller, Warren E., Elizabeth Douvan, William Crotty, and Jeane Kirkpatrick: *Convention Delegate Study of 1972: Women in Politics.*

Patterson, Thomas F.: *Presidential Campaign Impact on Voters: 1976 Panel, Erie, Pennsylvania, and Los Angeles.*

Patterson, Thomas E., and Robert D. McClure: *Televised Presidential Campaign Impact on Voters: 1972 Panel, Syracuse, New York.*

## Election Studies

Campbell, Angus, and Robert L. Kahn: *American National Election Study, 1948.*

Campbell, Angus, et al.: *American National Election Study, 1952.*

Campbell, Angus, et al.: *American National Election Study, 1956.*

Campbell, Angus, et al.: *American National Election Study, 1958.*

Campbell, Angus, et al.: *American National Election Study, 1960.*

Survey Research Center: *Minor American National Election Study, 1980.*

Political Behavior Program, Survey Research Center: *American National Election Study, 1982.*

Political Behavior Program, Survey Research Center: *American National Election Study, 1966.*

Political Behavior Program, Survey Research Center: *American National Election Study, 1968.*

Center for Political Studies: *American National Election Study, 1970.*

Miller, Warren, et al.: *American National Election Study, 1972.*

Miller, Warren, et al.: *American National Election Study, 1974.*

Miller, Warren, et al.: *American National Election Study, 1976.*

Center for Political Studies: *American National Election Series: 1972, 1974, 1978.*

Miller, Warren E., and National Election Studies/Center for Political Studies: *American National Election Study, 1978.*

Miller, Warren E., and National Election Studies/Center for Political Studies: *American National Election Study, Spring 1979.*

Miller, Warren E., and National Election Studies/Center for Political Studies: *American National Election Study, 1980*.

Survey Research Center: *American Panel Study: 1956, 1958, 1960*.

Campbell, Angus, and Homer Cooper: *Domestic Affairs Study, October 1954*.

Kovenock, David M., and James W. Prothro: *Comparative State Elections Project, 1968*.

Lazarfeld, Paul F., Bernard R. Berelson, and Hazel Gaudet: *Erie County Study, 1940*.

Lazarfeld, Paul F., Bernard R. Berelson, and William N. McPhee: *Elmira Community Study, 1948*.

National Opinion Research Center: *National Election Study, 1944*.

National Opinion Research Center: *National Election Study, 1948*.

Time Magazine: *Yankelovich Voter Study, 1972*.

Bureau of the Census: *Current Population Survey: Voter Supplement File, 1972*.

Bureau of the Census: *Current Population Survey: Voter Supplement File, 1974*.

Bureau of the Census: *Current Population Survey: Voter Supplement File, 1976*.

Bureau of the Census: *Current Population Survey: Voter Supplement File, 1978*.

Bureau of the Census: *Current Population Survey: Voter Supplement File, 1980*.

## Election Returns

Bartley, Numan V., and Hugh D. Graham: *Southern Primary and General Election Data, 1946–1972*.

Burnham, W. Dean, Jerome M. Clubb, and William Flanigan: *State-Level Presidential Election Data for the United States, 1824–1972*.

Heard, Alexander, and Donald S. Strong: *Southern Primary and General Election Data, 1920–1949*.

Inter-University Consortium for Political and Social Research: *Candidate and Constituency Statistics of Elections in the United States, 1788–1981*.

Inter-University Consortium for Political and Social Research: *Candidate Name and Constituency Totals, 1788–1980*.

Inter-University Consortium for Political and Social Research: *General Election Data for the United States, 1968–1980.*

Inter-University Consortium for Political and Social Research: *Referenda and Primary Election Materials.*

Inter-University Consortium for Political and Social Research: *Southern Primary Candidate Name and Constituency Totals, 1920–1972.*

Inter-University Consortium for Political and Social Research: *United States Historical Election Returns, 1788–1823.*

Inter-University Consortium for Political and Social Research: *United States Historical Election Returns, 1788–1980.*

Michigan Department of State: *Michigan Election Returns, 1972: Precinct-Level.*

## Ecological Data

Bureau of the Census: *County and City Data Book: 1952, 1956, 1967, 1982.*

Bureau of the Census: *County and City Data Book, 1972.*

Bureau of the Census: *County and City Data Book, 1977.*

Bureau of the Census: *County and City Data Book Consolidated File: City Data, 1944–1977.*

Bureau of the Census: *County and City Data Book Consolidated File: County Data, 1947–1977.*

Bureau of the Census: *United States Congressional District Data Books, 1961–1965.*

Bureau of the Census: *United States Congressional District Book for the Ninety-Third Congress, 1973.*

## Public Opinion

ABC News and the Washington Post: *ABC News/Washington Post Reaganomics Poll, February 1981.*

ABC News and the Washington Post: *ABC News/Washington Post Reagan Shooting Poll, March 1981.*

ABC News and the Washington Post: *ABC News/Washington Post Reagan 100 Days Poll, April 1981.*

CBS News: *CBS News Polls, 1977–1979.*

CBS News/The New York Times: *CBS News/New York Times Polls, 1977–1978.*

CBS News/The New York Times: *CBS News/New York Times Polls, 1979.*

CBS News/The New York Times: *CBS News/The New York Times National Surveys, 1981.*

Davis, James A., James S. Coleman, Norman H. Nie, John Riley, and Christopher Jencks: *NORC Amalgam Survey, December 1973.*

Louis Harris and Associates, Inc.: *Harris 1973 Confidence in Government Survey.*

Holm, John D.: *Watergate Hearings Panel Survey.*

Survey Research Center: *Perceptions of the 1963 Presidential Transition.*

## Congressional Data

Congressional Quarterly, Inc.: *Voting Scores for Members of the United States Congress, 1945–1978.*

Inter-University Consortium for Political and Social Research: *Roster of United States Congressional Officeholders and Biographical Characteristics of Members of the United States Congress, 1789–1980: Merged Data.*

Inter-University Consortium for Political and Social Research: *United States Congressional Roll Call Voting Records, 1789–1982 [97th Congress, First Session: House of Representatives]. United States Congressional Roll Call Voting Records, 1789–1982 [97th Congress, First Session: Senate].*

McKibbin, Carroll L.: *Biographical Characteristics of Members of the United States Congress, 1789–1978.*

## Miscellaneous

Janda, Kenneth: *Comparative Political Parties Data, 1950–1982.*

Milbrath, Lester: *Washington Lobbyists Survey, 1956–1957.*

Miller, Warren E., and Donald E. Stokes: *American Representatives Study, 1958.*

Verba, Sidney, and Norman Nie: *Political Participation in America, 1967.*

# Instructional Packages

Supplementary Empirical Teaching units in Political Science (SETUPS) for American Politics are computer-related modules designed for use in teaching introductory courses in American government and politics. The modules demonstrate the process of examining evidence and reaching conclusions and stimulate students to independent thinking. They enable untrained students to use the computer to analyze data on political behavior or to see the results of policy decisions by use of a simulation model. Manuals of the modules are distributed by the American Political Science Association; the ICPSR disseminates the machine-readable datasets or FORTRAN IV program sourcedecks designed to accompany them. The datasets can be supplied as OSIRIS files or in card-image format with SPSS job control cards if appropriate.

*Voting Behavior: The 1980 Election.* C. Anthony Broh and Charles L. Prysby. Washington, DC: American Political Science Association, 1981.
   This set introduces the study of voting behavior through the collection and analysis of survey data in the context of the latest presidential election. The dataset and exercises allow students to prepare their own research designs.

*Elections and the Mass Media.* David Blomquist. Washington, DC: American Political Science Association, 1981.
   The set reviews research on the influence of the media on voters and public policy in order to enable students to investigate these questions directly and explore new avenues of research.

*Campaign '80: The Public and the Presidential Selection Process.* Richard Joslyn and Janet Johnson. Washington, DC: American Political Science Association, 1981.
   This set explores research on public opinion and voter choice in the context of the 1980 presidential campaign. This SETUPS is drawn from a panel study and allows more complex data analysis.

# DIRECTORIES

A number of other institutions have data archives with files on presidential elections and activities. To locate them and their holdings, consult the following sources:

Sessions, Vivian S., ed. *Directory of Data Bases in the Social and Behavioral Sciences.* New York: Science Associates/International, Inc., 1974.
   This directory gives an extensive listing of 685 databases and centers in the United States. For each database, the following information is provided: (1) address; (2) director and principal staff; (3) data holdings; (4) storage media; and (5) avenue of access. It identifies over fifteen institutions with data holdings relating to election returns and electoral behavior. The work has a subject index, institutional index, and geographical index. The subject

index contains several relevant entries: Election Data, Election Returns, Election Studies, Electoral Data, and Electoral Studies.

*S S Data: Newsletter of Social Science Archival Acquisitions.* Iowa City: Laboratory for Political Research, University of Iowa, 1971– .
This *Newsletter* provides information on data acquired by archives throughout the United States and Canada. Participating archives supply descriptions of the dataset by (1) the original data collection agency and principal investigator and (2) the time period of the data, the population, and a descriptive paragraph explaining the nature of the study.

Several journals regularly contain articles using data files and identify what new datasets are available and the research in progress. These are *Social Science Information, Historical Methods Newsletter,* and the *Review of Public Data Use.* The last journal is especially useful for keeping up-to-date on Census Bureau developments and its distribution of data files. A second set of journals useful to anyone planning to use data files are those that focus on mathematical applications and quantitative research. They contain articles on statistical techniques as well as research findings based on the use of data files. These journals are:

*Social Science Research: A Quarterly Journal of Social Science Methodology and Quantitative Research*

*Sociological Methods and Research*

*Political Methodology*

*Mathematical Social Sciences*

*Quality and Quantity*

*Journal of Mathematical Sociology*

*Multivariate Behavior Research*

# GUIDES TO STATISTICAL METHODOLOGY

For students and researchers interested in using data files or compiling their own data, but who are not experienced in quantitative research, there are a number of excellent introductory guides to political statistics. The books listed below can provide explanations and illustrations of statistical techniques and methodologies and information for learning about more sophisticated analyses:

Alker, Hayward R. *Mathematics and Politics.* New York: Macmillan, 1965.

Buchanan, William. *Understanding Political Variables.* 2nd ed. New York: Scribner's, 1974.

Davis, Harold T. *Political Statistics.* Evanston: Principia Press of Illinois, 1954.

Golembiewski, Robert T., William A. Welsh, and William J. Crotty. *A Methodological Primer for Political Scientists.* Chicago: Rand McNally, 1969.

Gurr, Ted Robert. *Politometrics; An Introduction to Quantitative Macropolitics.* Englewood Cliffs, NJ: Prentice-Hall, 1972.

Hilton, Gordon. *Intermediate Politometrics.* New York: Columbia University Press, 1976.

Key, Valdimer Orlando. *A Primer of Statistics for Political Scientists.* New York: Crowell, 1966.

Tufte, E. *Data Analysis for Politics and Policy.* Englewood Cliffs, NJ: Prentice-Hall, 1972.

Rai, Kul B. *Political Science Statistics.* Boston: Holbrook Press, 1973.

# Secondary Sources

In this section, we identify a variety of secondary sources of additional data compilations, articles, and books on elections. Because election studies is a rapidly growing field, you should always check to see if there are any new bibliographies, data compilations, or journals.

## RESOURCE MATERIALS

Two multivolume sets on presidential elections give the researcher access to secondary and some primary material on elections since 1788.

Jensen, Merrill, and Robert A. Becker. *The Documentary History of the First Federal Elections, 1788–1790.* 3 vols. Madison: University of Wisconsin Press, 1976–1982.
    This set focuses on a time period for which there was previously little documentary material. Since the first elections are important both historically and politically, this material is extremely useful for researchers interested in electoral history.

Schlesinger, Arthur H., ed. *History of Presidential Elections, 1789–1968.* 4 vols. New York: Chelsea-McGraw-Hill, 1982.
    This comprehensive history of presidential elections, written by prominent historians and political scientists, covers the particular social and political climate of each election. The forty-five contributors were asked to analyze a presidential election and to select relevant documents illustrating their theses. An appendix in the fourth volume includes the popular and electoral vote by states, as well as all the party elections. Of special interest is an annotated bibliography, arranged by election, contained in the appendix.

# DATA SOURCEBOOKS

State agencies provide other important sources of election statistics. Within each state, various departments and organizations collect data relating to different aspects of campaigning and electioneering. The guides listed below identify where to find state election results, demographic data, and socioeconomic information.

Burnham, Walter Dean. *Sources of Historical Election Data: A Preliminary Bibliography.* East Lansing: Institute for Community Development and Services, Michigan University, 1963.
    This is a short annotated bibliography on election data divided into four sections (1) general sources of election returns; (2) state publication of election returns; (3) elections reported below the county level; and (4) demographic material. It is particularly useful for its bibliography of non-officially published compilations of election returns by state (e.g., Riker, Dorothy L., *Indiana Election Returns, 1816–1851.* [Indianapolis: Indiana State Historical Society, 1960].

Council of State Governments. *State Blue Books and Reference Publications (A Selected Bibliography).* Rev ed. Lexington: Council of State Governments, 1974.
    This is a listing, arranged alphabetically by states, of reference materials on the states and territories. Each state divides this material into three categories (1) Legislative and General State Government; (2) Digests or Summaries of Legislative Action; and (3) Guides, Statistics, etc. Each entry includes the source and place of publication, the date and frequency of publication, and the cost. An important addition is a table indicating the types of material included in the State Blue Books. An appendix contains a number of tables of comparative information. There is directory information, both current and historical, for the state level on the executive, judicial, and legislative branch and for the Federal government. A table records election returns, both current and historical. You can use this reference work to identify state sources of election statistics.

Press, Charles, and Oliver Williams. *State Manuals, Blue Books and Election Results.* Berkeley: Institute of Governmental Studies, University of California, 1962.
    This is a listing by states of source materials for official election results, legislative manuals, directories of state officials, and related information. Each entry presents an outline of the kind of information contained within each source. The place and frequency of publication is also noted.

Bureau of the Census. *Directory of Non-Federal Statistics for States and Local Areas: A Guide of Sources, 1969.* Washington, DC: U.S. Government Printing Office, 1970.
    This comprehensive listing of statistics covers all areas of study and is arranged by state, then by a topical breakdown within each state. Each state has a listing of material treating elections and voting. The materials are

presented in the following format: each document is described according to its (1) tabular detail; (2) areas to which data apply; (3) frequency of data; and (4) source document. The Census Bureau also publishes a *Directory of Federal Statistics for Local Areas: A Guide to Sources, 1976.*

Three works are compendiums of election survey data. They contain extensive data of a socioeconomic nature on voting behavior and political attitudes.

Black, Merle, and David M. Kovenock. *Political Attitudes in the Nation and the States.* Chapel Hill: Comparative State Elections Project, Institute for Research in Social Science, University of North Carolina, 1968.
    This volume data book of the Comparative State Elections Project presents over 200 survey variables in tables according to the thirteen states, six regional areas, and national frequencies. The introduction to the volume mentions the important interstate and interregional differences in political attitudes and behavior.

Kovenock, David M., and James W. Prothro. *Explaining the Vote: Presidential Choices in the Nation and the States.* Chapel Hill: Comparative State Elections Project, Institute for Research in Social Science, University of North Carolina, 1968.
    This volume grew out of the data gathered by a survey in the nation and thirteen states (Alabama; California; Florida; Illinois; Louisiana; Massachusetts; Minnesota; New York; North Carolina; Ohio; Pennsylvania; South Dakota; and Texas). In addition to the survey, a total of 7,673 respondents were interviewed. The volume analyzes the effect of numerous issues, including race; law and order; war and peace; the economy; and personal qualities of candidates, on the voter's decision and the election outcome. The effect of issues on voters' decisions are also compared to the factors of party identification, socioeconomic status, and ideology.

Miller, Warren E., Arthur H. Miller, and Edward J. Schneider. *American National Election Studies Data Sourcebook, 1952–1978.* Cambridge: Harvard University Press, 1980.
    The data compendium is the printed version of fourteen data archives available at the ICPSR. The surveys were conducted by the Survey Research Center and Center for Political Studies. Each of the studies contain information from 1,000 to 2,000 interviews with voters for elections from 1952 to 1978. Areas covered include the respondents' (1) expectations about outcome of election; (2) party identification; (3) interest in politics; (4) issue positions; (5) perception of interest groups; (6) assessment of major problems facing the country; (7) financial and class identity; (8) source of political information; (9) measures of political efficacy; (10) personal data; and (11) post election voting behavior.

# DATABASES

On-line searching for three of the reference tools mentioned in previous sections is available through various commercial vendors. The *American Statistics*

*Index* is available as ASI and the *Statistical Reference Index* as SRI. By doing a computer search on-line, you can identify documents with a variety of search terms, including the index terms, titles, keywords from the abstracts, issuing agency, and agency report number.

The data described in *Congressional District Business Patterns* are available on-line from two databases, EIS INDUSTRIAL PLANTS and EIS NON-MANUFACTURING ESTABLISHMENTS. These two databases, developed by Economic Information Systems, include data on more than 120,000 manufacturing plants and 350,000 nonmanufacturing businesses. The two databases cover 95 percent of all domestic manufacturing and about 65 percent of all nonmanufacturing business. Data are taken from journals, directories, corporate reports, Census Bureau publications, and information received from companies.

# BIBLIOGRAPHIES

When studying a presidential election, you should get as much background information as possible. Ever since the first presidential election, people have been analyzing the results and writing commentaries. A good way to begin a search for literature is to use the following bibliographies.

*The American Electorate: A Historical Bibliography.* Santa Barbara, CA: ABC-Clio, 1984.

This bibliography contains over 1,300 abstracts of articles on electoral history and politics, voting patterns, and individual elections and includes periodical literature published since 1963. It is organized by chapter according to a major subject, with entries arranged by author. There is also a rotated subject index.

Mauer, David J. *United States Politics and Elections: Guide to Information Sources.* Detroit: Gale Research Co., 1978.

This lengthy annotated bibliography includes citations to articles and books on electoral politics in general, presidential elections, and presidential candidates. It is arranged by chapter according to historical periods and contains a wealth of biographical materials on presidents and candidates. It also includes citations to important political issues and trends for each historical period.

Bone, Hugh A. "American Party Politics, Elections, and Voting Behavior." *Annals of the American Academy of Political and Social Science* 372 (1967): 124–137.

"Selected Bibliography in American Parties and Elections, 1967–1971: A Brief Annotation." *Annals of the American Academy of Political and Social Science* 402 (1972): 117–131.

These articles are concerned with the major literature in the areas of parties, elections, and voting behavior. Together they cover the period from 1961–1971. Both review books and monographs—texts, general works, historical articles, and new theoretical works. The two essays are especially useful for identifying major works and new trends of thought in the field of electoral politics.

Wynar, Lubomyr R., comp. *American Political Parties: A Selective Guide to Parties and Movements of the 20th Century.* Littleton, CO: Libraries Unlimited, Inc., 1969.

This work is a compilation of over 3,000 books, monographs, and unpublished dissertations on significant twentieth century American parties and movements. The arrangement is by subject and party. The book provides general background material related to elections, public opinion, parties, and political behavior.

Agranoff, Robert. *Elections and Electoral Behavior: A Bibliography.* De Kalb: Center for Governmental Studies, Northern Illinois University, 1972.

This bibliography is a listing of over 300 items dealing with theoretical and practical issues of elections. It is divided into four sections (1) electoral systems and voting rights; (2) candidate selection, nominations, party conventions; (3) voting behavior; and (4) electoral interpretation. Entries are not annotated, nor is the pagination given for either articles or books.

Smith, Dwight L., and Lloyd W. Garrison, eds. *The American Political Process; Selected Abstracts of Periodical Literature (1954–1971).* Santa Barbara, CA: ABC-Clio, 1974.

This work contains a lengthy section on American elections, including a subsection on presidential elections and campaigns. The abstracts in the work were taken from *Historical Abstracts* and *America: History and Life.*

The following bibliographies, while shorter and broader in scope, also contain many citations relating to elections and voting research.

Goehlert, Robert. *Coalition Theory and Formulation: A Bibliography.* Monticello, IL: Vance Bibliographies, 1981.

*Federal Elections: A Select Bibliography.* Monticello, IL: Vance Bibliographies, 1982.

*Reapportionment and Redistricting: A Selected Bibliography.* Monticello, IL: Vance Bibliographies, 1981.

*Voting Research and Modeling: A Bibliography.* Monticello, IL: Vance Bibliographies, 1981.

Steward, Alva W. *Congressional Reapportionment and Redistricting in the 1980's: A Preliminary Bibliography.* Monticello, IL: Vance Bibliographies, 1982.

Lutes, Terry. *Voting Behavior, 1968–1980.* Monticello, IL: Vance Bibliographies, 1981.

# PART IV

# Researching the Presidency

# CHAPTER 6

# Designing and Developing a Strategy

Attempting to develop a topic and research design on the presidency can be a frustrating and time-consuming process. Often, students have a difficult time in choosing a topic or narrowing it to a manageable size for a research paper. Even students who quickly find a topic are overwhelmed by the amount of material they find and lose the focus of their analyses. In this section, we present an outline on how to develop a topic, a research design, and a research strategy. What we emphasize is the interrelated nature of these processes; the topic and research design you develop can determine the kinds of materials you seek.

## APPROACHES

There is no single approach to the study of the presidency, nor is there any dominant theory. In fact, while an enormous amount of literature has been written about the presidency, there are few theoretical sources to which one can refer. However, it is important to be aware of some of the major approaches. Each approach has a distinct body of literature. You can use this literature to develop a topic and formulate a research design. Appendix 22, p. 270, identifies some of the major approaches to the study of the presidency and some of the key concepts used in that approach. The approaches and concepts listed there are by no means exhaustive or mutually exclusive.

What is important to realize is that the approach you take can shape the focus of your research, the assumptions you make, the methodology you use, and even the explanation of your results. For example, you can analyze a particular political decision using many of the above approaches, but the focus would differ with each approach. A legal analysis would emphasize the statutory history; an institutional approach would look at organization behavior; a political approach would focus on the environment; and a policy approach would look at the process. And in each case the kind of literature you draw upon—theoretical literature, previous research, and source material—would vary. The kind of resources a legal scholar would use would be quite different from the material someone using an organizational or bureaucratic approach would choose.

A student developing a topic on the presidency must keep in mind the kinds of approaches that have been used. You may wish to follow a particular approach or combine approaches. The topic you choose will demand a certain kind (or certain kinds) of approach. Consequently, there will be a body of literature to draw upon for further ideas, possible methodologies, and similar research designs.

# DEVELOPING A TOPIC

Developing a topic that is sufficiently narrow, manageable and original is not an easy task. A student often develops a topic from something heard in a lecture or read in an assignment that sparked his or her curiosity, i.e., Why was some decision significant? Why is some department so powerful? Topics eventually grow from some unanswered question a student thinks deserves further analysis and explanation. If you have an idea about something to investigate, you are well on your way. If you do not come across some statement you question, doubt, or think is too simple, then you must create a topic. The best strategy to follow is to browse through current newspapers, books, bibliographies, or an index to see what is being written about the presidency. Preliminary research and reading can help you develop a topic. A student should look for an interesting policy, event, decision, law, program, problem, process, individual agency, or group. Once you have a decision, event, or process you would like to analyze, evaluate, or explain the significance of, you can do some initial research to see what books and articles have been written about the particular topic. As you do preliminary research, develop questions regarding the particular person, problem or agency. This may involve combining one policy with another, or a person with an event, or a policy with a concept, such as fairness, equality, or justice. As you develop a topic, keep in mind that eventually you will need to define a proposition or hypothesis to prove or disprove. You should also think about describing the topic, such as when it takes place, who was involved, why was it considered a problem, who was affected, and so on. The more you think about a topic and outline the details, the easier it will be later to search thoroughly and systematically for materials.

# CONCEPTUALIZATION

Once you have a topic and before you begin to search for additional materials, you should think through a basic research design. This will help you organize your research strategy and clarify the topic. If the topic is too broad, it will become apparent. If a proposition can not be argued effectively, you will have to select other hypotheses. A research design should include a statement of the topic, a review of the literature, a definition of the hypotheses to be tested, a description of the operational design, and the methods of analysis and interpretation. The following includes some fundamental considerations to take into account when investigating possible research designs.

1. Research Topic

   What is the significance of the topic?

   What concepts can be used to describe the topic?

   Can the topic be analyzed?

   Are there any underlying assumptions in the approach I have chosen?

   Is the research project feasible?

2. Literature Review

   Has the topic been previously researched and how?

   What approaches have been used in prior research?

   How successful has prior research been in analyzing or explaining the topic?

   Is the topic related to any particular body of theory?

   How have the concepts been used in prior research?

3. Formulating Hypotheses

   What hypotheses can be used to test the proposition?

   What is the significance of these hypotheses to prior research?

   What terms can be used to define the concepts?

   How can the variables be measured?

4. Operational Design

   What are the units of analysis?

   What will be the operational design?

   Can the operational design be defended?

   What sources of data are available?

   How are the data to be collected?

5. Analysis and Interpretation

   What methodology will be used?

   What analytic tools can be used?

   What is the significance of the findings?

   How do the findings relate to prior research?

As this research design suggests, the use of data for testing a hypothesis is crucial. Students may gather their own data by surveys and interviews or do simulations and experimentations. Here we point to the numerous sources of published data, indexes, and written documents from which data can be generated. Appendix 23, p. 271, lists types of data sources or tools to use to find or collect data for nonreactive research. While students normally make good use of statistical compendia or find data by using indexes such as the *American Statistics Index,* many of the bibliographic tools cited throughout this book can be used to gather data. Since encyclopedias, directories, news indexes, document indexes, and similar reference tools are all running records, they can be used for collecting data. With a little imagination, these tools can be used to compile data on all sorts of activities.

The following books can be useful for developing a research design and for learning about various methodologies.

## Guides to Research Designs and Methodology

Blalock, Hubert M. *Conceptualization and Measurement in the Social Sciences.* Beverly Hills: Sage Publications, 1982.

Coogan, William H., and Oliver H. Woshinsky. *The Science of Politics: An Introduction to Hypothesis Formulation and Testing.* Washington, DC: University Press of America, 1982.

Garson, G. David. *Political Science Handbook.* Boston: Holbrook Press, 1976.

Glass, Gene V., Barry McGaw, and Mary L. Smith. *Meta-Analysis in Social Research.* Beverly Hills: Sage Publications, 1981.

Hartman, John J., and Jack M. Hedblom. *Methods for the Social Sciences: A Handbook for Students and Non-Specialists.* Westport, CT: Greenwood Press, 1979.

Katzner, Donald W. *Analysis Without Measurement.* New York: Cambridge University Press, 1983.

Kepple, Geoffrey. *Design and Analysis: A Researcher's Handbook.* 2nd ed. Englewood Cliffs, NJ: Prentice-Hall, 1982.

Kweit, Mary G., and Robert W. Kweit. *Concepts and Methods for Political Analysis.* Englewood Cliffs, NJ: Prentice-Hall, 1981.

Manheim, Jarol B, and Richard C. Rich. *Empirical Political Analysis: Research Methods in Political Science.* Englewood Cliffs, NJ: Prentice-Hall, 1981.

Meehan, Eugene J. *Reasoned Arguments in Social Science.* Westport, CT: Greenwood Press, 1981.

Miller, Delbert C. *Handbook of Research Design and Social Measurement.* 4th ed. New York: Longman, 1983.

Nachimas, David, and Chava Nachimas. *Research Methods in the Social Sciences.* 2nd ed. New York: St. Martin's Press, 1981.

Ostrom, Elinor, ed. *Strategies of Political Inquiry.* Beverly Hills: Sage Publications, 1982.

Outhwaite, William. *Concept Formation in Social Science.* Boston: Routledge, Kegan, Paul, 1983.

Patton, Michael Q. *Qualitative Evaluation Methods.* Beverly Hills: Sage Publications, 1980.

True, June A. *Finding Out: Conducting and Evaluating Social Research.* Belmont, CA: Wadsworth, 1983.

White, Louise G. *Political Analysis: Technique and Practice.* Monterey, CA: Brooks Cole, 1983.

Zeller, Richard A. *Measurement in the Social Sciences: The Link Between Theory and Data.* New York: Cambridge University Press, 1980.

Zisk, Betty H. *Political Research: A Methodological Sampler.* Lexington, MA: D. C. Heath, 1981.

# DESIGNING A SEARCH STRATEGY

There is no single search strategy for information about the presidency. In a sense, you actually conduct six separate searches, though in practice it is only one. As the research design outline indicates, you need to search for theoretical literature, previous research, primary sources, secondary sources, factual information, and statistical data. Appendix 24 p. 273, lists the kinds of material you would search for in each one of these cases. As the table shows, some materials belong in more than one literature search. The table is not exhaustive by any means, but is designed to help a student think of the kinds of materials he or she will need to search for in a complete information search.

In Appendices 25, p. 276, and 26, p. 278, we carry the search strategy one step further. The Table of Research Operations for Documents (Appendix 25) identifies what tools to use when searching for documents. The Table of Research Operations for Secondary Sources (Appendix 26) suggests tools to use when looking for other types of primary sources and secondary sources. Before conducting a literature search, it is best to develop a strategy by making a checklist of the kinds of materials you are looking for and the specific tools necessary to access those materials. This will enable you to conduct an efficient and methodical literature search. It is also important to think of which disciplines, i.e., history, law, psychology, etc., you might explore for materials, as well as the period you will cover (one year, a decade, etc.). Outlining such a strategy ahead of time will make your library search more efficient and productive.

Begin your search by checking several basic tools.

1. Search the library's subject catalog.
2. Search several indexes and abstracting services.

3. Search for any existing bibliographies on the specific topic.
4. Search guides to the literature and research guides to identify any special compilations, indexes, bibliographies, and other reference tools particularly germane to the topic.
5. Check bibliographies and footnotes in books, articles, dissertations, and materials you will use to begin your research. These can lead to important secondary sources, datasets, etc.

When designing the basic literature it is important to make a checklist of all of the possible terms, concepts, names, etc. that you will check for as subject headings. Such a list may include as many as a dozen or more possible subject terms. Since these headings vary from one another, as well as vary from a library's subject catalog, encyclopedias, and other tools, you need to think of related terms or synonyms to use from one tool to another. As you conduct a literature search, you will find which subject headings are most useful. But it is better to search under a variety of terms than just one or two. A common mistake is to look only under one or two headings, finding only a few citations, and assuming that little has been written about the subject. While that may indeed be the case, many times the materials are indexed under other headings.

# CONDUCTING A SEARCH

It is important to keep track of which tools you have checked and the subject headings you have used. Keeping a record of your research makes it easier to revise a strategy and remember which tools are available and which are not. Also, you can keep track of which sources and what kinds of information may prove beneficial if you need to refer back to a source to get additional citations. The most important thing to do when conducting a search is to take notes or make a record of where you find a particular citation. This will enable you to go back and check a citation, borrow an item on interlibrary loan, or expand a search by looking in earlier volumes of an index or under new subject headings. Keeping a record of the tools searched (which volumes or years, which subject headings, etc.) will save you time, help you revise a research project, and facilitate the writing of your research.

# Appendixes

# APPENDIX 1:
# House and Senate Rules and Manuals

## SENATE

U.S. Congress. Senate. Committee Rules and Administration. *Senate Manual Containing the Standing Rules, Orders, Laws and Resolutions Affecting the Business of the United States Senate.* Washington, DC: U.S. Government Printing Office, 1820– .

U.S. Congress. Senate. *Senate Procedure: Precedents and Practices.* Washington, DC: U.S. Government Printing Office, 1914– .

U.S. Congress. Senate. *Senate Legislative Procedural Flow (and Related House Action).* By Harold G. Ast. Washington, DC: U.S. Government Printing Office, 1978.

U.S. Congress. Senate. 96th Cong., 1st sess., *Enactment of a Law.* Washington, DC: U.S. Government Printing Office, 1979.

## HOUSE

U.S. Congress. House. *Constitution, Jefferson's Manual and the Rules of the House of Representatives.* Washington, DC: U.S. Government Printing Office, 1824– .

U.S. Congress. House. *Deschler's Procedures in the United States House of Representatives.* Washington, DC: U.S. Government Printing Office, 1977.

Hinds, Asher C. *Hinds' Precedents of the House of Representatives of the United States, Including Reference to Provisions of the Constitution, the Laws, and Decisions of the United States Senate.* 4 vols. Washington, DC: U.S. Government Printing Office, 1907.

Cannon, Clarence. *Cannon's Precedents of the House of Representatives of the United States, Including Reference to Provisions of the Constitution, the Laws, and Decisions of the United States Senate.* Vols. VI–XI. Washington, DC: U.S. Government Printing Office, 1935–1941.

U.S. Congress. House Committee on Rules. *Legislative Reorganization Act of 1970.* H.Rept. 1215. 91st Cong., 2d sess., Washington, DC: U.S. Government Printing Office, 1970.

U.S. Congress. House. Committee on Rules. *Guidelines for the Establishment of Select Committees.* 95th Cong., 1st sess., Washington, DC: U.S. Government Printing Office, 1977.

## APPENDIX 2:
## Records of Floor Proceedinᴏ⌐

### 1789-1824

*Annals of the Congress of the United States.* Washington, DC: Gales & Seaton, 1834-1856.

### 1824-1837

*Register of Debates in Congress.* Washington, DC: Gales & Seaton, 1825-1837.

### 1833-1873

*The Congressional Globe.* Washington, DC: Congressional Globe, 1835-1873.

### 1873-

U.S. Congress. *Congressional Record.* Washington, DC: U.S. Government Printing Office, 1874- .

### 1789-

U.S. Congress. Senate. *Journal of the Senate of the United States of America.* Washington, DC: U.S. Government Printing Office, 1789- .

### 1789-

U.S. Congress. House. *Journal of the House of Representatives of the United States of America.* Washington, DC: U.S. Government Printing Office, 1978- .

### 1828-

*Journal of the Executive Proceedings of the Senate of the United States of America.* Washington, DC: U.S. Government Printing Office, 1928- .

# APPENDIX 3:
# Indexes to Committee Hearings

### 1970–

*CIS/Index*. Bethesda: Congressional Information Service.

### 1830–1970

*CIS US Congressional Committee Hearings Index*. Bethesda: Congressional Information Service.

### 1959–

U.S. Congress. Senate. Secretary of the Senate. *Quadrennial Supplements to Cumulative Index of Congressional Committee Hearings (Not Confidential in Character); Quadrennial Supplement, Together With Selected Committee Prints in the United States Senate Library*. Washington, DC: U.S. Government Printing Office, 1963.

### 1935–1959

U.S. Congress. Senate. Secretary of the Senate. *Cumulative Index of Congressional Committee Hearings (Not Confidential in Character) from Seventy-Fourth Congress (January 3, 1935) Through Eighty-Fifth Congress (January 3, 1959) in the United States Senate Library*. Westport, CT: Greenwood Press, 1973.

### 1839–1935

Thomen, Harold O. *Supplement to the Index of Congressional Hearings Prior to January 3, 1935, Consisting of Hearings Not Catalogued by the U.S. Senate Library, from the Twenty-Fifth Congress, 1839, Through the Seventy-Third Congress, 1934*. Westport, CT: Greenwood Press, 1973.

### Prior to 1935

U.S. Congress. Senate. Secretary of the Senate. *Index of Congressional Committee Hearings (Not Confidential in Character) Prior to January 3, 1935, in the United States Senate Library*. Westport, CT: Greenwood Press, 1971.

### Prior to 1951

U.S. Congress. House. Clerk of the House of Representatives. *Index to Congressional Committee Hearings in the Library of the United States House of Representatives Prior to January 1, 1951*. Washington, DC: U.S. Government Printing Office, 1954.

## APPENDIX 4:
## Indexes to Committee Prints

### 1970–

*CIS Index*. Bethesda: Congressional Information Service.

### 1830–1969

*CIS US Congressional Committee Prints Index*. Bethesda: Congressional Information Service.

### 1911–1969

*A Bibliography and Indexes of United States Congressional Committee Prints: From the Sixty-first Congress, 1911 through the Ninety-first Congress, first session, 1969, in the United States Senate Library.* 2 vols. Edited by Rochelle Field; compiled by Gary Halvarson, et al. Westport, CT: Greenwood Press, 1976.

### 1917–1969

*A Bibliography and Indexes of United States Congressional Committee Prints: From the Sixty-fifth Congress, 1917 through the Ninety-first Congress, first session, 1969, not in the United States Senate Library.* Edited by Rochelle Field; compiled by Laura J. Kaminsky, Gary Halvarson, and Mark Woodbridge. Westport, CT: Greenwood Press, 1977.

# APPENDIX 5:
## Sources of Legislative Actions

| LEGISLATIVE ACTION | GUIDES TO LEGISLATIVE ACTIONS |
|---|---|
| Bill Is Introduced and Referred to Committee | *CIS/INDEX* |
| | *CIS Legislative History Annual*\* |
| | *Congressional Index* |
| | *Congressional Record* |
| | *CQ Weekly Report* |
| | *Digest of Public General Bills and Resolutions* |
| | *Federal Index* |
| | *National Journal* |
| Committee Holds Hearings | *CIS/INDEX* |
| | *CIS Legislative History Annual* |
| | *Congressional Index* |
| | *Congressional Monitor* |
| | *Congressional Record* |
| | *CQ Weekly Report* |
| | *Federal Index* |
| | *National Journal* |

*Continued on next page*

---

\*To be published as a third volume of *CIS/INDEX* starting with the 1984 edition.

## APPENDIX 5—*Continued*
## Sources of Legislative Actions

| LEGISLATIVE ACTION | GUIDES TO LEGISLATIVE ACTIONS |
|---|---|
| Committee Recommends Passage | *CIS/INDEX* |
| | *CIS Legislative History Annual* |
| | *Calendars of House and History of Legislation* |
| | *Congressional Index* |
| | *Congressional Monitor* |
| | *Congressional Record* |
| | *CQ Weekly Reports* |
| | *Federal Index* |
| | *National Journal* |
| | *U.S. Code Congressional and Administrative News* |
| Chamber Debates | *CIS/INDEX* |
| | *CIS Legislative History Annual* |
| | *Congressional Index* |
| | *Congressional Monitor* |
| | *Congressional Record* |
| | *CQ Weekly Report* |
| | *Federal Index* |
| | *National Journal* |
| Chamber Votes | *CIS/INDEX* |
| | *CIS Legislative History Annual* |

## APPENDIX 5—*Continued*
## Sources of Legislative Actions

| LEGISLATIVE ACTION | GUIDES TO LEGISLATIVE ACTIONS |
|---|---|
| | *Congressional Index* |
| | *Congressional Record* |
| | *Congressional Roll Call* |
| | *CQ Almanac* |
| | *CQ Weekly Report* |
| | *Federal Index* |
| | *House Journal* |
| | *National Journal* |
| | *Senate Journal* |
| Sent to Conference | *CIS/INDEX* |
| | *CIS Legislative History Annual* |
| | *Calendars of House and History of Legislation* |
| | *Congressional Index* |
| | *Congressional Monitor* |
| | *Congressional Record* |
| | *CQ Weekly Report* |
| | *Federal Index* |
| | *National Journal* |
| | *U.S. Code Congressional and Administrative News* |

*Continued on next page*

## APPENDIX 5—*Continued*
## Sources of Legislative Actions

| LEGISLATIVE ACTION | GUIDES TO LEGISLATIVE ACTIONS |
|---|---|
| Presidential Statements | *CIS/INDEX* |
| | *CIS Legislative History Annual* |
| | *CQ Weekly Report* |
| | *Federal Index* |
| | *National Journal* |
| | *Public Papers of the Presidents* |
| | *Weekly Compilation of Presidential Documents* |
| Law | *Calendars of House and History of Legislation* |
| | *CIS/INDEX* |
| | *CIS Legislative History Annual* |
| | *Congressional Index* |
| | *Congressional Record* |
| | *CQ Almanac* |
| | *CQ Weekly Report* |
| | *Digest of Public General Bills and Resolutions* |
| | *Federal Index* |
| | *National Journal* |
| | *Shepard's United States Citations: Statute Edition* |
| | *Statutes at Large* |

# APPENDIX 5—*Continued*
# Sources of Legislative Actions

| LEGISLATIVE ACTION | GUIDES TO LEGISLATIVE ACTIONS |
|---|---|
| | *United States Code Annotated* |
| | *United States Code Service* |
| Veto | *Calendars of House and History of Legislation* |
| | *CIS/INDEX* |
| | *CIS Legislative History Annual* |
| | *Congressional Index* |
| | *Congressional Record* |
| | *CQ Almanac* |
| | *CQ Weekly Report* |
| | *Federal Index* |
| | *House Journal* |
| | *Monthly Catalog* |
| | *National Journal* |
| | *Presidential Vetoes* |
| | *Public Papers of the Presidents* |
| | *Senate Journal* |
| | *Weekly Compilations of Presidential Documents* |
| Overriding a Veto | *CIS/INDEX* |
| | *CIS Legislative History Annual* |

*Continued on next page*

## APPENDIX 5—*Continued*
## Sources of Legislative Actions

| LEGISLATIVE ACTION | GUIDES TO LEGISLATIVE ACTIONS |
|---|---|
| | *Congressional Index* |
| | *Congressional Record* |
| | *Congressional Roll Call* |
| | *CQ Almanac* |
| | *CQ Weekly Report* |
| | *Federal Index* |
| | *House Journal* |
| | *National Journal* |
| | *Senate Journal* |

# APPENDIX 6:
## Research Chart for *Statutes at Large* and *U.S. Code**

| REFERENCE | U.S. STATUTES AT LARGE | U.S. CODE | U.S. CODE SUPPLEMENT | ADDITIONAL FINDING AIDS |
|---|---|---|---|---|
| 1. Revised Statutes Section (e.g., Rev. Stat. 56) | Revised Statutes, 1873, were published as pt. 1, vol. 18, U.S. Statutes at Large 2d ed. published in 1878 | Use tables in U.S.C. Popular Names and Tables volume to find U.S.C. section; verify text; then— | Check latest U.S.C. Supplement for recent changes; verify text. | Check Table 3 in latest U.S.C.C.A.N. for changes during current period; if Code section is included, verify text in same publication or in slip law. |
| 2. a. For the date of a law any year up to and through year of last edition of U.S.C. | Use Stat. volume for that year to check the List of Laws; get law number and verify page number from list; then— | Use tables in U.S.C. Popular Names and Tables volume to find U.S.C. section; verify text; then— | Check latest U.S.C. Supplement for recent changes; verify text. | Check Table 3 in latest U.S.C.C.A.N. for changes during current period; if Code section is included, verify text in same publication or in slip law. |
| 2. b. For any year after year of last edition of U.S.C. and through year of latest Supplement | Use Stat. volume for that year to check the list of Public Laws; get law number and verify page number from List; then— | | Use tables in latest U.S.C. Supplement to find U.S.C. section; verify text. | Check Table 3 in latest U.S.C.C.A.N. for changes during current period; if Code section is included, verify text in same publication or in slip law. |
| 2. c. For current year | | | | Use slip law or U.S.C.C.A.N. text to get law number, Stat. citation, |

*Continued on next page*

# APPENDIX 6—Continued
## Research Chart for *Statutes at Large* and *U.S. Code*

| REFERENCE | U.S. STATUTES AT LARGE | U.S. CODE | U.S. CODE SUPPLEMENT | ADDITIONAL FINDING AIDS |
|---|---|---|---|---|
| | | | | and to verify subject matter; also use Table 2, U.S.C.C.A.N. to find U.S.C. classification |
| 3. a. For name of Law: any year up to and through year of last edition of U.S.C. (e.g. | | Use Acts Cited by Popular Name index (in U.S.C. Popular Names and Tables volume) to obtain Stat. and U.S.C. citations; verify both; then— | Check latest U.S.C. Supplement for recent changes; verify text. | Check Table 3 in latest U.S.C.C.A.N. for changes during current period; verify any changes in same publication or in slip law. Other sources: Index of Popular Name Acts Affected in U.S. Statutes at Large Laws Affected Tables, 1956–1970 and 1971–1975; Table of Federal Statutes by Popular Names in U.S. Supreme Court Reports; Shepard's Acts and Cases by Popular Name; U.S.C.A. Popular Name Table; U.S.C.S. tables volume. |
| 3. b. For any year after year of last edition of U.S.C. and through | | | Use Acts Cited by Popular Name Index preceding Tables in U.S.C. Supplement to | Check Table 3 in latest U.S.C.C.A.N. for changes during current period; verify |

year of latest
Supplement

obtain Stat. and U.S.C.
citation; verify both; then—

any changes in same
publication or in slip law.
Other sources: Index of
Popular Name Acts Affected
in U.S. Statutes at Large
Laws Affected Tables,
1956–1970 and 1971–1975;
Table of Federal Statutes by
Popular Names in U.S.
Supreme Court Reports;
Shepard's Acts and Cases by
Popular Name; U.S.C.A.
Popular Name Table;
U.S.C.S. tables volume.

3. c. For current year

Use House Calendar index
and numerical list to get bill
number, then law number if
assigned; or U.S.C.C.A.N.
Index or Table 10; use slip
law or U.S.C.C.A.N. text to
get Stat. Citation and U.S.C.
classification, and to verify
date and subject matter; also,
with law number, use
Table 2, U.S.C.C.A.N. to
find U.S.C. classification.

4. a. For the number of a
law any year up to and

You will need additional
information, such as the

Use tables in U.S.C. Popular
Names and Tables volume to

Check latest U.S.C.
Supplement for recent

Check Table 3 in latest
U.S.C. for changes during

*Continued on next page*

# APPENDIX 6—Continued
## Research Chart for Statutes at Large and U.S. Code

| REFERENCE | U.S. STATUTES AT LARGE | U.S. CODE | U.S. CODE SUPPLEMENT | ADDITIONAL FINDING AIDS |
|---|---|---|---|---|
| through year of last edition of U.S.C. and the law— does not have a numerical prefix | Congress, the year, or the Stat. volume— year used then use the Stat. volume to check the List of Public Laws; get and verify page number from List; then— | find U.S.C. section, verify text; then— | changes; verify text. | current period; if Code section is included, verify text in same publication or in slip law. |
| 4. b. For a number of a law for any year up to and through year of last edition of U.S.C. and the law— does have a numerical prefix | Use Stat. volume for the Congress indicated by the numerical prefix; check the list of Public Laws; get and verify page number from List; then— | Use tables in U.S.C. Popular Names and Tables volume to find U.S.C. section; verify text; then— | Check latest U.S.C. Supplement for recent changes; verify text. | Check Table 3 in latest U.S.C.C.A.N. for changes during current period; if Code section is included, verify text in same publication or in slip law. |
| 4. c. For any year after last edition of U.S.C. and through year of latest Supplement | Use Stat. volume for the Congress indicated by the numerical prefix; check the List of Public Laws; get and verify page number from List; then— | | Use tables in latest U.S.C. Supplement to find U.S.C. | Check Table 3 in latest U.S.C.C.A.N. for changes during current period; if Code section is included, verify text in same publication or in slip law. |

| | | | | |
|---|---|---|---|---|
| 4. d. For current year | | | | Use slip law or U.S.C.C.A.N. text to get Stat. citation, U.S.C. classification, and to verify date and subject matter; also, with law number, use Table 2, U.S.C.C.A.N. to find U.S.C. classification. |
| 5. a. For Stat. Citation any year up to and through year of last edition of U.S.C. | Use Stat. volume to get date and law number; verify subject matter, then— | Use tables in U.S.C. Popular Names and Tables volume to find U.S.C. section; verify text; then— | Check latest U.S.C. Supplement for recent changes; verify text; then— | Check Table 3 in latest U.S.C.C.A.N. for changes during current period; if Code section is included, verify text in same publication or in slip law. |
| 5. b. For any year after year of last edition of U.S.C. and through year of latest Supplement | Use Stat. volume to get date and law number; verify subject matter, then— | | Use tables in latest U.S.C. Supplement to find U.S.C. | Check Table 3 in latest U.S.C.C.A.N. for changes during current period; if Code section is included, verify text in same publication or in slip law. |
| 5. c. For current year | | | | Use slip law or U.S.C.C.A.N. text to verify subject matter, date, U.S.C. classification and law number. Table 2, U.S.C.C.A.N. also may be used to find U.S.C. classification. |

*Continued on next page*

# APPENDIX 6—Continued
## Research Chart for Statutes at *Large* and *U.S. Code*

| REFERENCE | U.S. STATUTES AT LARGE | U.S. CODE | U.S. CODE SUPPLEMENT | ADDITIONAL FINDING AIDS |
|---|---|---|---|---|
| 6. a. For the U.S.C. Citation for any year up to and through year of last edition of U.S.C. | | Check section in U.S.C. to verify subject matter and determine appropriate Stat. citation; verify text against Stat. volume; then— | Check latest U.S.C. Supplement for recent changes; verify text; then— | Check Table 3 in latest U.S.C.C.A.N. for changes during current period; if Code section is included, verify text in same publication or in slip law. |
| 6. b. For any year after year of last edition of U.S.C. and through year of latest Supplement | | | Check section in latest U.S.C. Supplement to verify subject matter and determine appropriate Stat. citation; verify text against Stat. volume then— | Check Table 3 in latest U.S.C.C.A.N. for changes during current period; if Code section is included, verify text in same publication or in slip law. |
| 6. c. For current year | | | | Check Table 3 in latest U.S.C.C.A.N.; if Code section is included, get page number on which text of law appears and get law number from that page (Code citation should appear as a marginal note), then verify Stat. citation and subject matter from slip law. |

*This chart is an abridged version of the table appearing in the Office of Federal Register publication entitled, *How to Find U.S. Statutes and U.S. Code Citations.*

# APPENDIX 7:
# Bill Status Table

| REFERENCE TOOL | SECTION OR INDEX |
|---|---|
| *CIS/Index* | Bill Numbers |
| *Congressional Record* | History of Bills and Resolutions |
| *Congressional Record, Daily Digest* | Subject index of bills acted upon |
| *Congressional Index* | Bill Status Tables |
| *Digest of Public General Bills* | Synopsis of bills |
| *Federal Index* | Calendar of Legislation |
| *House of Representative Calendars* | Numerical order of Bills and Resolutions which have passed either or both Houses, and Bills now pending on the Calendar |

## APPENDIX 8:
## Locating Legislative Histories

| REFERENCE TOOL | TABLE/INDEX |
| --- | --- |
| *Calendars of the House and History of Legislation* | Index Key and History of Bill |
| *CIS/ANNUAL* | Index of Bill, Report and Document Number |
| *CIS Legislative History Annotated Directories* | Table of Contents |
| *CIS Legislative History Annual*\* | Subject or Title Index |
| *Congressional Index* | Bill Status Tables |
| *Congressional Record, Daily Digest* | History of Bills Enacted into Law |
| *CQ Almanac* | Subject Index |
| *Digest of Public General Bills and Resolutions* | Public Law Listing |
| *Federal Index* | Calendar of Legislation |
| *House Journal* | History of Bills and Resolutions |
| *Senate Journal* | History of Bills and Resolutions |
| *Slip Law* | Legislative History |
| *Statutes at Large* | Guide to Legislative History of Bills Enacted into Public Law |
| *U.S. Code Annotated* | Annotations and Legislative History |
| *U.S. Code Congressional and Administrative News* | Table of Legislative History |
| *U.S. Code Service* | Annotations and Legislative History |

*To be published as a third volume of *CIS/INDEX* starting with the 1984 edition.

## APPENDIX 9:
## Indexes to Federal Statutes

| | SUBJECT | POPULAR NAME | BILL OR CHAPTER TO LAW | TRANSFER TABLES |
|---|---|---|---|---|
| *Statutes at Large* | ● | ● | ● | |
| *United States Code* | ● | ● | | ● |
| *United States Code Annotated* | ● | ● | | ● |
| *United States Code Service* | ● | ● | ● | ● |
| *Federal Index* | ● | | | |
| *Shepard's United States Citations* | ● | ● | | ● |
| *Shepard's Act and Cases by Popular Name* | | ● | | |
| *United States Supreme Court Report, Lawyer's Edition* | ● | ● | | |
| *United States Code Congressional and Administrative News* | | ● | ● | ● |
| *Congressional Index* | | ● | ● | |
| *United States Law Week* | | ● | | |
| *Congressional Record, Daily Digest* | | | ● | |
| *Digest of Public General Bills* | | | ● | |

## APPENDIX 10:
## Sources of Treaty Information

| ACTION | SOURCE |
|---|---|
| Initial Negotiations | *Department of State Bulletin* |
| | *Federal Index* |
| | *Public Affairs Information Service Bulletin* |
| | *Weekly Compilation of Presidential Documents* |
| Presidential Approval | *Department of State Bulletin* |
| | *Federal Index* |
| | *Public Affairs Information Service Bulletin* |
| Transmittal to Senate | *Congressional Record* |
| | *CQ Weekly Report* |
| | *Federal Index* |
| | *Senate Executive Journal* |
| | *Weekly Compilation of Presidential Documents* |
| Senate Foreign Relations Committee Action | *CIS/Index* |
| | *Congressional Index* |
| | *Congressional Record* |
| | *Congressional Record, Daily Digest* |
| | *CQ Weekly Report* |
| | *Monthly Catalog* |
| | *Senate Executive Journal* |

## APPENDIX 10—*Continued*
## Sources of Treaty Information

| ACTION | SOURCE |
|---|---|
| Senate Action | *Congressional Index* |
| | *Congressional Record* |
| | *CQ Weekly Report* |
| | *Federal Index* |
| | *Senate Executive Journal* |
| Withdrawal | *Congressional Record, Daily Digest* |
| | *Federal Index* |
| | *Senate Executive Journal* |
| | *Weekly Compilation of Presidential Documents* |
| Ratification | *Department of State Bulletin* |
| | *Federal Index* |
| | *Public Affairs Information Service Bulletin* |
| | *Weekly Compilation of Presidential Documents* |
| Promulgation | *Department of State Bulletin* |
| | *Federal Index* |
| | *Statutes at Large* |
| | *Shepard's United States Citations* |
| | *Treaties in Force* |
| | *United States Code Annotated* |

*Continued on next page*

## APPENDIX 10—*Continued*
## Sources of Treaty Information

ACTION                                    SOURCE

United States Code
   Congressional and Administrative
   News

United States Treaties and other
   International Agreements

Weekly Compilation of Presidential
   Documents

## APPENDIX 11:

## Subsequent Actions for Treaties and Executive Agreements

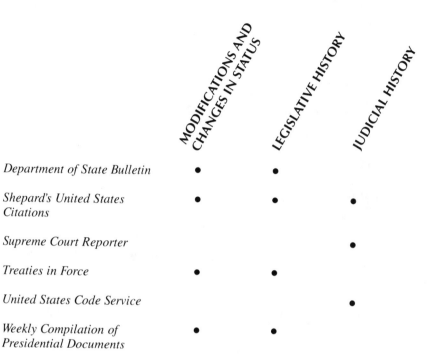

|  | MODIFICATIONS AND CHANGES IN STATUS | LEGISLATIVE HISTORY | JUDICIAL HISTORY |
|---|:---:|:---:|:---:|
| *Department of State Bulletin* | ● | ● | |
| *Shepard's United States Citations* | ● | ● | ● |
| *Supreme Court Reporter* | | | ● |
| *Treaties in Force* | ● | ● | |
| *United States Code Service* | | | ● |
| *Weekly Compilation of Presidential Documents* | ● | ● | |

## APPENDIX 12:
## Executive Office of the President Since 1939

The White House Office, 1939– .

Council on Personnel Administration, 1939–1940

Office of Government Reports, 1939–1942

Liaison Office for Personnel Management, 1939–1943

National Resources Planning Board, 1939–1943

Bureau of the Budget, 1939–1970

Office of Emergency Management, 1940–1954

Committee for Congested Production Areas, 1943–1944

War Refugee Board, 1944–1945

Council of Economic Advisers, 1946– .

National Security Council, 1947– .

Central Intelligency Agency, 1947– .

National Security Resources Board, 1947–1953

Telecommunications Adviser to the President, 1951–1953

Office of Director of Mutual Security, 1951–1954

Office of Defense Mobilization, 1952–1959

Permanent Advisory Committee on Government Organization, 1953–1961

Operations Coordinating Board, 1953–1961

The President's Board of Consultants on Foreign Intelligence Activities, 1956–1961

Office of Civil and Defense Mobilization, 1958–1962

National Aeronautics and Space Council, 1958–1973

## APPENDIX 12—*Continued*
## Executive Office of the President Since 1939

The President's Foreign Intelligence Advisory Board, 1961–1977

Office of Emergency Planning, 1962–1973

Office of United States Trade Representation, 1963– .

Office of Economic Opportunity, 1964–1975

Office of Emergency Preparedness, 1965–1973

National Council on Marine Resources and Engineering Development, 1966–1971

Council on Environmental Quality, 1969– .

Council for Urban Affairs, 1969–1970

Office of Intergovernmental Relations, 1969–1973

Office of Management and Budget, 1970– .

Domestic Council, 1970–1978

Office of Telecommunications Policy, 1970–1977

Council on International Economic Policy, 1971–1977

Office of Consumer Affairs, 1971–1973

Special Action Office for Drug Abuse Prevention, 1971–1975

Federal Property Council, 1973–1977

Council on Economic Policy, 1973–1974

Energy Policy Office, 1973–1974

Federal Energy Office, 1973–1974

Council on Wage and Price Stability, 1974– .

*Continued on next page*

**APPENDIX 12—Continued**
**Executive Office of the President Since 1939**


Energy Resource Council, 1974–1977

Office of Science and Technology Policy, 1976– .

Office of Administration, 1977– .

Domestic Policy Staff, 1978–1981

Office of Policy Development, 1981– .

# APPENDIX 13:
# Databases and Corresponding Indexes

| DATABASE | INDEX |
|---|---|
| | *ABC POL SCI* |
| | *ABS Guide to Recent Literature in Social and Behaviorial Sciences* |
| AMERICA: HISTORY AND LIFE | *America: History and Life* |
| ASI | *American Statistics Index* |
| | *Applied Science and Technology Index* |
| | *Annual Legal Bibliography* |
| | *Arts and Humanities Citation Index* |
| BIOGRAPHY MASTER INDEX | *Bio-Base* |
| | *British Humanities Index* |
| | *Business Periodical Index* |
| CIS | *CIS/Index* |
| | *Communications Abstracts* |
| COMPREHENSIVE DISSERTATION INDEX | *Comprehensive Dissertation Index* |
| CONGRESSIONAL RECORD ABSTRACTS | *Congressional Record* |
| | *Contents of Current Legal Periodicals* |
| EIS INDUSTRIAL PLANTS | |
| | *Current Law Index* |
| EIS NON MANUFACTURING ESTABLISHMENTS | |

*Continued on next page*

## APPENDIX 13—*Continued*
## Databases and Corresponding Indexes

| DATABASE | INDEX |
| --- | --- |
| ENCYCLOPEDIA OF ASSOCIATIONS | *Encyclopedia of Associations* |
| FEDERAL INDEX | *Federal Index* |
| FEDERAL REGISTER ABSTRACTS | *Federal Register* |
| GPO MONTHLY CATALOG | *Monthly Catalog of Government Publications* |
| | *Humanities Index* |
| GPO PUBLICATIONS REFERENCE FILE | *GPO Publications Reference File* |
| | *Index to Legal Periodicals* |
| | *Index to Periodical Articles Related to Law* |
| | *International Bibliography of Political Science* |
| | *International Political Science Abstracts* |
| | *Journalism Abstracts* |
| LEGAL RESOURCE INDEX | *Legal Resource Index* |
| LEXIS | |
| | *Monthly Digest of Legal Articles* |
| MAGAZINE INDEX | *Magazine Index* |
| NATIONAL NEWSPAPER INDEX | *National Newspaper Index* |
| NEWSEARCH | |
| PAIS INTERNATIONAL | *Public Affairs Information Service Bulletin* |

# APPENDIX 13—*Continued*
# Databases and Corresponding Indexes

| DATABASE | INDEX |
|---|---|
| PSYCINFO | *Psychological Abstracts* |
| | *Reader's Guide to Periodical Literature* |
| | *Sage Public Administration Index* |
| | *Social Sciences Index* |
| SOCIAL SCISEARCH | *Social Sciences Citation Index* |
| SOCIOLOGICAL ABSTRACTS | *Sociological Abstracts* |
| USPSD | *United States Political Science Documents* |
| WESTLAW | *Writings on American History* |

## APPENDIX 14:
## Sources of Presidential Documents

| | Speeches | Proclamations | Executive Orders | Addresses to Congress | Vetoes |
|---|---|---|---|---|---|
| Federal Register | | • | • | | |
| Congressional Record | • | • | • | • | • |
| Department of State Bulletin | • | • | | • | |
| Statutes at Large | | • | | | |
| Journals of House & Senate | | | | • | • |
| Weekly Compilation of Presidential Documents | • | • | • | • | • |
| Code of Federal Regulations | | • | • | | |
| Serial Set | | | | | |
| Presidential Executive Orders | | | • | | |
| Public Papers of the President | • | | • | • | |
| Senate/House Documents | | | | | • |
| US Code Congressional & Administrative News | | • | • | | |

# APPENDIX 14—*Continued*
## Sources of Presidential Documents

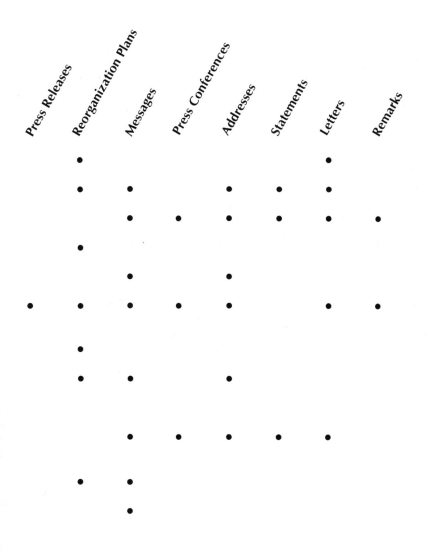

# APPENDIX 15:
## Sources of Presidential Actions

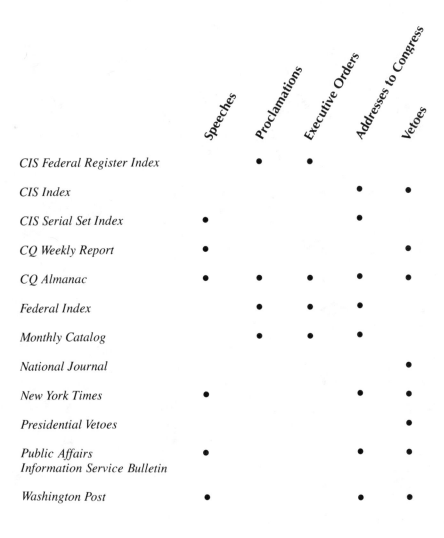

| | Speeches | Proclamations | Executive Orders | Addresses to Congress | Vetoes |
|---|---|---|---|---|---|
| *CIS Federal Register Index* | | • | • | | |
| *CIS Index* | | | | • | • |
| *CIS Serial Set Index* | • | | | • | |
| *CQ Weekly Report* | • | | | | • |
| *CQ Almanac* | • | • | • | • | • |
| *Federal Index* | | • | • | • | |
| *Monthly Catalog* | | • | • | • | |
| *National Journal* | | | | | • |
| *New York Times* | • | | | • | • |
| *Presidential Vetoes* | | | | | • |
| *Public Affairs Information Service Bulletin* | • | | | • | • |
| *Washington Post* | • | | | • | • |

# APPENDIX 15—*Continued*
## Sources of Presidential Actions

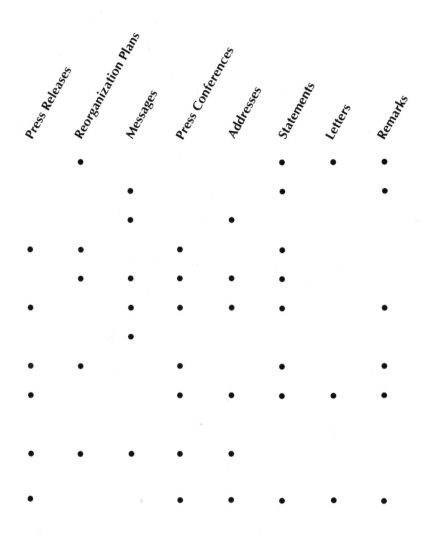

## APPENDIX 16:
## Sources of Presidential Speeches

| CURRENT | RETROSPECTIVE |
|---|---|
| *CQ Weekly Report* | *Annals of Congress* |
| *Department of State Bulletin* | *CIS US Serial Set Index* |
| *Federal Index* | *Congressional Globe* |
| *House Journal* | *Congressional Record* |
| *New York Times* | *Monthly Catalog* |
| *Public Affairs Information Service Bulletin* | *Public Papers of the President* |
| *Senate Journal* | *Register of Debates* |
| *Washington Post* | *Richardson's Compilation of Messages and Papers . . .* |
| *Weekly Compilation of Presidential Documents* | |

# APPENDIX 17:
## Sources of Presidential Messages

| CURRENT | RETROSPECTIVE |
|---|---|
| CIS / Index | American State Papers |
| Congressional Record | Annals of Congress |
| CQ Weekly Report | CIS US Serial Set Index |
| Department of State Bulletin | Comprehensive Index to Publications of the U.S. |
| Federal Index | Government |
| House Journal | Congressional Globe |
| Monthly Catalog | Descriptive Catalog of Government Publications of the U.S. |
| Public Affairs Information Service Bulletin | Document Catalog |
| Senate Journal | Public Documents of the First Fourteen Congresses |
| United States Code Congressional and Administrative News | Register of Debates |
| Weekly Compilation of Presidential Documents | Richardson's Compilation of Messages and Papers |

## APPENDIX 18:
## Sources of Presidential Proclamations and Executive Orders

| CURRENT | RETROSPECTIVE |
|---|---|
| CIS Federal Register Index | Codification of Presidential Proclamations and Executive Orders |
| CIS Index to the Code of Federal Regulations | |
| | Document Catalog |
| Code of Federal Regulations | |
| | Index Analysis of Federal Statutes |
| Federal Index | |
| | Index to Federal Statutes |
| Federal Register | |
| | Lord's List of Index of Presidential Orders |
| IHS Index to the Code of Federal Regulations | |
| | Lord's Presidential Executive Orders |
| Monthly Catalog | |
| Statutes at Large | Presidential Executive Orders |
| United States Code Congressional and Administrative News | Richardson's Compilation of Messages and Papers |
| Weekly Compilation of Presidential Documents | |

# APPENDIX 19:
## Terms of Presidents by Year and Congress

| PRESIDENT | PARTY | YEAR | CONGRESS |
|-----------|-------|------|----------|
| Reagan | R | 1982–1983 | 98th |
| Reagan | R | 1980–1981 | 97th |
| Carter | D | 1978–1979 | 96th |
| Carter | D | 1977–1978 | 95th |
| Ford | R | 1975–1976 | 94th |
| Nixon | R | 1973–1974 | 93d |
| Nixon | R | 1971–1972 | 92d |
| Nixon | R | 1969–1970 | 91st |
| Lyndon Johnson | D | 1967–1968 | 90th |
| Lyndon Johnson | D | 1965–1966 | 89th |
| Lyndon Johnson | D | 1963–1964 | 88th |
| Kennedy | D | | |
| Kennedy | D | 1961–1962 | 87th |
| Eisenhower | R | 1959–1960 | 86th |
| Eisenhower | R | 1957–1958 | 85th |
| Eisenhower | R | 1955–1956 | 84th |
| Eisenhower | R | 1953–1954 | 83d |
| Truman | D | 1951–1952 | 82d |
| Truman | D | 1949–1950 | 81st |
| Truman | D | 1947–1948 | 80th |
| Truman | D | 1945–1946 | 79th |

*Continued on next page*

## APPENDIX 19—*Continued*
## Terms of Presidents by Year and Congress

| PRESIDENT | PARTY | YEAR | CONGRESS |
|---|---|---|---|
| Franklin Roosevelt | D | 1943–1944 | 78th |
| Franklin Roosevelt | D | 1941–1942 | 77th |
| Franklin Roosevelt | D | 1939–1940 | 76th |
| Franklin Roosevelt | D | 1937–1938 | 75th |
| Franklin Roosevelt | D | 1935–1936 | 74th |
| Franklin Roosevelt | D | 1933–1934 | 73d |
| Hoover | R | 1931–1933 | 72d |
| Hoover | R | 1929–1931 | 71st |
| Coolidge | R | 1927–1929 | 70th |
| Coolidge | R | 1925–1927 | 69th |
| Coolidge | R | 1923–1925 | 68th |
| Harding | R | 1921–1923 | 67th |
| Wilson | D | 1919–1921 | 66th |
| Wilson | D | 1917–1919 | 65th |
| Wilson | D | 1915–1917 | 64th |
| Wilson | D | 1913–1915 | 63d |
| Taft | R | 1911–1913 | 62d |
| Taft | R | 1909–1911 | 61st |
| Theodore Roosevelt | R | 1907–1909 | 60th |
| Theodore Roosevelt | R | 1905–1907 | 59th |
| Theodore Roosevelt | R | 1903–1905 | 58th |

# APPENDIX 19—*Continued*
## Terms of Presidents by Year and Congress

| PRESIDENT | PARTY | YEAR | CONGRESS |
|---|---|---|---|
| Theodore Roosevelt | R | 1901–1903 | 57th |
| McKinley | R | | |
| McKinley | R | 1899–1901 | 56th |
| McKinley | R | 1897–1899 | 55th |
| Cleveland | D | 1895–1897 | 54th |
| Cleveland | D | 1893–1895 | 53d |
| B. Harrison | R | 1891–1893 | 52d |
| B. Harrison | R | 1889–1891 | 51st |
| Cleveland | D | 1887–1889 | 50th |
| Cleveland | D | 1885–1887 | 49th |
| Arthur | R | 1883–1885 | 48th |
| Arthur | R | 1881–1883 | 47th |
| Garfield | R | | |
| Hayes | R | 1879–1881 | 46th |
| Hayes | R | 1877–1879 | 45th |
| Grant | R | 1875–1877 | 44th |
| Grant | R | 1873–1875 | 43d |
| Grant | R | 1871–1873 | 42d |
| Grant | R | 1869–1871 | 41st |
| Andrew Johnson | R | 1867–1869 | 40th |

*Continued on next page*

## APPENDIX 19—*Continued*
## Terms of Presidents by Year and Congress

| PRESIDENT | PARTY | YEAR | CONGRESS |
|---|---|---|---|
| Andrew Johnson | R | 1865–1867 | 39th |
| Lincoln | R | 1863–1865 | 38th |
| Lincoln | R | 1861–1863 | 37th |
| Buchanan | D | 1859–1861 | 36th |
| Buchanan | D | 1857–1859 | 35th |
| Pierce | D | 1855–1857 | 34th |
| Pierce | D | 1853–1855 | 33d |
| Fillmore | W | 1851–1853 | 32d |
| Fillmore | W | 1849–1851 | 31st |
| Taylor | W | | |
| Polk | D | 1847–1849 | 30th |
| Polk | D | 1845–1847 | 29th |
| Tyler | W | 1843–1845 | 28th |
| Tyler | W | 1841–1843 | 27th |
| William Harrison | W | | |
| Van Buren | D | 1839–1841 | 26th |
| Van Buren | D | 1837–1839 | 25th |
| Jackson | D | 1835–1837 | 24th |
| Jackson | D | 1833–1835 | 23d |
| Jackson | D | 1831–1833 | 22d |
| Jackson | D | 1829–1831 | 21st |

# APPENDIX 19—*Continued*
## Terms of Presidents by Year and Congress

| PRESIDENT | PARTY | YEAR | CONGRESS |
|-----------|-------|------|----------|
| John Q. Adams | C | 1827–1829 | 20th |
| John Q. Adams | C | 1825–1827 | 19th |
| Monroe | DR | 1823–1825 | 18th |
| Monroe | DR | 1821–1823 | 17th |
| Monroe | DR | 1819–1821 | 16th |
| Monroe | DR | 1817–1819 | 15th |
| Madison | DR | 1815–1817 | 14th |
| Madison | DR | 1813–1815 | 13th |
| Madison | DR | 1811–1813 | 12th |
| Madison | DR | 1809–1811 | 11th |
| Jefferson | DR | 1807–1809 | 10th |
| Jefferson | DR | 1805–1807 | 9th |
| Jefferson | DR | 1803–1805 | 8th |
| Jefferson | DR | 1801–1803 | 7th |
| John Adams | F | 1799–1801 | 6th |
| John Adams | F | 1797–1799 | 5th |
| Washington | F | 1795–1797 | 4th |
| Washington | F | 1793–1795 | 3d |
| Washington | F | 1791–1793 | 2d |
| Washington | F | 1789–1791 | 1st |

*Party symbols: C—Coalition; D—Democratic; DR—Democratic-Republican; F—Federalist; R—Republican; W—Whig

## APPENDIX 20:
## Presidential Election Returns

| YEAR | CANDIDATE | PARTY | ELECTORAL VOTE | POPULAR VOTE |
|------|-----------|-------|----------------|--------------|
| 1980 | Ronald Reagan | R | 489 | 42,797,153 |
| | Jimmy Carter | D | 49 | 34,434,100 |
| 1976 | Jimmy Carter | D | 297 | 40,829,046 |
| | Gerald R. Ford | R | 240 | 39,146,006 |
| 1972 | Richard M. Nixon | R | 520 | 47,170,179 |
| | George McGovern | D | 17 | 29,171,791 |
| 1968 | Richard M. Nixon | R | 301 | 31,785,480 |
| | Hubert Humphrey | D | 191 | 31,275,166 |
| 1964 | Lyndon B. Johnson | D | 486 | 43,129,566 |
| | Barry Goldwater | R | 52 | 27,178,188 |
| 1960 | John F. Kennedy | D | 303 | 34,226,731 |
| | Richard M. Nixon | R | 219 | 34,108,157 |
| 1956 | Dwight D. Eisenhower | R | 457 | 35,590,472 |
| | Adlai E. Stevenson | D | 73 | 26,022,752 |
| 1952 | Dwight D. Eisenhower | R | 442 | 33,936,234 |
| | Adlai E. Stevenson | D | 89 | 27,314,992 |
| 1948 | Harry S Truman | D | 303 | 24,179,345 |
| | Thomas E. Dewey | R | 189 | 21,991,291 |

# APPENDIX 20—*Continued*
## Presidential Election Returns

| YEAR | CANDIDATE | PARTY | ELECTORAL VOTE | POPULAR VOTE |
|------|-----------|-------|----------------|--------------|
| 1944 | Franklin D. Roosevelt | D | 432 | 25,606,585 |
|      | Thomas E. Dewey | R | 99 | 22,014,745 |
| 1940 | Franklin D. Roosevelt | D | 449 | 27,307,819 |
|      | Wendell Willkie | R | 82 | 22,321,018 |
| 1936 | Franklin D. Roosevelt | D | 523 | 27,752,869 |
|      | Alfred M. Landon | R | 8 | 16,674,665 |
| 1932 | Franklin D. Roosevelt | D | 472 | 22,809,638 |
|      | Herbert C. Hoover | R | 59 | 15,758,901 |
| 1928 | Herbert C. Hoover | R | 444 | 21,391,993 |
|      | Alfred E. Smith | D | 87 | 15,016,169 |
| 1924 | Calvin C. Coolidge | R | 382 | 15,718,211 |
|      | John W. Davis | D | 136 | 8,385,283 |
| 1920 | Warren G. Harding | R | 404 | 16,143,407 |
|      | James M. Cox | D | 127 | 9,130,328 |
| 1916 | Woodrow Wilson | D | 277 | 9,127,695 |
|      | Charles E. Hughes | R | 254 | 8,533,507 |
| 1912 | Woodrow Wilson | D | 435 | 6,296,547 |
|      | Theodore Roosevelt | P | 88 | 4,118,571 |

*Continued on next page*

## APPENDIX 20—*Continued*
## Presidential Election Returns

| YEAR | CANDIDATE | PARTY | ELECTORAL VOTE | POPULAR VOTE |
|------|-----------|-------|----------------|--------------|
| 1908 | William H. Taft | R | 321 | 7,675,320 |
|      | William J. Bryan | D | 162 | 6,412,294 |
| 1904 | Theodore Roosevelt | R | 336 | 7,628,461 |
|      | Alton B. Parker | D | 140 | 5,084,223 |
| 1900 | William McKinley | R | 292 | 7,218,491 |
|      | William J. Bryan | D | 155 | 6,356,734 |
| 1896 | William McKinley | R | 271 | 7,102,246 |
|      | William J. Bryan | D | 176 | 6,492,559 |
| 1892 | Grover Cleveland | D | 277 | 5,555,426 |
|      | Benjamin Harrison | R | 145 | 5,182,690 |
| 1888 | Benjamin Harrison | R | 233 | 5,447,129 |
|      | Grover Cleveland | D | 168 | 5,537,857 |
| 1884 | Grover Cleveland | D | 219 | 4,879,507 |
|      | James G. Blaine | R | 182 | 4,850,293 |
| 1880 | James A. Garfield | R | 214 | 4,453,295 |
|      | Winfield S. Hancock | D | 155 | 4,414,082 |
| 1876 | Rutherford B. Hayes | R | 185 | 4,036,572 |
|      | Samuel J. Tilden | D | 184 | 4,284,020 |

# APPENDIX 20—*Continued*
## Presidential Election Returns

| YEAR | CANDIDATE | PARTY | ELECTORAL VOTE | POPULAR VOTE |
|------|-----------|-------|----------------|--------------|
| 1872 | Ulysses S. Grant | R | 286 | 3,596,745 |
| | Horace Greeley | D | 3 | 2,843,446 |
| 1868 | Ulysses S. Grant | R | 214 | 3,013,421 |
| | Horatio Seymour | D | 80 | 2,706,829 |
| 1864 | Abraham Lincoln | R | 212 | 2,206,938 |
| | George B. McClellan | D | 21 | 1,803,787 |
| 1860 | Abraham Lincoln | R | 180 | 1,865,593 |
| | Stephen Douglas | D | 12 | 1,382,713 |
| 1856 | James Buchanan | D | 174 | 1,832,955 |
| | John C. Fremont | R | 114 | 1,339,932 |
| 1852 | Franklin Pierce | D | 254 | 1,601,117 |
| | Winfield Scott | W | 42 | 1,385,453 |
| 1848 | Zachary Taylor | W | 163 | 1,360,967 |
| | Lewis Cass | D | 127 | 1,222,342 |
| 1844 | James K. Polk | D | 170 | 1,338,464 |
| | Henry Clay | W | 105 | 1,300,097 |
| 1840 | William H. Harrison | W | 234 | 1,274,624 |
| | Martin Van Buren | D | 60 | 1,127,781 |

*Continued on next page*

## APPENDIX 20—*Continued*
## Presidential Election Returns

| YEAR | CANDIDATE | PARTY | ELECTORAL VOTE | POPULAR VOTE |
|---|---|---|---|---|
| 1836 | Martin Van Buren | D | 170 | 765,483 |
| | William H. Harrison | W | 73 | 739,795 |
| 1832 | Andrew Jackson | D | 219 | 687,502 |
| | Henry Clay | NR | 49 | 530,189 |
| 1828 | Andrew Jackson | D | 178 | 647,286 |
| | John Q. Adams | NR | 83 | 508,064 |
| 1824 | John Q. Adams | C | 84 | 108,740 |
| | Andrew Jackson | D | 99 | 153,544 |
| 1820 | James Monroe | R | 231 | |
| | John Q. Adams | C | 1 | |
| 1816 | James Monroe | R | 183 | |
| | Rufus King | F | 34 | |
| 1812 | James Madison | DR | 128 | |
| | De Witt Clinton | | 89 | |
| 1808 | James Madison | DR | 122 | |
| | C. C. Pinckney | F | 47 | |
| 1804 | Thomas Jefferson | DR | 162 | |
| | C. C. Pinckney | F | 14 | |

# APPENDIX 20—*Continued*
## Presidential Election Returns

| YEAR | CANDIDATE | PARTY | ELECTORAL VOTE | POPULAR VOTE |
|------|-----------|-------|----------------|--------------|
| 1800 | Thomas Jefferson | DR | 73 | |
| | Aaron Burr | DR | 73 | |
| 1796 | John Adams | F | 71 | |
| | Thomas Jefferson | DR | 68 | |
| 1792 | George Washington | F | 132 | |
| | John Adams | F | 77 | |
| 1789 | George Washington | F | 69 | |
| | John Adams | F | 34 | |

*Party symbols: C—Coalition; D—Democratic; DR—Democratic-Republican; F—Federalist; IR—Independent Republican; NR—National Republican; P—Progressive; R—Republican; W—Whig

## APPENDIX 21:
## Sources of Election Data

| | YEARS | Total Vote | Percentage of Vote |
|---|---|---|---|
| Petersen | 1792–1960 | ● | ● |
| Burnham | 1836–1892 | ● | |
| Robinson | 1896–1944 | ● | |
| *America at the Polls* | 1920–1964 | ● | ● |
| Runyon | 1948–1968 | ● | |
| Cox | 1910–1970 | ● | ● |
| *America Votes* | 1955– | ● | ● |
| *CQ Guide and Supplement* | 1789–1976 | ● | ● |

## APPENDIX 21—*Continued*
## Sources of Election Data

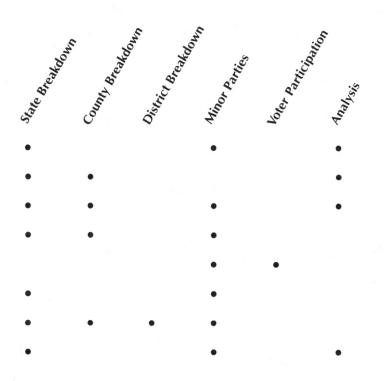

| State Breakdown | County Breakdown | District Breakdown | Minor Parties | Voter Participation | Analysis |
|---|---|---|---|---|---|
| • | | | • | | • |
| • | • | | | | • |
| • | • | | • | | • |
| • | • | | • | | |
| | | | • | • | |
| • | | | • | | |
| • | • | • | • | | |
| • | | | • | | • |

**APPENDIX 22:**

## Approaches to Studying the Presidency

| APPROACHES | SOME KEY CONCEPTS |
|---|---|
| Historical | Constitutional and statutory powers and structures |
| Institutional | Organizational roles, structures, processes |
| Legal | Constitutional and statutory powers and structures |
| Policy | Formulation, output, impact, evaluation |
| Political | Power relations, leadership, and elites |
| Psychological | Personality, style, character |
| Social Choice | Bargaining, voting, rationality, and collective action |
| Sociological | Socialization, recruitment, group theories |

# APPENDIX 23:

# Data Sources to Aid in the Location and Collection of Data for Nonreactive Research

| CATEGORY | TYPE | EXAMPLE |
|---|---|---|
| Political Records | Elections | *America Votes* |
| | Voting | *American National Election Studies Data Sourcebook* |
| | Roll Calls | *Congressional Roll Call* |
| | Ratings | *CQ Weekly Report* |
| | Budgetary | *Budget of the U.S. Government* |
| Mass Media | Newspapers | *The New York Times* |
| | Public Opinion | *Gallup Polls* |
| | News Letters | *First Monday* |
| | Magazines | *Newsweek* |
| Directories | Industrial Sales | *Congressional District Business Patterns* |
| | Institutional | *Encyclopedia of Associations* |
| | Political | *Politics in America* |
| | Biographical | *Who's Who in American Politics* |
| Written Materials | Documents | *Congressional Record* |
| | Platforms | *National Party Platforms* |
| | Speeches | *Public Papers of the Presidents* |

*Continued on next page*

## APPENDIX 23—*Continued*
## Data Sources to Aid in the Location and Collection of Data for Nonreactive Research

| CATEGORY | TYPE | EXAMPLE |
|---|---|---|
| Indexes | Document | *CIS/Index* |
| | Television | *CBS News Index* |
| | Newspaper | *New York Times Index* |
| | Statistical | *American Statistics Index* |

## APPENDIX 24:
## Types of Literature Searches

| | |
|---|---|
| Theoretical Literature | Articles |
| | Books |
| | Dissertations |
| | Encyclopedias |
| | Handbooks |
| | Bibliographies |
| | Databases |
| Previous Research | Articles |
| | Books |
| | Dissertations |
| | Encyclopedias |
| | Handbooks |
| | Bibliographies |
| | Research Guides |
| | Databases |
| Primary Research Sources | Documents |
| | Newspapers |
| | Legal Newspapers |
| | Memoirs |
| | Published Private Papers |

*Continued on next page*

**APPENDIX 24—*Continued***
## Types of Literature Searches

|  |  | Archival Material |
|  |  | Newsletters |
|  |  | TV Archives |
| Secondary Research Sources |  | Articles |
|  |  | Books |
|  |  | Dissertations |
|  |  | News Magazines |
|  |  | News Digests |
|  |  | Encyclopedias |
|  |  | Bibliographies |
|  |  | Research Guides |
|  |  | Databases |
| Factual Information |  | Almanacs |
|  |  | Dictionaries |
|  |  | Encyclopedias |
|  |  | Handbooks |
|  |  | Chronologies |
|  |  | Statistical Compendia |
|  |  | Biographical Directories |
|  |  | Institutional Directories |
|  |  | Factbooks |

# APPENDIX 24—*Continued*
## Types of Literature Searches

Statistical Data

Almanacs

Databases

Electoral Compendia

Voting Compendia

Public Opinion Polls

Data Archives

Statistical Abstracts

Statistical Indexes

## APPENDIX 25:
## Table of Research Operations for Documents

| TYPE OF DOCUMENT | SOURCES |
|---|---|
| Constitutional Law and Cases | *Constitution of the United States* |
| | *Landmark Briefs and Arguments of the Supreme Court of the U.S.* |
| | *United States Code* |
| | *United States Code Annotated* |
| | *United States Code Service* |
| Congressional Documents | *Congressional Record* |
| | *House Journal* |
| | *Senate Journal* |
| | *Serial Set* |
| | *United States Code Congressional and Administrative News* |
| Statutory Law | *Shepard's United States Citations: Statutes Edition* |
| | *Slip Law* |
| | *United States Code* |
| | *United States Code Annotated* |
| | *United States Code Congressional and Administrative News* |
| | *United States Statutes at Large* |
| Presidential Documents | *Code of Federal Regulations* |
| | *Congressional Record* |
| | *Federal Register* |

## APPENDIX 25—*Continued*
## Table of Research Operations for Documents

| TYPE OF DOCUMENT | SOURCES |
|---|---|
| | *Public Papers of the President* |
| | *Serial Set* |
| | *Statutes at Large* |
| | *United States Code Congressional and Administrative News* |
| | *Weekly Compilation of Presidential Documents* |
| Administrative Law | *Code of Federal Regulations* |
| | *Federal Register* |
| Court Decisions | *Records and Briefs of Tape Recordings of Oral Arguments* |
| | *Supreme Court Reporter* |
| | *United States Law Week* |
| | *United States Reports* |
| | *United States Supreme Court Reports* |
| Treaties | *Bevan's* |
| | *Treaties and Other International Acts Series* |
| | *Treaties in Force* |
| | *United States Treaties and Other International Agreements* |

## APPENDIX 26:
## Table of Research Operations for Secondary Sources

| TYPE OF MATERIAL | TYPE OF INFORMATION NEEDED | RESOURCE |
| --- | --- | --- |
| Social Science Reference Literature | Surveys | *Guide to Library Resources in Political Science: American Politics* |
| | | *Guide to Reference Materials in Political Science* |
| | | *Information Sources of Political Science* |
| | | *Literature of Political Science* |
| | | *Research Resources: Guide to the Social Sciences* |
| Document Reference Literature | Surveys and Explanations | *Congressional Publications* |
| | | *Government Publications: A Guide to Bibliographic Tools* |
| | | *Government Publications and Their Use* |
| | | *Introduction to United States Public Documents* |
| | | *United States Government Publications* |
| | | *U.S. Government Publications Relating to the Social Sciences* |

## APPENDIX 26—*Continued*
## Table of Research Operations for Secondary Sources

| TYPE OF MATERIAL | TYPE OF INFORMATION NEEDED | RESOURCE |
|---|---|---|
| Legal Reference Literature | Surveys and Explanations | *Effective Legal Research* |
| | | *Fundamentals of Legal Research* |
| | | *How to Find the Law* |
| | | *Legal Research in a Nut Shell* |
| | | *Legislative Analysis: How to Use Statutes and Regulations* |
| General Information | Current Events | *CQ Weekly Report* |
| | | *National Journal* |
| | | *Facts on File* |
| | | *Keesing Contemporary Archives* |
| | | *New York Times* |
| | | *Washington Post* |
| | Newspaper Indexes | *National Newspaper Index* |
| | | *Newsbank Urban Affairs Library* |
| | | *Newspaper Index* |
| | Political Terms | *American Political Dictionary* |

*Continued on next page*

## APPENDIX 26—*Continued*
## Table of Research Operations for Secondary Sources

| TYPE OF MATERIAL | TYPE OF INFORMATION NEEDED | RESOURCE |
|---|---|---|
| | | *Dictionary of American Government* |
| | | *Dictionary of American History* |
| | | *Dictionary of American Politics* |
| | Legal Terms | *Ballantine Law Dictionary* |
| | | *Black's Law Dictionary* |
| | | *Law Dictionary* |
| | | *Law Dictionary and Concise Encyclopedia* |
| | | *Quick Legal Terminology* |
| | Topic Survey for Politics | *Encyclopedia of American History* |
| | | *Handbook of Political Science* |
| | | *International Encyclopedia of the Social Sciences* |
| | Topic Surveys for Law | *American Jurisprudence* |
| | | *Corpus Juris Secundum* |
| | | *Legal Encyclopedia and Dictionary* |

# APPENDIX 26—*Continued*
## Table of Research Operations for Secondary Sources

| TYPE OF MATERIAL | TYPE OF INFORMATION NEEDED | RESOURCE |
|---|---|---|
| | | *The Guide to American Law* |
| | Topic Surveys of National Politics | *Congress and the Nation* |
| | | *CQ Almanac* |
| | | *Editorial Research Reports* |
| | | *Facts on File Yearbooks* |
| | | *Guide to Current American Government* |
| | Quick Facts and Figures | *Information Please Almanac* |
| | | *Official Associated Press Almanac* |
| | | *World Almanac and Book of Facts* |
| | Information Directories | *Federal Regulatory Directory* |
| | | *Researcher's Guide to Washington* |
| | | *Washington Information Directory* |
| | | *Washington Pocket Directory* |
| | Biographical Directories | *Dictionary of American Biography* |

*Continued on next page*

## APPENDIX 26—*Continued*
## Table of Research Operations for Secondary Sources

| TYPE OF MATERIAL | TYPE OF INFORMATION NEEDED | RESOURCE |
|---|---|---|
| | | *Taylor's Encyclopedia of Government Officials* |
| | | *Who's Who in American Politics* |
| | | *Who's Who in Government* |
| | Biographical Indexes | *Bio-Base* |
| | | *Biographical Dictionaries Master Index* |
| | | *Biography and Genealogy Master Index* |
| | | *Biography Index* |
| | Locator Aids for Dissertations | *American Doctoral Dissertations* |
| | | *Comprehensive Dissertation Index* |
| | | *Dissertation Abstracts International* |
| | TV Coverage | *CBS News Index* |
| | | *Television News Index* |
| | Recent Articles | *Humanities Index* |
| | | *Magazine Index* |

# APPENDIX 26—*Continued*
## Table of Research Operations for Secondary Sources

| TYPE OF MATERIAL | TYPE OF INFORMATION NEEDED | RESOURCE |
|---|---|---|
| | | *Reader's Guide to Periodical Literature* |
| | | *Social Sciences Index* |
| General Data | Locator Aids | *American Statistics Index* |
| | | *Bureau of Census Catalog* |
| | | *Statistical Reference Index* |
| | Data Compendiums | *County and City Data Book* |
| | | *Historical Statistics of the United States* |
| | | *Statistical Abstract of the United States* |
| | Statistical Directories | *Directory of Federal Statistics for Local Areas* |
| | | *Directory of Non-Federal Statistics* |
| | | *Federal Statistical Directory* |
| | | *Guide to U.S. Government Statistics* |
| | | *State Blue Books and Reference Publications* |

*Continued on next page*

**APPENDIX 26—*Continued***
**Table of Research Operations for Secondary Sources**

| TYPE OF MATERIAL | TYPE OF INFORMATION NEEDED | RESOURCE |
|---|---|---|
| | | *State Manuals, Blue Books and Election Results* |
| | Public Opinion | *Gallup Opinion Index Report* |
| | | *Gallup Poll: Public Opinion, 1935–1971* |
| | | *Gallup Poll: Public Opinion, 1972–1977* |
| | | *Harris Survey Yearbook of Public Opinion* |
| | | *Public Opinion* |
| Presidential Activities | Locator Aids to Documents | *Cumulated Indexes to the Public Papers of the President* |
| | | *Federal Index* |
| | | *Public Papers of the President* |
| | | *Weekly Compilation of Presidential Documents* |
| | Quick Facts | *Book of the Presidents* |
| | | *Facts About the Presidents* |
| | | *World Book of America's Presidents* |

## APPENDIX 26—*Continued*
## Table of Research Operations for Secondary Sources

| TYPE OF MATERIAL | TYPE OF INFORMATION NEEDED | RESOURCE |
|---|---|---|
| | Biographical Information | *Biographical Directory of the United States Executive Branch* |
| | | *Political Profile Series* |
| | Bibliographies | *The American Presidency: A Historical Bibliography* |
| | | *The American Presidency: A Guide to Information Sources* |
| | | *Evolution of the Modern Presidency* |
| | | *Presidents: A Catalog of Doctoral Dissertations* |
| | | *Presidents of the U.S. 1789–1962* |
| | Recent Articles | *ABC POL SCI* |
| | | *America: History & Life* |
| | | *British Humanities Index* |
| | | *Humanities Index* |
| | | *Index to Legal Periodicals* |

*Continued on next page*

**APPENDIX 26—*Continued***
## Table of Research Operations for Secondary Sources

| TYPE OF MATERIAL | TYPE OF INFORMATION NEEDED | RESOURCE |
| --- | --- | --- |
| | | *International Bibliography of Political Science* |
| | | *International Political Science Abstracts* |
| | | *Social Sciences Citation Index* |
| | | *Social Sciences Index* |
| | | *United States Political Science Documents* |
| | | *Writings on American History* |
| Campaigning | Identifying Information about Interest Groups | *Directory of Registered Federal and State Lobbyists* |
| | | *Directory of Washington Representatives of American Associations and Industry* |
| | | *Encyclopedia of Associations* |
| | | *Greenwood Encyclopedia of American Institutions* |
| | | *National Trade and Professional Associations of the U.S.* |

# APPENDIX 26—*Continued*
## Table of Research Operations for Secondary Sources

| TYPE OF MATERIAL | TYPE OF INFORMATION NEEDED | RESOURCE |
| --- | --- | --- |
| | | *Washington Lobbyists / Lawyers Directory* |
| | | *Washington Representatives* |
| | Identify Information about PACS | *PACS Americana* |
| | | *PAC Handbook* |
| | | *Political Action Register* |
| | | *Tyke's Register of Political Action Committees* |
| | Recent Articles | *Applied Science and Technology Index* |
| | | *Business Periodical Index* |
| | | *Communication Abstracts* |
| | | *Journalism Abstracts* |
| | Party Information | *Political Parties: A Cross National Survey* |
| | | *Political Parties and Civic Action Groups* |
| | | *Political Parties of the World* |
| | | *World Encyclopedia of Political Systems* |

*Continued on next page*

**APPENDIX 26—*Continued***

**Table of Research Operations for Secondary Sources**

| TYPE OF MATERIAL | TYPE OF INFORMATION NEEDED | RESOURCE |
|---|---|---|
| | Bibliographies | *American Political Parties* |
| | | *American Political Process* |
| | | *The Democratic and Republican Parties in America* |
| | | *The Image Makers* |
| | | *Political Campaigns* |
| | | *Political Campaign Communication* |
| Elections | Returns Data | *America at the Polls* |
| | | *America Votes* |
| | | *Presidential Elections Since 1789* |
| | | *CQ Guide to U.S. Elections* |
| | | *Sourcebook of American Presidential Campaign and Election Statistics* |
| | | *State and National Voting in Federal Elections* |
| | | *Statistical History of the American Presidential Elections* |

## APPENDIX 26—*Continued*
## Table of Research Operations for Secondary Sources

| TYPE OF MATERIAL | TYPE OF INFORMATION NEEDED | RESOURCE |
|---|---|---|
| | District Data | *Congressional District Business Patterns* |
| | | *Congressional District Data Book* |
| | | *Historical Atlas of United States Congressional Districts* |
| | Bibliographies | *The American Electorate* |
| | | *American Politics and Elections* |
| | | *Elections and Electoral Behavior* |
| | | *United States Politics and Elections* |
| | Recent Articles | *ABC POL SCI* |
| | | *Social Sciences Citation Index* |
| | | *Social Science Index* |
| | | *Public Affairs Information Service Bulletin* |
| | | *United States Political Science Documents* |
| Treaties | Locator Aids | *Treaties in Force* |

*Continued on next page*

**APPENDIX 26—*Continued***
## Table of Research Operations for Secondary Sources

| TYPE OF MATERIAL | TYPE OF INFORMATION NEEDED | RESOURCE |
|---|---|---|
| | | *UST Cumulative Index, 1776–1949* |
| | | *UST Cumulative Index, 1950–1970* |
| | Current Validity | *Department of State Bulletin* |
| | | *Shepard's United States Citation: Statute Edition* |
| | | *Treaties in Force* |
| | | *United States Treaties and International Agreements* |
| | Bibliographies | *American Foreign Relations: A Guide to Information Sources* |
| | | *Guide to American Foreign Relations Since 1700* |
| | | *Guide to the Diplomatic History of the U.S.* |
| | Recent Articles | *ABC POL SCI* |
| | | *Humanities Index* |
| | | *Public Affairs Information Service Bulletin* |
| | | *Social Sciences Index* |

# APPENDIX 26—*Continued*
## Table of Research Operations for Secondary Sources

| TYPE OF MATERIAL | TYPE OF INFORMATION NEEDED | RESOURCE |
| --- | --- | --- |
| | | *United States Political Science Documents* |
| | | *Writings on American History* |
| Congressional Activities | Locator Aids for Documents | *CIS/Index* |
| | | *CIS Legislative History Annual** |
| | | *Congressional Index* |
| | | *Digest of Public General Bills* |
| | | *Federal Index* |
| | | *United States Code Congressional and Administrative News* |
| | Current Events | *CQ Weekly Report* |
| | | *National Journal* |
| | | *New York Times* |
| | | *Washington Monthly* |
| | | *Washington Post* |
| | Biographical Directories | *Almanac of American Politics* |
| | | *Biographical Directory of the American Congress* |

*Continued on next page*

*To be published as a third volume of *CIS/INDEX* starting with the 1984 edition.

## APPENDIX 26—*Continued*
## Table of Research Operations for Secondary Sources

| TYPE OF MATERIAL | TYPE OF INFORMATION NEEDED | RESOURCE |
|---|---|---|
| | | *Congressional Directory* |
| | | *Politics in America* |
| | Bibliographies | *The American Political Process* |
| | | *American Politics and Elections* |
| | | *United States Congress: A Bibliography* |
| | Recent Articles | *ABC POL SCI* |
| | | *Index to Legal Periodicals* |
| | | *Public Affairs Information Service Bulletin* |
| | | *Social Sciences Index* |
| | | *United States Political Science Documents* |
| Statutory Law | Locator Aids for Laws | *CIS Index* |
| | | *Monthly Catalog* |
| | | *Shepard's Acts and Cases by Popular Name* |
| | | *Statutes at Large* |
| | | *United States Code* |

# APPENDIX 26—*Continued*
## Table of Research Operations for Secondary Sources

| TYPE OF MATERIAL | TYPE OF INFORMATION NEEDED | RESOURCE |
| --- | --- | --- |
| | | *United States Code Annotated* |
| | | *United States Code Service* |
| | Current Events | *CQ Weekly Report* |
| | | *Major Legislation of Congress* |
| | | *National Law Week* |
| | | *National Journal* |
| | | *U.S. Law Week* |
| | Recent Articles | *Current Law Index* |
| | | *Index to Legal Periodicals* |
| | | *Legal Resource Index* |
| | | *Public Affairs Information Service Bulletin* |
| | | *Social Sciences Index* |
| | | *United States Political Science Documents* |
| Court Decisions | Locator Aid for Supreme Court | *U.S. Supreme Court Decisions: Index* |
| | | *U.S. Supreme Court Digest* |

*Continued on next page*

## APPENDIX 26—*Continued*
## Table of Research Operations for Secondary Sources

| TYPE OF MATERIAL | TYPE OF INFORMATION NEEDED | RESOURCE |
|---|---|---|
| | | *U.S. Supreme Court Reports, Lawyers' Edition* |
| | Current Events | *Legal Times of Washington* |
| | | *Nation Law Journal* |
| | | *U.S. Law Week* |
| | Recent Articles | *Contents of Current Legal Periodicals* |
| | | *Current Law Index* |
| | | *Index to Legal Periodicals Related to Law* |
| | | *Legal Resource Index* |
| | | *Monthly Digest of Legal Articles* |
| Administrative Law | Locator Aids | *CIS Federal Register Index* |
| | | *Federal Register* |
| | | *IHS Index to the Code of Federal Regulations* |
| | | *Index to the Code of Federal Regulations* |
| | | *Shepard's United States Administrative Citations* |

# APPENDIX 26—*Continued*
# Table of Research Operations for Secondary Sources

| TYPE OF MATERIAL | TYPE OF INFORMATION NEEDED | RESOURCE |
|---|---|---|
| | Current Events | *Legal Times of Washington* |
| | | *National Journal* |
| | | *National Law Week* |
| | | *Regulation* |
| | Recent Articles | *Current Law Index* |
| | | *Index to Legal Periodicals* |
| | | *Index to Periodical Literature Related to Law* |
| | | *Legal Resource Index* |
| | | *Public Affairs Information Service Bulletin* |
| | | *Sage Public Administration Abstracts* |
| | | *United States Political Science Documents* |
| Constitutional Law | Bibliographies | *American Constitutional Development* |
| | | *Selected Bibliography of American Constitutional Law* |

*Continued on next page*

## APPENDIX 26—*Continued*
## Table of Research Operations for Secondary Sources

| TYPE OF MATERIAL | TYPE OF INFORMATION NEEDED | RESOURCE |
|---|---|---|
| | | *U.S. Constitution: A Guide to Information Sources* |
| | Recent Articles | *ABC POL SCI* |
| | | *Current Law Index* |
| | | *Humanities Index* |
| | | *Index to Legal Periodicals* |
| | | *Legal Resource Index* |
| | | *Social Sciences Citation Index* |
| | | *Social Sciences Index* |
| | | *United States Political Science Documents* |
| Executive Office | Locator Aids for Documents | *CIS Index* |
| | | *GPO Sales Publication Reference File* |
| | | *Guide to Publication of Executive Branch* |
| | | *Monthly Catalog* |
| | | *Public Affairs Information Service Bulletin* |
| | Current Events | *CQ Weekly Report* |

# APPENDIX 26—*Continued*
# Table of Research Operations for Secondary Sources

| TYPE OF MATERIAL | TYPE OF INFORMATION NEEDED | RESOURCE |
|---|---|---|
| | | *Legal Times of Washington* |
| | | *National Journal* |
| | | *U.S. Law Week* |
| | Recent Articles | *Public Affairs Information Service Bulletin* |
| | | *Sage Public Administration Abstracts* |
| | | *Social Sciences Index* |
| | | *United States Documents* |
| Advisory Committees and Boards | Locators Aid for Reports | *GPO Sales Publication Reference File* |
| | | *Monthly Catalog* |
| | | *Popular Names of U.S. Government Reports* |
| | | *Public Affairs Information Service Bulletin* |
| | Identifying Commissions | *Bibliography of Presidential Commissions . . .* |
| | | *Encyclopedia of Governmental Advisory Organizations* |

*Continued on next page*

**APPENDIX 26—*Continued***

## Table of Research Operations for Secondary Sources

| TYPE OF MATERIAL | TYPE OF INFORMATION NEEDED | RESOURCE |
|---|---|---|
| | | *Guide to Presidential Advisory Commissions, 1973–1981* |
| | | *New Governmental Advisory Organizations* |
| | | *U.S. Government Manual* |
| Citations | Explanation and Description | *Corpus Juris Secundum* |
| | | *Effective Legal Research* |
| | | *Radin Law Dictionary* |

# Bibliography

Aeschbacher, W. D. "Presidential Libraries: New Dimension in Research Facilities." *Midwest Quarterly* 6 (January 1965): 205–214.

Album, Michael T. "Government Control of Richard Nixon's Presidential Material." *Yale Law Journal* 87 (July 1978): 1601–1635.

Benadom, Gregory A., and Robert U. Goehlert "The CIA: Its History, Organization, Functions and Publications." *Government Publications Review* 6 (1979): 195–212.

Bernstein, Barton. "Who Owns History?" *Inquiry Magazine* 1 (May 1978): 6–8.

Berry, J. "No More Presidential Libraries." *Library Journal* 99 (Nov 1974): 2787.

Boque, Allan G. "The Historian and Social Science Data Archives in the United States." *American Behavioral Scientist* 19 (April 1979): 419–442.

Brooks, Philip C. "The Harry S Truman Library—Plans and Reality." *American Archivist* 25 (January 1962): 25–37.

Brooks, Philip C. "Understanding the Presidency: The Harry S Truman Library." *Prologue* 1 (Winter 1969): 3–12.

Buck, Elizabeth Hawthorn. "General Legislation for Presidential Libraries." *American Archivist* 18 (October 1955): 337–341.

Cappon, Lester J. "Why Presidential Libraries?" *Yale Review* 68 (Autumn 1978): 11–34.

Cochrane, J. L. "U.S. Presidential Libraries and the History of Political Economy." *History of Political Economy* 8 (Fall 1976): 412–427.

Cole, J. L. "Presidential Libraries." *Journal of Librarianship* 4 (April 1974): 115–129.

Connor, Robert D. W. "The FDR Library." *American Archivist* 3 (April 1940): 83–92.

Cook, J. Frank. "Private Papers of Public Officials." *American Archivist* 38 (July 1975): 299–324.

Dickerson, Reed. *Materials on Legal Drafting.* St. Paul: West Pub. Co., 1981.

Drewry, Elizabeth B. "The Role of Presidential Libraries." *Midwest Quarterly: A Journal of Contemporary Thought* 7 (October 1965): 53–65.

Feis, Herbert. "The President's Making of History." *Atlantic Monthly* 224 (September 1969): 64–65.

Fenn, D. H. "Launching the John F. Kennedy Library." *American Archivist* 42 (October 1979): 429–442.

Fisher, Louis. "Research Tools for Public Law." *Teaching Political Science* (Spring 1982): 134–138.

Flato, Linda. "Automation at the White House." *Datamation* 24 (Jan 1978): 190–193.

Fridley, Russell. "Should Public Papers be Private Property?" *Minnesota History* 44 (Spring 1974): 37–39.

Geselbracht, Raymond H., and Daniel J. Reed. "The Presidential Library and the White House Liaison Office." *American Archivist* 46 (Winter 1983): 69–71.

Graebner, Norman A. *Records of Public Officials.* New York: American Assembly, Columbia University Press, 1975.

Grover, Wayne C. "The Presidential Library System." *Palimpsest* 43 (Aug 1962): 387–392.

Ham, F. Gerald. "Public Ownership of the Papers of Public Officials." *American Archivist* 37 (April 1974): 357.

Hanson, R. "Hail to the Chiefs: Our Presidential Libraries." *Wilson Library Bulletin* 55 (April 1981): 576–583.

Heclo, Hugh. *Studying the Presidency: A Report to the Ford Foundation.* New York: Ford Foundation, 1979.

Herbert, Elise S. "How Accessible Are the Records in Government Records Centers?" *Journalism Quarterly* 52 (Spring 1975): 23–29.

Hirshon, Arnold. "Recent Developments in the Accessibility of Presidential Papers and Other Presidential Historical Materials." *Government Publications Review* 6 (1979): 343–358.

Hirshon, Arnold. "The Scope, Accessibility and History of Presidential Papers." *Government Publications Review* 1 (Fall 1974): 363–390.

Holmes, Oliver W. "Public Records—Who Knows What They Are?" *American Archivist* 14 (January 1960): 3–26.

"Hoover Library Dedicated." *Library Journal* 87 (September 1962): 3013.

Horn, David E. "Who Owns Our History?" *Library Journal* 100 (April 1975): 635–639.

Jacobs, Richard F. "The Status of the Nixon Presidential Historical Materials." *American Archivist* 38 (July 1975): 337.

Johnson, Nancy P. "Legal Statistics." *Legal Reference Services Quarterly* 1 (Summer/Fall 1981): 3–16.

Jones, H. G. "Presidential Libraries: Is There a Case for a National Presidential Library?" *American Archivist* 38 (July 1975): 325–328.

Jones, H. G. *The Records of a Nation: Their Management, Preservation, and Use.* New York: Atheneum Press, 1969.

Kahn, Herman. "The Long-Range Implications for Historians and Archivists of Charges Against the Franklin D. Roosevelt Library." *American Archivist* 34 (July 1971): 265–275.

Kahn, Herman. "The Presidential Library—New Institution." *Special Libraries* 50 (March 1959): 106–113.

Kegan, E. H. "A Becoming Regard to Posterity." *American Archivist* 40 (January 1977): 5–15.

"Kennedy Memorial Library." *Library Journal* 88 (January 1964): 210.

Kirkendell, Richard S. "Presidential Libraries: One Researcher's Point of View." *American Archivist* 25 (October 1962): 441–448.

Kirkendell, Richard S. "A Second Look at Presidential Libraries." *American Archivist* 29 (July 1966): 371–386.

Lagerquist, Philip D. "The Harry S Truman Library as a Center for Research on the American Presidency." *College and Research Libraries* 25 (January 1964): 32–36.

Leland, Waldo G. "The Creation of the Franklin D. Roosevelt Library." *American Archivist* 18 (January 1955): 11–29.

Lewis, Finlay. "Presidential Papers: An Attempt to Own History." *Nation* 19 (October 1974): 366–369.

Lloyd, David D. "The Harry S Truman Library." *American Archivist* 18 (April 1955): 99–110.

Lloyd, David D. "Presidential Papers and Presidential Libraries." *Manuscripts* 8 (Fall 1955): 4–9.

Lovely, Louise. "Evolution of Presidential Libraries." *Government Publication Review* 6 (1979): 27–35.

McCallum, Sue Vest. "Legal Research for Non-Law Librarians." *Government Publications Review* 6 (1979): 263–274.

McCoy, Donald R. "The Beginnings of the Franklin D. Roosevelt Library." *Prologue* 7 (Fall 1975): 137–150.

McDonough, John, R. Gordon Hoxie, and Richard Jacobs. "Who Owns Presidential Papers?" *Manuscripts* 27 (Winter 1975): 2–11.

McKay, P. R. "Presidential Papers: A Property Issue." *Library Quarterly* 52 (January 1982): 21–40.

Middleton, H. "Lyndon B. Johnson Presidential Library." *Texas Libraries* 39 (Winter 1977): 181–191.

Moorehead, Joe. "Federal Advisory Committees and Access to Public Information: A Status Report." *Government Publications Review* 2 (Winter 1975): 1–8.

Morton, Louis. "A Proposal for a Government Wide Historical Office." *Prologue* 3 (Spring 1971): 3–11.

Nelson, Anna K. "Government Historical Offices and Public Records." *American Archivist* 41 (October 1978): 405–412.

Nelson, Anna K. "Public Documents Commission: Politics and Presidential Records." *Government Publications Review* 9 (September–October 1982): 443–445.

O'Neill, James E. "Will Success Spoil the Presidential Libraries?" *American Archivist* 36 (July 1973): 339–351.

Patch, B. W. "Access to Official Papers and Information." *Editorial Research Reports* 1 (June 1963): 417–433.

Peat, W. Leslie. "Non-Legal Reference Books for Law Libraries." *Legal Reference Services Quarterly* 1 (Spring 1981): 13–32.

"The Presidency in the Information Age: New Directions." *Bulletin of the American Society for Information Science* 5 (December 1978): 13–27.

"The Records of Public Officials." *American Archivist* 38 (July 1975): 329–336.

Reid, Warren R. "Public Papers of the Presidents." *American Archivist* 25 (October 1962): 435–439.

Relyea, Harold C. "Opening Government to Public Scrutiny: A Decade of Federal Efforts." *Public Administration Review* (January–February 1975): 3–9.

Rhoads, James B. "Who Should Own the Documents of Public Officials?" *Prologue* 7 (Spring 1975): 32–35.

Rothwell, C. F. "Resources and Records in Hoover Institute and Library." *American Archivist* 18 (April 1955): 141–150.

Rourke, F. E. "Presidential Power: The Convenience of Secrecy." *Nation* 24 (July 1972): 39–42.

Rowland, Buford. "The Papers of the Presidents." *American Archivist* 13 (July 1950): 195–211.

Schick, F. L. *Presidential Libraries.* New York, Bowker, 1968.

Schlesinger, Arthur M. "Who Owns a President's Papers?" *Manuscripts* 27 (Summer 1975): 178–182.

Seymour-Ure, Colin. "Presidential Power, Press Secretaries and Communication." *Political Studies* 28 (June 1980): 253–270.

Seymour-Ure, Colin. "Who Speaks for the President? Problems of Control in Presidential Information." *Communication* 5 (1980): 267–274.

Shelley, Fred. "Manuscripts in the Library of Congress: 1800–1900." *American Archivist* 11 (January 1948): 3–19.

Shelley, Fred. "The Presidential Papers Program of the Library of Congress." *American Archivist* 25 (October 1962): 429–433.

Smith, T. A. "Before Hyde Park: The Rutherford B. Hayes Library." *American Archivist* 43 (Fall 1980): 485–488.

Spencer, Patricia L. "Separation of Powers—Bills of Attainder—Presidential Papers—Chief Executive's Right to Privacy." *Akron Law Review* 11 (Fall 1977): 378–386.

Stewart, William J. "Opening Closed Material in the Roosevelt Library." *Prologue* 7 (Winter 1975): 137–150.

Taylor, D. "Eisenhower Library Will Be a Historical Research Center." *Kansas Library Bulletin* 32 (March 1963): 12–14.

Travgott, Michael W., and Jerome M. Clubb. "Machine-Readable Data Production by the Federal Government: Access to and Utility for Social Research." *American Behavioral Scientists* 19 (April 1976): 387–408.

U.S. National Historical Publications Commission. *A Report to the President Containing a Proposal.* Washington, DC: U.S. Government Printing Office, 1963.

U.S. National Study Commission on Records and Documents of Federal Officials. *Final Report.* Washington, DC: U.S. Government Printing Office, 1977.

Vose, Clement E. "Presidential Papers as a Political Science Concern." *PS* 8 (Winter 1975): 8–18.

Walter, Robert. "What Did Ziegler Say, and When Did He Say It?: A Catalogue of Public Relations Ploys." *Columbia Journalism Review* 13 (September–October 1974): 30–35.

Weisberger, Bernard A. "The Paper Trust." *American Heritage* 22 (April 1971): 38–41.

# Author Index

# Title Index